Spare Time Guides, No. 4

SPARE TIME GUIDES:
Information Sources for Hobbies and Recreation, No. 4

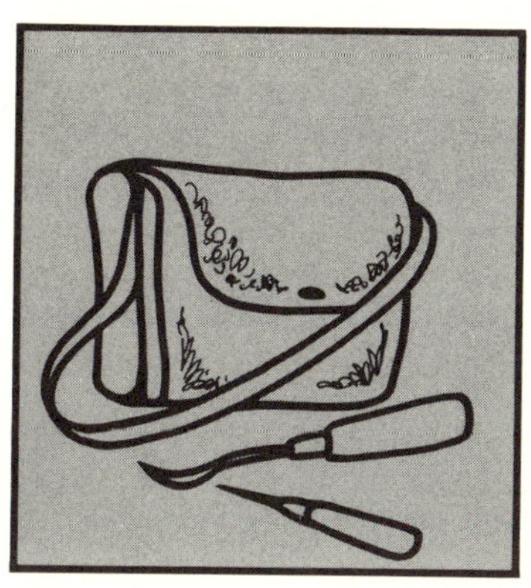

Crafts for Today:
Ceramics, Glasscrafting, Leatherworking, Candlemaking, and Other Popular Crafts

ROLLY M. HARWELL and
ANN J. HARWELL

1974
Libraries Unlimited, Inc.
Littleton, Colorado

10300

Library of Congress Card Number 73-92979
International Standard Book Number 0-87287-067-7

LIBRARIES UNLIMITED, INC.
P.O. Box 263
Littleton, Colorado 80120

CONTENTS

To previous joint projects:

Coleman,
Bin,
and Ross

INTRODUCTION

The Spare Time Guides series was conceived with a dual purpose—to provide libraries with selective annotated lists of recommended books on specific hobbies and recreational activities, and to help craftsmen and do-it-yourselfers learn more about their hobbies and crafts.

Today's intense interest in crafts of all sorts is the result of a number of factors: increased leisure time; a revulsion against store-bought, mass-manufactured, and/or shoddy goods; a recognition of the therapeutic value of working with the hands; and an eagerness to be part of a current trend.

Whatever the origins, however, the popularity of crafts today has encouraged a flurry of publishing activity that can only be confusing in its multiplicity. Librarians are engulfed by announcements of crafts books, but the books are reviewed only sporadically. The reviewing media that serve librarians devote little space to books on crafts and leisure time activities, and a search of hobby and craft magazines reveals only a few book reviews. Librarians need evaluations of these books, since budgets are too tight to allow indiscriminate purchasing. Individual craftsmen, on the other hand, face the opposite problem: they are seldom flooded with publishers' announcements, but they suffer from this by remaining unaware of new publications that might well be of great value. In too many cases librarians and hobbyists alike must rely on the exaggerated claims of advertisers or other equally unsatisfactory channels for information about these important books.

It is in hopes of improving all aspects of this situation that the present volume—and, indeed, the entire Spare Time Guides series—was conceived. Librarians will find that it has value not only as a selection aid but as a reference source to help patrons locate books on a particular craft. Teachers and those who always need new crafts projects that children can manage will find a plethora of projects books suggested here. Individual craftsmen seeking to advance from beginning to intermediate level or beyond will find that the annotations can guide them to manuals, handbooks, and how-to books at all levels.

The term "crafts" encompasses many media and a wide range of ability levels. The potter's thrown jug is perhaps more appealing than the pot produced in a child's first attempt to work with clay—but both the potter and the child are practicing a craft. Carving a menagerie or a crèche is on a different level from whittling one's first simple whistle—but both acts belong to the craft of woodworking. And between these extremes there are craftsmen at all levels of experience, skill, and talent. The elements that are common to all these craftsmen are enthusiasm and a delight not only in the finished product but in the very process of creating. It is for all these creators that this book is designed—for these creators and for the librarians who cater to their needs.

SCOPE

Reflecting the wide range of skills of those who enjoy working in one craft or another, this guide includes books aimed at rank beginners, those designed for intermediate-level craftsmen, and those that the professional will best be able to utilize to the fullest extent.

The first section, General Crafts, will provide novices with an overview of possibilities in many crafts areas, while the subdivision of that section, Projects Books, lists many books aimed at beginners and/or children. These books will be of value primarily to teachers, leaders of children's crafts groups, and parents.

The section of pottery and ceramics books, on the other hand, although it lists many beginning books, contains a greater number of entries for intermediate and advanced level books—aimed at experienced or professional craftsmen. This same principle is true for other chapters as well: e.g., the section on paper crafts contains proportionately more books designed for beginners and/or young people than do the sections on jewelry or plastics.

The specific crafts covered in this book range from beadworking to woodworking, and, as the title of the book indicates, they encompass most of the "crafts for today"—i.e., crafts that are currently experiencing a revival of interest. Because this volume is the first attempt to provide comprehensive bibliographic guidance in the area of crafts books, it seemed essential to include as many of today's crafts as possible; this wide scope will make *Crafts for Today* even more useful to librarians and teachers. Two forthcoming volumes of the Spare Time Guides series will cover needlework and macrame—two other crafts that are attracting great numbers of today's craftsmen and hobbyists.

Although an emphasis has been placed on books of recent vintage (from 1965 through 1973), there are examples of older works as well. Such works were carefully considered before being included, and several factors were taken into account. First, it is often the case that nothing has been published that supersedes it. Second, even a book that has been largely replaced by a more recent work often contains specific material that retains its value. This is particularly true of crafts encyclopedias and projects books, which can contribute that variety of new projects so essential to children's crafts programs. And lastly, the shelves of small libraries often hold a number of these older works (even pre-1960), and their inclusion here will help the craftsman locate them and determine their usefulness for his particular needs.

BIBLIOGRAPHIC DESCRIPTION

Entries provide the following information, when available: author, title, edition statement, place of publication, publisher, date, pagination, price, Library of Congress card number, and International Standard Book Number. It should be pointed out here that the prices given are those found in the publishers' current catalogs. But today's inflationary trend renders prices obsolete within a few months, so one should probably be prepared for an occasional "upward revision" of the prices listed.

The annotations provided for books are long and detailed. Where appropriate, comparisons often are made between similar books. In addition, many of the annotations make reference to additional books: works that are of less importance, that are older, or that have been announced for publication but were unavailable for examination.

Information provided for periodicals includes title, address, year of founding, frequency, and price, with short annotations that describe the focus, purpose, and/or audience of the publication.

ARRANGEMENT

Aside from the first section, General Crafts, the arrangement of the volume is alphabetical by craft. As we organized the book, it seemed most efficient to define some activities in terms of the end results (e.g., "Jewelry") and others in terms of the medium (e.g., "Paper" or "Leather"). Books that deal with a variety of crafts are listed in the section "General Crafts," which is further subdivided to reflect the intent and format of particular books. Each of the books in the "Miscellaneous" section is limited to a specific craft—but a craft that is supported by only a minimum of literature. Within each section, entries are alphabetical by main entry (usually author).

The table of contents provides an outline of the entire book, while the author-title-subject index affords access to books and periodicals. Books that are discussed in annotations are designated in the index with the letter "n" (i.e., 256n).

The list of publications includes the major national periodicals that will be of use to those interested in learning more about specific crafts.

Organizations listed include only the major national (and a few international) associations in the crafts areas covered in this volume. Not all crafts lend themselves to such formal structure, of course. There are numerous local and regional groups that could prove very helpful to beginning and advanced craftsmen. Hobby shops and crafts studios can often provide specific information on local groups.

There is an alphabetical list of all publishers whose books are listed in this guide, with their addresses.

ACKNOWLEDGEMENTS

Finally, acknowledgement must be made to several individuals and corporate entities who were instrumental in the preparation of this volume. First, a thank you to the publishers who have been so cooperative in furnishing review copies of their books—not only for this volume but for all the volumes of the Spare Time Guides series.

It must be pointed out that the collective nagging of the Libraries Unlimited personnel contributed not a little to the relatively early completion of the book. Sally Wynkoop, in particular, deserves notice for her encouragement and advice.

January 1974   Rolly M. Harwell
                                                  Ann J. Harwell

Crafts for Today

GENERAL CRAFTS

GENERAL REFERENCE

1. **American Crafts Guide: A Comprehensive Directory to Craft Shops, Galleries, Crafts Schools, Museums and Studios of Individual Craftsmen Across the United States**, San Jose, Calif., Gousha Publications, 1973. 222p. $3.95pa. LC 72-97826.

The directory is arranged alphabetically by state and subdivided by craft categories (batik, ceramics, glass, rugs). Two important subdivisions are schools and instructions, and supplies. Omitted are painters and galleries devoted to fine arts (except graphics and sculpture) and souvenir-type shops. Each entry lists name, address, phone, and brief description of the specialties crafted or taught. Although a work of this sort is never comprehensive, the information provided here will give craftsmen a useful starting place for locating specific shops, schools, etc.

2. Kroncke, Grete. **Mounting Handicraft: Ideas and Instructions for Assembling and Finishing**. New York, Van Nostrand Reinhold, 1971. 96p. illus. index. (Scandinavian Craft Series). $4.50. LC 72-123380.

The aim of this book is "to show with clear instructions and step-by-step instructions the very pleasing effects that may be achieved by imaginative mounting of handicraft articles." It deals not only with mounting paintings and collages but with making embroidered fabrics into pillows, wall hangings, handbags, purses, etc. Other objects made from handicraft materials are covered boxes, book covers, sewing baskets. An excellent book whose detailed instructions and line drawings provide explicit directions for mounting favorite needlework and art projects. Recommended for public libraries.

3. Lovell, Eleanor C., and Ruth M. Hall, comps. **Index to Handicrafts, Modelmaking, and Workshop Projects**. Boston, F. W. Faxon, 1936. 476p. $14.00.

This index is based on the collection of references accumulated in the Minneapolis Public Library over the 12-year period preceding its publication. It covers a field of miscellaneous and previously unorganized materials on handicrafts and amateur shop work projects, including practical and decorative wood and metal work, modelmaking and other forms of handicrafts. Needlework, radio, and strictly art subjects have been excluded. Only articles giving practical information and the necessary drawings or diagrams for construction have been selected. There are over 2,000 subject entries, alphabetically arranged. The number of references under each entry varies considerably, though some entries have quite extensive references. Projects from approximately 400 books and journals have been indexed. A list of these books and periodicals, with full bibliographic information, precedes the index.

4. Lovell, Eleanor C., and Ruth M. Hall, comps. **Index to Handicrafts, Modelmaking and Workshop Projects: First Supplement**. Boston, F. W. Faxon, 1950. 593p. $14.00.

This supplement brings up to date the original "Index" described above. The same procedure is followed with respect to selection and scope. Projects from 37 periodicals and approximately 400 books published between 1934 and 1942 are indexed.

5. Lovell, Eleanor C., and Ruth M. Hall, comps. **Index to Handicrafts, Modelmaking and Workshop Projects: Second Supplement**. Boston, F. W. Faxon, 1950. 593p. $14.00.

A supplement to the supplement, this volume brings up to date the original and supplement described above, indexing projects from approximately 400 volumes and 45 periodicals published between 1942 and 1950. The bibliography, however, contains certain items published earlier that were missed in the preceding volumes.

6. Turner, Harriet P., and Amy Winslow, comps. **Index to Handicrafts, Model Making, and Workshop Projects: Third Supplement, 1950-1961**. Boston, F. W. Faxon, 1965. 914p. $14.00. LC 36-27324.

This Third Supplement to the Index was initiated by the Baltimore Chapter of the ALA Reference Services Division and was carried out under its sponsorship. The period covered is 1950 to 1961 (with the addition of a few titles published earlier) and the index was limited to material available through the Enoch Pratt Free Library of Baltimore. Because of the phenomenal increase in "do-it-yourself" publications over the 12 years since the preceding supplement, only craft magazines not indexed in the *Readers' Guide to Periodical Literature* were included. This limited the number of periodicals in the bibliography to 14, though the number of books from which project references were taken was almost doubled. Generally, the criteria for selection were the same as in previous volumes.

7. Alt, E. Winifred, comp. **Index to Handicrafts, Model Making, and Workshop Projects: Fourth Supplement, 1962-1967**. Boston, F. W. Faxon, 1969. 468p. $14.00. LC 36-27324. SBN 87305-096-7.

This Fourth Supplement to the Index covers the period from 1962 to 1967. Its scope has been increased by the inclusion of titles available from the Baltimore Public Library System. The periodicals indexed are the same as those in the Third Supplement—i.e., those not indexed in the *Readers' Guide to Periodical Literature*. Basically the coverage remains the same as in previous volumes; however, "art" books are indexed if the text gives extensive practical directions for the use of tools and equipment. Electronic devices are included, but not radio and television technology; construction of photographic equipment, but not its use; specific needlework items such as purses, hats, bags, but not basic sewing, embroidery or knitting instructions. Cookery and gardening continue to be omitted.

The Faxon Indexes are of exceptional practical value to the reference librarian in answering "how-to-make-it" questions. In addition, the extensive bibliography contained in each volume—though not organized in a manner convenient for reference—is a useful guide to the literature published on crafts during the last 40 years.

8. Miles, Walter. **Design for Craftsmen**. Garden City, N.Y., Doubleday, 1962. 224p. illus. $5.95. LC 62-16692.

A practical guide helpful to the professional, the amateur artist, and the craftsman as well as to the homemaker, the designer, and the decorator in any field. This is a collection of visual designs taken from all ages and places and applicable to work in many craft areas. The designs are organized into three sections according to whether they originate in nature, in geometry, or simply in freeform invention. They are derived from many civilizations, from famous artists, and from the worlds of microscopic beings and the IBM computer. Design applications are illustrated in a number of black and white photographs. An excellent collection.

9. Moseley, Spencer, Pauline Johnson, and Hazel Koenig. **Crafts Design: An Illustrated Guide**. Belmont, Calif., Wadsworth, 1962. 435p. illus. $19.90. LC 61-13693.

This standard text emphasizes the importance of design in the areas of weaving, bookbinding, leather, clay, decorated textiles, mosaics, and enamelling. Two aspects of design are treated for each craft: a study of the works of master craftsmen and artists in the field, and a systematic explanation of technical processes, including step-by-step directions.

10. Rick, Frank M. **Dictionary of Discards**. New York, Avenel Books; distr. P.O. Box 642 FDR, New York, N.Y. 10022, Resourceful Research, 1952. 143p. $3.50.

The dictionary suggests uses for all types of discards. Types of waste material are listed alphabetically: alarm clocks, crankcase oil, newspapers, etc. Some of the suggested ideas and projects will be useful to teachers and students; however, many are well known or obvious. Illustrated with line drawings.

11. Sattler, Helen Roney. **Recipes for Art and Craft Materials**. New York, Lothrop, Lee and Shepard, 1973. illus. $4.50. LC 73-4950. ISBN 0-688-41557-1.

An essential work for all crafts group leaders or teachers, not to mention parents. It includes recipes for pastes, modelling materials, papier mâché, paints, and inks.

12. Weiss, Mark, comp. and ed. **The Best Things in Life Are Free: A Directory of Free Craft and Hobby Materials**. New York, Drake, 1972. 165p. $3.95pa. ISBN 0-87749-296-4.

This is a guide to free catalogs, instruction sheets, and patterns. Arrangement is by almost 50 areas: eggcraft, crewel, collecting (gold and silver, firearms, comic books, antiques, Indian relics), quilting, shellcraft, macrame, etc. Instructions on ordering are included at the front of the book. Some of the items listed are available for nominal postage and handling fees, rather than "free."

ENCYCLOPEDIC WORKS

13. **Craft Techniques in Occupational Therapy**. Washington, Government Printing Office, 1971. 496p. (Department of the Army, No. TM 8-290).

An encyclopedic introduction to various crafts used in occupational therapy, this technical manual provides information on a number of crafts. Included in the 15 chapters are art and design (including charcoal and pastels, finger painting, oils, stenciling, watercolor), ceramics, mosaics, plastics, metalwork and jewelry, weaving, macrame, braiding and hooking rugs, needlework, leather, printing, woodworking, and engines. Pages are numbered consecutively within chapters, and the looseleaf format, although of doubtful utility to libraries, makes it easy to divide for distribution.

The largest amount of space is devoted to woodworking (136 pages), with 55 pages for leather and 50 pages for ceramics. Each section provides an introduction defining the craft, sometimes with historical notes. Tools and equipment are pictured, and the function of each is described. Line drawings illustrate basic processes and techniques; the illustrations are large and of excellent quality for the purpose. The therapeutic value of each craft is defined for different types of patients. Except for these notes, there is little to indicate the actual purpose of the manual. The final chapter is a description of the therapeutic value of play for children. An excellent introduction to a wide variety of crafts.

14. Di Valentin, Louis, and Maria Di Valentin. **Practical Encyclopedia of Crafts**. New York, Sterling, 1971. 543p. illus. index. $20.00. LC 71-126844. ISBN 0-8068-5150-8.

The editors of this "encyclopedia" chose to eliminate crafts that require expensive or elaborate equipment, familiar crafts (such as sewing), and crafts that they considered fads. The result is a compendium of information on a number of traditional crafts, organized either by the materials with which the craftsman works or by areas of activities. These ten categories, arranged alphabetically, are: Art Materials (crayon craft, fresco), Clay (claywork, ceramics, mosaics, sculpture), Fabrics (batik, burlap, felt, macrame, needlecraft, tie and dye, weaving), Metal and Glass (metal crafting, enamelwork, nail sculpture, repoussage, stained glass, tin-can craft, wire craft), Natural Materials (basketry, ikebana, lapidary, scrimshaw, stone carving), Paper (papercraft, bookbinding, cardboard, coloring paper, origami, paper flowers, scissorscraft), Plastics and Leather (acrylic, beads, candles, leather, plastic foam, sculpture and collage in plastic), Print (etching and other intaglio prints, potato printing, rubbings, screen process printing, woodblock), Scrap Material (collage, corrugated carton crafts, decoupage, mask making, matchbox crafting, mobiles, musical instruments, papier mâché, scrapcraft), Wood (woodworking, dollmaking, kite making, puppets and marionnettes, and wood carving and whittling). Information is provided, within subdivisions, on the techniques and methods of making simple projects. Thus, in the section on "Claywork," under the subtopic "coil building" the reader is instructed in how to make a clay pot using the coil technique. Under "ceramics" there is a short section on history, clay bodies and the various processes associated with ceramic work (wedging, preparing the clay, forming, throwing, drying, finishing, etc.). Drawings illustrate the processes under discussion.

The authors assume no knowledge on the part of the reader, with the result that all articles are basic introductions to the craft. Some, however, are more useful than others (under "Fresco" we find out what fresco is, but there is little information here to permit us to start our own fresco). For the most part, however, basic fundamentals of each of the crafts are presented in sufficient detail and instructions are clear enough to provide the reader with a rudimentary knowledge of a particular craft. The bibliography provides further references for those who wish to pursue the topic, and the directory of suppliers will be helpful. Children and adults may find the book interesting reading; it should be an aid to teachers who need information about projects involving a number of different craft areas. Recommended for school and public libraries.

15. Hayes, Joy, and Elizabeth Russell. **Simple Homecrafts**. New York, Drake, 1973. illus. $7.95.

The 15 crafts covered here include patchwork, flowers (of both paper and fabric), and macrame. The authors' approach is to delineate the history of the craft and the materials used, and then to suggest projects (including instructions and patterns for specific items).

16. Hellegers, Louisa B., and Anne E. Kallem, comps. **Family Book of Crafts**. New York, Sterling, 1973. 576p. illus. index. $20.00. LC 72-95199. ISBN 0-8069-5250-4.

Billed as a "companion volume" to Sterling's *Practical Encyclopedia of Crafts* (see entry 14), this work provides information on over 50 crafts, with specific projects given for each. The three main divisions of the book are "The *Medium* Is the Thing," "The *Thing* Is the Thing," and "The *Process* Is the Thing." Many of the projects are the ones suggested in the corresponding book of Sterling's Little Crafts Book Series, but this encyclopedic collection will probably have more appeal than the individual books of the series, as far as teachers and group leaders are concerned.

Instructions, which are quite clear, are illustrated with line drawings and black and white photographs. The projects—and, indeed, the crafts—covered vary greatly in levels of difficulty, but this could be considered an advantage rather than a handicap, if the book is to serve teachers.

17. Ickis, Marguerite, and Reba Esh. **The Book of Arts and Crafts**. New York, Dover, 1973. 275p. illus. index. $2.00pa.

More than 1,000 projects are suggested here, for the edification of teachers, camp counselors, parents, scoutmasters, or anyone who continually needs new ideas for crafts items. The index groups crafts according to their use (for boys, for girls, for church groups, for little children, etc.). From peach-pit necklaces to carved candles to willow whistles—this book has detailed instructions that even novices can follow. In addition, there are general directions for mixing and making glues, clays, dyes, paints, and other basic materials.

18. Karlen, Tommy. **Basic Craft Techniques**. New York, Drake, 1973. 505p. illus. $7.95. LC 72-10492. ISBN 0-87749-419-3.

Provides basic information on a wide variety of crafts. Illustrations amplify the straightforward text.

19. Lindbeck, John R., and others. **Basic Crafts**. Peoria, Ill., Charles A. Bennett, 1969. 274p. illus. index. $7.12 (text ed.).

This general crafts book introduces the reader to six different craft areas: metal work, graphic arts, plastic crafts, woodcraft, leathercraft, and ceramics. It was primarily designed as a text for high school students. The instructions are clear but are more of an informative nature than a practical nature. It describes the various processes involved in each of the crafts, discussing tools used and operations necessary, but it does not give practical how-to guidance. This presumably is left up to the teacher who demonstrates in the shop. Still, it is an informative text with a vast amount of information that should benefit the student. The introductory section provides information on design principles, sketching, layout, and shop safety. The final section is devoted to simple projects in each of the crafts. Many black and white photographs, and a few in color. A good high school text, recommended for use in general craft courses and for the applied arts collection of school libraries.

20. Mattil, Edward L. **Meaning in Crafts**. 3rd ed. Englewood Cliffs, N.J., Prentice-Hall, 1971. 133p. illus. $8.50.

This book, written for adults who work with children, is intended to aid in the development of crafts programs in elementary school programs.

The author introduces the teacher to a number of different craft areas, with short descriptions of the materials used in each. For example, under modelling and sculpturing, he describes non-hardening modelling clay, common earth clay, "salt ceramic" (water, cornstarch, and salt), wire sculpture, toothpicks and soda straws, white soap, paraffin, concrete, plaster, wood, etc., with suggestions on their use and the range of their possibilities. Other chapters include descriptions of printmaking, puppets, painting, holiday activities, papier mâché, and weaving, and there is a potpourri chapter on miscellaneous craft projects. Instructions are brief, in keeping with the author's idea of allowing the child full freedom once he becomes familiar with a basic technique. Few specific projects are described, but the author does manage to make a great many suggestions for projects. Recommended for school libraries.

21. Pluckrose, Henry, ed. **The Book of Crafts**. Chicago, Regnery, 1971. $8.95.

Presents basic how-to-do-it instructions for about 30 contemporary crafts—e.g., leatherwork, needlework, coppertooling, puppetry. Advice on the proper tools and selection of materials accompanies examples and instructions for making finished works.

22. Schwartz, Alvin. **Hobbies: An Introduction to Crafts, Collections, Nature Study, and Other Life-Long Pursuits**. New York, Simon and Schuster, 1972. 345p. illus. $9.95.

Crafts, collections, nature study hobbies, science projects, and amateur communications hobbies—a selection of 25 in all—are discussed in this introductory work. Equipment and techniques are explained. Although the descriptions for some of the hobbies are detailed enough to suffice for a beginner, in most cases this book provides only an overview of the hobby's possibilities. A bibliography at the end of each chapter, however, lists sources for further study.

23. Voss, Gunther. **Reinhold Craft and Hobby Book**. New York, Van Nostrand Reinhold, 1963. 360p. illus. index. $10.95. LC 63-19223.

Mr. Voss's book is designed to introduce the home craftsman to the skills needed to work in a variety of materials. There are 20 chapters. The first three deal with the tools and materials with which the craftsman will be working, discussing wood, metal, and plastics in detail, and describing the techniques of using and caring for tools. A short glossary of terms concludes the beginning chapters. The remaining chapters, which deal with different crafts, describe the basic processes associated with each. Woodworking, block printing, metalworking, bookbinding, weaving and hand-printing fabrics, basketmaking, ceramics, lampmaking, mosaics, jewelry making, toymaking, puppetry, and electrical work are treated in separate chapters, with the emphasis on fundamental processes. Drawings illustrate tools and their use. Additional chapters provide ideas and instructions for making Christmas decorations, for outdoor sporting equipment (crossbow, boomerang, etc.), and for nature hobbies (an aquarium and a terrarium). Many project suggestions are found in each of the chapters. This practical handbook of basic processes will be of excellent utility to the home craftsman.

24. Young, Jean. **Woodstock Craftsman's Manual**. New York, Praeger, 1973. 253p. illus. $10.00. LC 76-185655.

This manual's main use will be to encourage people (and especially young people, in view of the title) to begin being craftsy. Its emphasis on creativity will stimulate readers' inspiration in such areas as batik, macrame, pottery, candlemaking, leatherworking, etc. Instructions and photographs are not always as detailed as they should be, however, so more specific beginning texts will be needed to supplement the information provided here.

25. Zarchy, Harry. **Creative Hobbies**. New York, Knopf, 1960. 299p. illus. index. $3.75.

Clear text and explanatory diagrams provide the reader with the basic procedures in nine different craft areas: stagecraft, woodcarving, lampmaking, whittling, papercraft, silkscreen printing, bookbinding, plastics, and shellcraft. Though no one will become master of any of these fields by reading Mr Zarchy's book, it does teach the fundamental procedures necessary for making a start. Some crafts are, of course, more satisfactorily treated than others, such as the chapter devoted to lampmaking. The treatment of paper, however, is very unsatisfactory, considering more up-to-date and fuller treatments in other books. The choice of hobby areas is peculiar, combining, as it does, stagecraft and lampmaking in the same book. Nevertheless, this does provide a basic introduction to each of the crafts. There is a short bibliography of each area.

26. Zechlin, Ruth. **Complete Book of Handcrafts**. 2nd ed. Newton Centre, Mass., Branford, 1968. 347p. illus. index. $8.75. LC 68-12559.

Like most crafts books that cover many topics, this one varies in the sufficiency and quality of information provided for a specific craft. In general, however, the step-by-step instructions and the illustrations furnish more than adequate guidance to the 16 crafts covered (ranging from needlework to bookbinding and mosaics).

PROJECTS BOOKS

27. Aspden, George. **Model Making in Paper, Cardboard and Metal**. New York, Van Nostrand Reinhold, 1964. 88p. illus. $7.50.

The author, who has had experience teaching at every level from junior high on up, is concerned with encouraging creative model making rather than with slavish imitation, a concern that dictates the form of this book. The models range from bulls and horses to queens, exotic fish, birds, and insects. Instructions are given for making the basic model, and measurements and diagrams are included. Full-page illustrations, some in color, show the completed model, followed by suggestions for variations and further projects. Many variations are illustrated in half-tones, color drawings, and photographs. Instructions and descriptions of tools and techniques for working with paper, cardboard, and metal are included. All the projects are imaginative and some are extremely handsome. Recommended for high school students, art teachers, and adults who want an inexpensive and satisfying hobby. The most recent book by Mr. Aspden is *One Piece of Card* (Taplinger, 1973. $6.50).

28. Choate, Judith, and Jane Green. **Scrapcraft: 50 Easy-to-Make Handicraft Projects**. Garden City, N.Y., Doubleday, 1973. 64p. (Crafts for Children Series). $4.95.

Another work designed for the very young hobbyist. Anyone whose store of ideas has been depleted will welcome this collection of simple projects. Materials include tin cans, macaroni, and other household odds and ends.

29. Clapper, Edna, and John Clapper. **Pack-O-Fun Treasury of Crafts, Gifts, and Toys**. New York, Hawthorn Books, 1971. 256p. illus. index. $4.95. LC 74-161643.

The authors describe how to make hundreds of different toys and gifts from ordinary household materials. These projects should provide pastime activities for a myriad of children. Projects include such favorites as puppets and puppet theatres, paper bag hats and animals, etc. The nine chapters include such topics as toys and novelties; scraps; wood, cork, and leather; native crafts; decorative ideas; Christmas crafts; and gifts. Most of the projects suggested are simple; small children may need adult help, but luckily parents will find the projects appealing. Recommended for public libraries. The same authors have prepared *Pack-O-Fun Craft Projects: Make It Yourself with Odds and Ends* (Hawthorn, 1972. $4.95). It lists hundreds of projects that use discards, scraps, and oddments.

30. Dank, Michael Carlton. **Scrap Craft**. New York, Dover, 1969. (Repr. of 1946 edition published under the title **Adventures in Scrap Craft**). 376p. illus. index. $2.50.

This reprint tells in great detail how to make all those things that people used to make in craft classes at summer Bible school. The 105 objects to be made are arranged under the materials they need: mop and broom handles, wood scraps, tin cans, sheet metal scraps, felt, etc. Some of these materials are no longer available (wooden cigar boxes and cheese boxes, for instance) but other materials can be substituted. Although some toys are included, most of the projects are either useful domestic objects (such as wall plaques, desk blotters, or a serving tray) or jewelry (brooches, lapel pins, necklaces, bracelets). Directions are extremely detailed, for those who must be told every step, and are supplemented by drawings and plans. The projects are primarily intended for children. Information on tools and the shop are included.

31. Duvall, Carol. **Wanna Make Something Out of It? How to Turn Household Junk into Useful Craft Projects**. Los Angeles, Calif., Nash, 1972. illus. $6.95. ISBN 0-8402-1277-1.

As the subtitle implies, this book gives directions for inexpensive projects made with discarded (or discardable) household objects.

32. Egge, Ruth Stearns. **How to Make Something from Nothing**. New York, Coward-McCann, 1968. 224p. illus. index. $5.95. LC 68-23371.

Like Ms. Duvall's book, this one has ideas for ways to use household discards to create objects of dubious aesthetic appeal, which will probably in turn be discarded. But those looking for ways to keep children occupied can't always afford to be particular about the finished project.

33. Fleming, Gerry. **Scrap Craft for Youth Groups**. New York, John Day, 1969. 216p. illus. $6.95. LC 68-24143.

This book is intended to provide inexpensive project suggestions for group leaders who need to come up with new ideas. The suggestions are arranged under various headings—puppetry, artificial flowers, egg carton fun, pictures, tin-can craft, table decorations, spools, sticks, etc. Under each heading there are lists of materials and directions for making several different projects; all are made from scrap materials, as the title indicates, and all are relatively easy to make. The large format makes the book suitable for use with a group. Projects should appeal to children up to the age of 10 or so.

34. Frankel, Lilian, and Godfrey Frankel. **Creating from Scrap**. New York, Sterling, 1962. 127p. illus. index. $2.95.

This little book offers approximately 90 projects arranged under such chapter headings as "Creating for Your Room." Included are gardening ideas, useful gadgets, things to wear, decorations, musical toys, and toys and games. All can be made by children, though a few may appeal to adults as well. Children can follow the simply written directions, all of which are accompanied by line drawings of the projects. Projects include such articles as pencil holder, nail keg stool, eggshell planter, napkin rings, book ends, bird feeder, wig, bottle band (musical), eggshell mosaics, parachute, button pictures, papier mâché bowls, etc. A few of the projects may require adult supervision for children under 10.

35. Griswold, Lester, and Kathleen Griswold. **The New Handicraft**: **Processes and Projects**. 10th ed. New York, Van Nostrand Reinhold, 1972. 462p. illus. index. $9.95; $4.95pa.

After a short introduction to the elements of design, the authors describe the basic techniques involved in 11 different crafts, including basketry; bookbinding; ceramics; fabric, wood, and paper decorating; lapidary; leather; plastics; weaving; and woodworking. Several of the chapters are preceded by a short history of the craft, and all describe, however briefly, the basic techniques, processes, materials, and tools needed for the craft. Within each chapter also are projects designed to introduce the various crafts. Some portions of this tenth edition have been revised and expanded—namely, those on lapidary, bookbinding, and basketry. The descriptions of the various crafts are of necessity brief but, within the confines of the text, fairly complete. Under "Ceramics" we find a complete description of the potter's craft from preparation of the clay to firing and kiln construction. The interested amateur should be able to satisfy his initial curiosity through these chapters though, of course, he will have to go elsewhere to gather more details about the individual crafts.

36. Hershoff, Evelyn Glanz. **It's Fun to Make Things from Scrap Materials**. New York, Dover, 1964. (Reprint of 1944 edition). 373p. illus. index. $2.25. LC 64-25093. ISBN 0-486-21251-3.

This project book is basically intended for children—or for their long-suffering mothers who must answer the question, "What can I do now?" Using simple and easily available materials such as rubber bands, thumbtacks, milk bottle tops, handkerchiefs, boxes, clothespins, old combs, etc., the author tells how to make hundreds of toys, games, decorations, gifts, musical instruments, and just odds and ends. Since this is a reprint of a 1944 edition (entitled *Scrap Fun for Everyone*), some of the materials then easily available are not around today (cheese boxes, for example). In most cases, however, other materials can be substituted.

37. Jordan, Eve. **Arts and Crafts at Home**. New York, House of Collectibles, 1973. 191p. illus. $1.95pa. ISBN 0-87637-148-9.

Designed for novices to arts and crafts, for leaders of youth groups, for art teachers, and for "rainy-day mothers," this book is indeed arts and crafts at home. There are many recipes for clay, paste, and doughs to sculpt, and most of the equipment needed is readily available at home. Chapters cover printing, paste, paint, dough (with a separate chapter on edible doughs), clay, sculpture, and mosaics. The last two chapters cover "art parties" (including a Christmas tree decorating party), and a community art fair. A mine of information, for a small price.

38. Kampmann, Lothar. **Creating with Found Objects**. New York, Van Nostrand Reinhold, 1973. 72p. illus. (Art Media Series). $5.95. LC 72-2792. ISBN 0-442-24249-2.

Like Mr. Kampmann's other titles in this series, this work emphasizes the development of a child's creativity. Among the "found" objects are stones, bottle tops, and string.

39. Laskin, Joyce N. **Arts and Crafts Activities Desk Book**. West Nyack, N.Y., Parker, 1972. 255p. illus. index. $9.95.

This book is intended for teachers of elementary and intermediate grades who need activity ideas correlated to classroom instruction in a wide variety of subjects. For example, there are activities dealing with food and nutrition, community helpers, nature study, music and dance, animal study, the human body, etc. The chapter on the community and its helpers suggests projects for building a community of milk cartons, helpers made of spools, a train made of waxed paper cartons, a fire engine of the same, a mailbox, a model airport, community helper hats, etc. Each of the sections offers experience in a wide variety of materials and techniques, and the range of activities appeals to varying degrees of ability. Visual guides are provided, along with lists of materials needed for each project and step-by-step instructions for construction. Follow-up activities and classroom management hints are suggested. Highly recommended for teachers of elementary and intermediate grades.

40. Lavaivre, Noelle. **A Book Full of Ideas**. New York, St. Martin's Press, 1973. illus. $7.50.

The projects presented here are based on a new way of looking at familiar objects. Leaves, pebbles, and other prosaic materials become the basis of creative undertakings. The color photographs and the line drawings contribute greatly to the book's attractiveness.

41. LeFevre, Gregg. **Junk Sculpture**. New York, Sterling, 1973. 48p. illus. index. (Little Craft Book Series). $2.95. LC 72-95204. ISBN 0-8069-5258-X.

Sterling's Little Craft Book Series includes some 50 books on a variety of crafts. They serve older children as well as younger ones who have parental guidance. This junk sculpture book was prepared with the aid of a class of sixth-graders, some of whose creations are pictured. Types of junk that can be used are egg cartons, fruit trays, plastic bottles, "mixed media," TV dinner trays, tin cans, etc. Some of the suggested projects are ingenious and attractive; others look a lot like junk sculpture, although it is obvious that all were prepared with enthusiasm. Instructions are clear, and methods of mounting and hanging the projects are indicated.

42. Musselman, Virginia W. **Learning About Nature Through Crafts**. Harrisburg, Pa., Stackpole Books, 1969. illus. index. $3.95. LC 78-85646.

After an introduction to tools, supplies, and equipment, this book is divided into seven parts according to the natural materials used in constructing the projects. Thus, there are sections on tree trimmings, seeds, ferns and mosses, fruits and nuts, flowers, beach objects, and foods (for indoor projects). At the beginning of the book, over 157 crafts projects are indexed. Each section, however, offers much more than the projects; for example, the section on tree trimmings provides a nature lesson on trees and their identification and categorization. The projects suggested after this informative "lesson" are all made from materials obtained from trees. Each of the sections follows this same general outline. The information provided on nature is excellent, and the approach, relating crafts and nature study, is highly recommended. Suitable for scout troops and other nature-oriented children's organizations. A list of nature books, magazines, and organizations is appended.

43. Nickell, Molli. **This Is Baker's Clay: A New Sculpture/Craft Medium**. New York, Drake, 1973. illus. $7.95. LC 73-5550. ISBN 0-87749-525-4.

Devoted to the use, possibilities, and techniques of baker's clay.

44. **Painting, Printing, and Modeling**. New York, Franklin Watts, 1972. 169p. illus. (Color Crafts Series). $5.95.

The fifth book in the Color Crafts Series. Designed for children in grades 2 through 7, this book has four main sections: painting and drawing, modeling, mosaics, and printing and engraving. Directions, which are clearly presented, are augmented by brightly colored drawings and photographs. The projects use such media as wax crayons, poster paints, india ink, and modeling clay; they are appealing but simple enough for beginners.

45. Portchmouth, John. **Creative Crafts for Today: A Source Book of Materials and Activities**. New York, Viking, 1970. 190p. illus. index. $6.95. LC 75-86968.

Any group leader or teacher whose ideas need occasional refreshing will find inspiration among the hundreds of projects suggested here. In addition to scrap-craft projects (using tin cans, buttons, and similar around-the-house items), the suggestions in this sourcebook also cover clay, printmaking, and plaster.

46. Pownall, Glen. **Fun Crafts**. New ed. New York, Drake, 1973. illus. $3.95. LC 72-10514. ISBN 0-87749-326-X.

47. Pownall, Glen. **Simple Crafts**. New ed. New York, Drake, 1973. illus. $3.95. LC 72-10509. ISBN 0-87749-327-8.

These two new editions of Mr. Pownall's works cover the usual basic crafts. *Simple Crafts* is designed for children, while *Fun Crafts* is a manual of today's handicrafts that will appeal to adults and children alike.

48. Schwalbach, James. **Fun-Time Crafts**. Chicago, Children's Press, 1949. 32p. illus. $2.25. ISBN 0-516-03211-9.

Not so much a how-to book as a what-to-do-with book. The author describes a number of materials (dough clay, gesso, finger paints, paste) that can be simply made. There are suggestions for making whistles, kites, paper-bag masks, junk jewelry, purses, party decorations, tops, Christmas tree decorations, etc. Colorfully illustrated but with few step-by-step directions. Most of the projects, however, are simple and the illustrations suffice. Ages 8 to 11.

49. Stribling, Mary Lou. **Art from Found Materials Discarded and Natural**. New York, Crown, 1970. 244p. illus. index. $7.95; $3.95pa.

Among the found materials used by the author are threads, fibers, feathers; fabrics and paper; scrap metal and tin cans; old bottles and plastic discards; stones, bones, seeds, lava rocks, and other natural materials. Also used are more common materials like clay, plaster, and papier mâché. From these and many other materials the author proves her own ability to fashion artistic objects from common throwaways. After a chapter called "Art: Found and Refound," in which the author defines the term "found art" and discusses its potential for the artist/craftsman, she divides her work into chapters dealing with the various materials from which the artist is to create. There are many examples of finished products, plus instructions and suggestions for working with each kind of material. The range of the author's activities is especially appealing and should make the book of particular interest to housewives with an artistic bent as well as to practicing artists who want to widen their own activities. All illustrations are black and white (except the frontispiece), but this does not seriously detract from the book and it does keep the price within reason. A temperature equivalent chart of ceramic cones is included, as well as a list of suppliers, a bibliography, and a glossary of terms. An excellent book for all would-be artists. Highly recommended for all public libraries.

50. Sunset Editorial Staff. **Sculpture with Simple Materials**. Menlo Park, Calif., Lane Books, 1972. 96p. illus. $1.95.

This is a how-to book devoted to construction and sculpting in three-dimensional forms in a variety of materials (including wire, papier mâché, clay, wood and stone, and odds and ends). There are also chapters on casting and treatment of the surface of three-dimensional objects. Each chapter shows the creation of relatively simple projects which the student may complete with no great effort. There is ample information on each type of construction to allow the reader to initiate his own projects. Therefore, this will be a welcome idea book for do-it-yourselfers and for teachers and craft directors with small or large charges.

51. Waltner, Willard, and Elma Waltner. **Hobbycraft for Juniors**. New York, Lantern Press, 1967. 138p. illus. $4.95.

Here is a collection of 36 projects to be made by young children (up to grade 4). Directions include a list of materials and tools, plus step-by-step instructions. Diagrams provide supplementary help, and photographs of finished projects accompany the text. Projects include gift items, puzzles, decorative objects, jewelry, toys, and others. This book would be suitable for work with groups and for classroom activity ideas.

52. Waltner, Willard, and Elma Waltner. **The New Hobbycraft Book**. New
York, Lantern Press, 1963. 144p. illus. $5.60.

In this book the Waltners describe how to make a number of objects in
a variety of categories (including mini-games, fishing lures, periscope, bank,
bookends, circus wagon, wastebasket, Indian moccasins, popcorn tree, etc.).
All are for children, and the language of the text is simple enough that (with
some help from older brothers and sisters) any child from the fourth grade up
should be able to make at least some of the projects. Some are science-
oriented, some involve origami, and others are games and toys. At any rate,
the book provides a wide variety of things to do and to make. Recommended
for elementary school libraries.

53. Waltner, Willard, and Elma Waltner. **A New Look at Old Crafts**. New
York, Lantern Press, 1971. 142p. illus. $5.60. LC 70-143700.

A compilation of some 20 projects, each using a different craft
technique. Seven of the projects are reprinted from such periodicals as *Boy's
Life* or *Twelve/Fifteen* (a Methodist Publishing House journal). Projects
include a batik wall hanging, apple-head dolls, chessmen made from nuts and
bolts, bead sculpture pictures, and a "patto-rama multiscope," which is a
kaleidoscope—by far the most interesting of the suggestions. Instructions for
most of the techniques can be found in greater detail in books devoted
exclusively to one craft.

54. Waltner, Willard, and Elma Waltner. **Wonders of Hobbycraft**. New
York, Lantern Press, 1962. 144p. illus. $5.60.

In this book the Waltners provide instructions for making 26 different
projects which should appeal to children up to age 12. Projects include a
letter holder, mini-kites, bookbinding, carving, trays, bird-feeder, sundial,
planter, dolls, and drums. The projects involve a number of crafts, including
woodworking, metal forming, repoussage, upholstering, and several others.
Recommended to crafts groups in clubs, and to school and public libraries.

55. Waltner, Willard, and Elma Waltner. **Year Round Hobbycraft**. New
York, Lantern Press, 1968. 144p. illus. $4.95. LC 68-23984.

This children's book is organized about the 12 months of the year.
After a brief introduction to the month and how it was named, including a
bit of lore about the month, the authors give two projects for each month.
Projects are intended to be appropriate to the month or season, but they are
not in any sense restricted to the time of the year. In addition to
how-to-make-it articles, the authors also suggest games and tell what to do on
days when children can't think of something for themselves. Projects and

games are all simple to construct, and the simple style of the text makes the book appropriate for elementary school children up to grade 6. Photographs of projects are included and directions are supplemented by illustrative diagrams and drawings.

56. Weiss, Harvey. **The Gadget Book**. New York, Crowell, 1971. 60p. illus. $4.50. LC 70-132307. ISBN 0-690-32124-4.

This little book should appeal to any gadget-minded child from 10 to 14. Mr. Weiss tells how to construct 24 useful or worthless gadgets that remind one of Rube Goldberg. Here we have a sunbeam alarm clock (the sun is focused through a magnifying glass onto a candle that supports a board holding marbles; as the candle softens, the marbles are released and fall onto a bell); a spool cannon; a monorail system (for sending messages, deliveries, or people); games; a burglar alarm; a flashlight; a block and tackle; and many other fascinating workable gadgets. Unless kids have changed, this should have wide appeal. But maybe the fun was in thinking them up yourself. Recommended for public libraries.

57. **Wire, Wood, and Cork**. New York, Franklin Watts, 1972. 171p. illus. (Color Crafts Series). $5.95.

As in most of the books in this series, the projects are graduated from simplest to most complex. Children in grades 2 through 7 can follow the step-by-step instructions and drawings on their own (although the very youngest may need adult supervision). The 70 projects range from toothpick towers to jewelry.

58. Wirtenberg, Patricia Z. **All-Around-the-House Art and Craft Book**. Boston, Houghton Mifflin, 1968. 103p. illus. $5.95. LC 68-28058.

Wall hangings, pictures, and sculpture are the usual products of the undertakings suggested here. The book is divided by location of the material used ("From the Kitchen," "From the Laundry," "From the Yard," etc.). Some of the end results are of doubtful utility or aesthetic appeal, but beauty is probably in the eye of the creator. At any rate, there are enough worthwhile suggestions for techniques (helpfully illustrated with numerous black and white photos) to warrant an expenditure of $5.95.

59. Wiseman, Ann. **Making Things: The Hand Book of Creative Discoveries**. Boston, Little, Brown, 1973. 159p. illus. $6.95; $3.95pa.

Another useful book of projects from inexpensive or salvageable materials. This one, attractively hand-lettered, gives directions and diagrams for over 100 items—some decorative, some utilitarian. Bibliography. Recommended for teachers, crafts directors, or harassed parents during the rainy season.

FOLK CRAFTS

60. D'Amato, Janet, and Alex D'Amato. **American Indian Craft Inspirations**. New York, M. Evans; distr. Philadelphia, Lippincott, 1972. 224p. illus. $7.95.

An ideal guide for adapting Indian crafts to today's needs. The authors first describe Indian methods and designs for each project, then give detailed instructions for making beaded jewelry; jewelry from metal, bone, and seed; leather items; wall decorations; and sand paintings. In view of the recent resurgence of interest in Indian crafts, this should be an essential work for both amateur and experienced craftsmen.

61. Eaton, Allen H. **Handicrafts of the Southern Highlands**. New York, Russell Sage Foundation, 1937; repr. New York, Dover, 1973. 370p. illus. index. $5.00pa. LC 72-77661. ISBN 0-486-22211-X.

This reprint of a study of mountain handicrafts is divided into three main parts: the handicrafts of pioneer days, their revival and present-day (1937) use, and the rural handicraft movement. The second of these parts is the largest, with chapters on spinning and weaving, quilting, native dyes, furniture, baskets, whittling and woodcarving, dolls and toys, musical instruments, pottery, etc. It is not a how-to book, but it presents a worthwhile historical study of native crafts. A preface by Ralph Rinzler and an introduction by Rayna Green have been added to the Dover edition.

62. Fisher, Leonard Everett. **The Homemakers**. New York, Franklin Watts, 1973. 48p. illus. (Colonial Americans). $3.95. LC 73-5692. ISBN 0-531-01047-3.

Those interested in old-time techniques will welcome this book. It describes the Colonial techniques used in making cider, brooms, candles, and soap.

63. **The Foxfire Book: Hog Dressing, Log Cabin Building, Mountain Crafts and Foods, Planting by the Signs, Snake Lore, Hunting Tales, Faith Healing, Moonshining, and Other Affairs of Plain Living**. Garden City, N.Y., Doubleday, 1972. 384p. illus. $8.95; $3.50pa. LC 70-163087.

This treasure-trove of old-time crafts is a collection of material from *Foxfire* magazine, prepared by high school students in Georgia. It covers all the topics mentioned in the subtitle, and then some. Articles were prepared from tape-recorded interviews with Southern Appalachian folk. An excellent compendium that reminds us how things were done and why. The sequel to *Foxfire* is *Foxfire 2* (Doubleday, 1973. $10.00; $4.50pa.), with all new material. Both books are highly recommended.

64. Hunt, Ben. **Ben Hunt's Big Indiancraft Book**. New York, Bruce, 1969. 187p. illus. index. $7.95.

Compiled from Ben Hunt's *Indian and Camp Handicraft* and *Indiancraft*, this book is especially suitable for scout troops. It will also be useful for anyone who wishes to know something about the craft techniques practiced by the Indians. There are chapters on tools and equipment, Indian clothing, Indian design and decoration, headdresses and necklaces, Indian ceremonies, and hunting, war, and games. Additional chapters describe how to make equipment used by Northern Indians, crafts practiced by Indian women, musical instruments, and work equipment. Because of the wide scope of the book, treatment of various subjects is of necessity limited, but drawings and photographs in most cases are sufficient if an experienced craftsman is available for consultation. An excellent book, as are most of Ben Hunt's books. His most recent one is *The Complete How-to Book of Indiancraft* (Collier, 1973. $2.95pa.).

65. Hunt, W. Ben, and J. F. (Buck) Burshear. **American Indian Beadwork**. Beverly Hills, Calif., Bruce, 1951; repr. New York, Collier, 1971. 63p. illus. $3.95. LC 75-185636.

This book, according to the authors, is not an exhaustive study of design and methods, but a handicraft guide for those interested in the fundamentals of construction and ideas for design. In the first of its three sections the authors give a short history of Indian beadwork and describe the methods by which the Indians create their bead objects. The second section illustrates in black and white photographs the types of objects made using beadwork. Section three provides 14 full-page color plates showing the bead design of objects from various tribes. Excellent for anyone who wants to attempt to make authentic-looking Indian bead objects. A similar work, but one intended primarily for children, is Robert Hofsinde's *Indian Beadwork* (Morrow, 1958. $3.78).

66. Kinney, Jean, and Cle Kinney. **21 Kinds of American Folk Art and How to Make Each One**. New York, Atheneum, 1972. 121p. illus. $6.95.

In each section of this book the author describes a particular type of craft activity. Whether all would be considered "folk art" is problematic. Among the activities described are Eskimo carvings, pottery, basketry, American woodcarving, dolls, rugmaking, stencil work, glass painting, scrimshaw, and many others. After describing each of these folk activities the author suggests a particular project for the reader. Directions are general, for the most part, leaving much to the potential craftsman, but the projects are simple and easily made. This might be an interesting book for use with social studies groups in the lower grades. In most cases the information about the craft is little more than a description of the form plus some historical notes. Photographs (in black and white) are quite good. An older work, and one with a more historical approach, is Betsey B. Creekmore's *Traditional American Crafts* (Hearthside, 1968. $10.00. LC 68-8517).

67. Miller, Marjorie. **Indian Art and Crafts**. Los Angeles, Nash, 1972. 118p. illus. $2.45pa.

A how-to guide for American Indian craft. The author explains the processes and describes the tools used by Southwestern Indians in their craftwork. Included among the crafts described are silver work, dolls, rugs, and pottery. The author describes the methods that Indians use in making many objects, always in such a way that the reader, by using the same method, may achieve the same result. The text is interestingly written, and details of the various crafts seem authentic.

68. Newsome, Arden J. **Crafts and Toys from Around the World**. New York, Messner, 1972. 95p. illus. $5.75. LC 78-180532. ISBN 0-671-32489-6.

These 35 toys, games, and decorations from all over the world are intended for young readers (under 10 or 11). The author begins with an introduction describing the elementary skills the child will use in making the projects. Instructions are then given for projects, arranged by country. Included among these are such favorites as tangram (Chinese), Easter eggs (Czech), a May basket (England), puppets (Italian), etc. Illustrated by line drawings. A list of suppliers is included.

69. Slayton, Mariette Paine. **Early American Decorating Techniques: Step-by-Step Directions for Mastering Traditional Crafts**. New York, Macmillan, 1972. 244p. $12.95.

Craftsmen interested in authentic techniques and patterns will find this work essential. There are 27 full-size patterns of Colonial designs, to be applied on rockers, mirrors, etc. Directions are clear and concise for stencilling (on tin, wood, or velvet), lace-edge painting, and the use of gold leaf. The author, an artist, is a member of the Historical Society of Early American Decoration. Lists of equipment and suppliers, plus a bibliography, are appended.

70. Tanner, Clara Lee. **Southwest Indian Craft Arts**. Tucson, University of Arizona Press, 1968. 206p. illus. bibliog. index. $15.00. LC 66-24299.

Such prominent Indian crafts as pottery, jewelry, and textiles are covered here, with photographs (some in color) and drawings to augment the text. The author discusses the current status of these and less important crafts. Appended is a bibliography of standard works in the field. A newly announced work is Marian Harvey's *Crafts of Mexico* (Macmillan, 1973. $12.95).

71. Waltner, Willard, and Elma Waltner. **Hobbycraft Around the World**. New York, Lantern Press, 1966. 143p. illus. $4.95. LC 66-11074.

Here the Waltners provide instructions for making a number of projects on national themes. There are 27 projects in all, ranging from lace doilies to Japanese scroll paintings. In addition to directions, and the step-by-step photographs, there is an introduction to each project with historical notes on the craft or principle involved. Instructions are extremely clear and the projects themselves range from simple objects with aesthetic appeal (a popcorn mosaic) to objects that will offer some challenge to the creator. There are game projects, toymaking projects, jewelry, printing, kites, musical instruments, and many more. This represents a good selection with wide appeal to children in grades 3 to 6.

GIFTS AND HOLIDAY DECORATIONS

72. Carlis, John. **How to Make Your Own Greeting Cards**. New York, Watson-Guptill, 1968. 142p. illus. index. $8.95. ISBN 0-8230-2425-3.

This book for all ages tells how to get ideas for and how to make greeting cards and cards for special occasions. Techniques used in making cards include offset tracing, rubbings, blot prints, stamped prints, linocuts, woodcuts, monotypes, etching, stencil, silk screen, light printing, gelatin prints, tempera batik, and collage. Technical information for all types is included, with line drawings that illustrate details. There are numerous photos of both simple and sophisticated cards. An excellent comprehensive text for people of varying talents and imagination. This general text with wide appeal is recommended for public libraries.

73. Creekmore, Betsey B. **Making Gifts from Oddments and Outdoor Materials**. New York, Hearthside, 1970. 224p. illus. index. $7.95. LC 78-113260.

Here is a gift-making book for adults. Ms. Creekmore abandons the popsicle sticks and old spools and leads the reader into making a variety of objects that are decorative and highly artistic. At the same time the home artist can learn a great deal about nature. There are projects for dried and cured flowers, berries and foliage, grass flowers, pine cones, shucks and a variety of other natural materials. She tells how to make topiary plants, holiday wreaths, and other decorations. In addition, there is a chapter on herbs and seasonings blended at home for gifts, scented gifts (sachets, pomanders), and candle crafts. The gift ideas cover a variety of different craft areas, so the author describes how to use one's talents in a number of different areas. More photographs would have been welcome, though the one color section serves quite well to show the quality of the author's work. An excellent book with excellent ideas. The appendix lists sources of supply and provides a table of ways to dry and preserve various types of flowers and foliage.

74. Hautzig, Esther. **Let's Make More Presents: Easy and Inexpensive Gifts for Every Occasion**. New York, Macmillan, 1973. 150p. illus. $5.95.

Most of the gifts suggested can be made for under a dollar. Children can easily follow the directions, and the finished products are actually useful and good-looking.

75. Kenneway, Eric. **Making Pop-Up Greeting Cards**. New York, Drake, 1973. $3.95. LC 72-11266. ISBN 0-87749-437-1.

The cards suggested use simple materials and equipment (paper, ruler, crayons, scissors, etc.) and are designed so that even beginners can follow the instructions.

76. Lewis, Felicity. **How to Make Presents from Odds and Ends**. New York, Van Nostrand Reinhold. 64p. illus. $3.95.

Another book showing ways to get the children to use up your otherwise discardable household items. The finished products can then be presented as gifts.

77. Logan, Elizabeth. **Scrap Craft: Ideas for Holidays and Parties**. New York, Scribner's, 1973. 224p. illus. $12.50. LC 72-7730. ISBN 0-684-13206-0.

Holidays throughout the year are covered, with a total of 33 child-oriented projects. Materials are the usual odds and ends: tin cans, spools, string, wire, scraps of material. Full-size patterns are included where necessary. Good source for elementary school teachers.

78. McCann, Karen Carlson, with Sue T. Garmon. **Party and Holiday Decorations You Can Make**. Garden City, N.Y., Doubleday, 1970. 94p. illus. index. $4.95.

This book tells the reader what to make and how to make it, offering suggestions for favors, centerpieces, and decorations of all sorts for special and not-so-special occasions. All projects use inexpensive materials and require only a little effort and a certain amount of imagination. The directions include simple line drawings, and there are a few photographs. The same authors prepared *Creative Home Decorations You Can Make* (Doubleday, 1968), which provides terse instructions on making centerpieces, papier mâché items, kitchen brighteners, etc. A more recent title that provides a sale-oriented approach to home and decorative crafts is Dorothea S. Britton's *The Complete Book of Bazaars* (Coward, McCann and Geoghegan, 1973. $7.95).

79. Metcalfe, Edna, comp. **The Trees of Christmas**. Nashville, Abingdon Press, 1969. 188p. illus. index. $7.95. LC 73-79158. ISBN 0-687-42590-5.

Beautiful traditional tree decorations are pictured and explained here, with a short history of the particular tradition and directions for making the ornaments. Many of the trees pictured are foreign, but five American approaches to tree-trimming are also given. An excellent book for the careful craftsman who loves Christmas.

80. Purdy, Susan. **Holiday Cards for You to Make**. Philadelphia, Lippincott, 1967. 64p. illus. index. $4.69.

This little book, primarily intended for children or their teachers, tells how to make special occasion cards using a number of techniques—transfer prints, potato prints, linoleum prints, roller prints, stencil, and silk screen. In addition, there are original ideas for cards, such as pressed flower cards, pop-up cards, jigsaw cards, etc., and a special section on making envelopes. The book is colorfully designed and should be very appealing to children. Recommended for primary grades.

81. Waltner, Willard, and Elma Waltner. **Holiday Hobbycraft**. New York, Lantern Press, 1964. 142p. illus. $5.60. LC 64-10341.

As the title suggests, this is a collection of specific projects, using a variety of techniques, arranged chronologically by holiday (a cardboard log cabin for Lincoln's Birthday, a bleach-bottle piggy bank for St. Patrick's day, a Purim rattle, four Easter projects, etc., through "Santa's Goodie Sleigh"). Numerous photographs, line drawings, and patterns amplify the instructions. Many of the projects have been reprinted from the crafts sections of various young people's periodicals.

BEADS

82. La Croix, Grethe. **Beads Plus Macrame: Applying Knotting Techniques to Beadcraft**. New York, Sterling, 1971. 48p. illus. index. (Little Craft Book Series). $2.95.

This book deals with more aspects of beadcraft than the title implies: bead collages, glued beads, sewn beads, and even pinned beads are discussed. A rather long section treats the use of beads with embroidery. The macrame section shows how to make a number of relatively simple beaded macrame pieces—purses, picture frames, jewelry, belts, and bottle covers. Instructions are simple and clear, supplemented by occasional step-by-step illustrations.

83. La Croix, Grethe. **Creating with Beads**. New York, Sterling, 1969. 48p. illus. index. (Little Craft Book Series). $2.95. LC 69-19487. ISBN 0-8069-5124-9.

The author offers step-by-step diagrams for a variety of beading techniques. Photographs, some in color, show finished projects. In addition, this book contains a section on embroidering with beads, with photos of some fine examples of this age-old craft. Ample, simple instructions make this of particular use to the beginner, though the photographs may also inspire those with some experience in beadwork. A work devoted exclusively to embroidering with beads is Natalie Gilstoff's *Fashion Bead Embroidery* (Branford, 1971. $6.50).

84. Nathanson, Virginia. **The Art of Making Bead Flowers and Bouquets**. New York, Hearthside, 1967. illus. index. $8.95. LC 67-27169.

This book is devoted entirely to the Victorian art of bead flower making. Illustrations and instructions are clear and easily understood, and directions for making a great many different flowers are included. One of the most comprehensive books dealing with beadcraft. Highly recommended.

85. Nathanson, Virginia. **New Patterns for Bead Flowers and Decorations**. New York, Hearthside, 1969. 210p. illus. index. $8.95. LC 73-92495. ISBN 0-8208-0333-2.

This sequel to Ms. Nathanson's earlier work, *The Art of Making Bead Flowers and Bouquets*, introduces the reader to a fresh garden of flowers including anthurium, aster, bittersweet, calla lily, peony, and others. She begins, however, with a step-by-step description of the fundamental techniques of beadwork. Moreover, additional chapters treat miniature flowers, potted plants (including an unusual Ming tree and a double-ball topiary). Two final chapters provide instructions for making Christmas ornaments and bead flowers for the bride. A comprehensive text that will be especially appealing to those who know Ms. Nathanson's earlier work.

86. Nathanson, Virginia. **The Pearl and Bead Boutique Book**. New York, Hearthside, 1972. 190p. illus. index. $8.95. LC 71-163560.

Although this work overlaps somewhat with Ms. Nathanson's earlier works, it nevertheless provides a wide variety of bead projects. As usual, her instructions are easy to follow, and the illustrations consist of both photographs and line drawings.

87. Osterland, Virginia. **Bouquests from Beads**. New York, Scribner's, 1971. illus. index. $12.50. LC 78-143938.

Full instructions and step by step diagrams are provided for 44 different bead flowers, arranged alphabetically by name. Beautiful color photographs illustrate a number of finished examples. Besides the directions for making flowers, the author also provides full explanation of arrangement principles, with illustrations of bead flower arrangements. A final chapter deals with special ideas for Christmas. This makes an excellent supplement to Ms. Nathanson's works. It is highly recommended for public libraries, in spite of the somewhat steep price.

88. Wasley, Ruth, and Edith Harris. **Bead Design: A Comprehensive Course for Beginner and Experienced Craftsmen**. New York, Crown, 1970. 216p. illus. index. $7.95; $3.95pa. LC 74-93401.

Like Ms. Nathanson's works, this one deals with bead flowers; thus, it is not the "comprehensive course" indicated in the subtitle. As a text for making bead flowers, however, it is successful: directions and illustrations are clear and easy to follow. Useful both for beginners (including children, with adult guidance) and for experienced beadworkers.

89. White, Mary. **How to Do Bead Work**. Doubleday Page and Company, 1904; repr. New York, Dover, 1972. 142p. illus. $1.75pa. LC 76-183981. ISBN 0-486-20697-1.

Although the quality of the illustrations in this book is poor, the author describes how to make several types of bead objects of traditional design, using traditional methods. She discusses strung beads, how to do bead weaving on a loom, diagonal weaving without a loom, beadwork on canvas, and primitive beadwork. Separate chapters describe methods of making candle shades and knotted and crocheted bags and purses of late Victorian design. A final chapter describes beadwork that a child might be able to do. The directions are complete. Though the reader may possibly have to adapt the directions for modern materials, it is consoling to note that some things have changed very little. It is indeed unfortunate that the illustrations are not clearer and more attractive, since they might be more enticing to prospective beadworkers. Recommended for public libraries as a supplementary text. Herder and Herder's Play Craft Series includes H. Hornung's *Bead Necklaces* (1969, $1.25pa.), with a number of projects suitable for children.

CANDLES

90. Carey, Mary. **Step-by-Step Candlemaking**. New York, Golden Press, 1972. 64p. illus. $4.95.

Specifically designed for the beginner, this work concentrates on basic equipment and supplies, rules for safety, and the casting of simple candles. Projects are explained in detail, and numerous photographs reinforce the instructions.

91. Chisholm, K. Lomneth. **The Candlemaker's Primer**. New York, Dutton, 1973. illus. $7.95. ISBN 0-525-07308-6.

Primarily for the beginner, as the title would indicate, this guide discusses dipped as well as molded candles. Experienced candlemakers may find a few helpful hints. Some readers may be disconcerted, however, by the fact that the information presented and the style of writing do not seem consistently addressed to a single audience.

92. Collins, Paul. **Introducing Candlemaking**. New York, Taplinger, 1972. 100p. illus. $6.95. LC 72-563. ISBN 0-8008-4199-9.

Candlemaking is an art whose practitioners quickly progress from rank beginner to producer of marketable—or at least admirable—products. This book, with a simplified, step-by-step text, introduces the candlemaker to all sorts of candles: round, cone-shaped, striped, dipped, and branched. Molds used vary from discarded bottles to paper containers. A scheduled addition to the family of candle books is *Tall Book of Candle Crafting*, by Gary Guy (Sterling, 1973. $7.95).

93. Heller, Beatrice. **Introduction to Candle Making: A Step-by-Step Guide**. Los Angeles, Nash, 1972. 118p. illus. index. $2.45pa. ISBN 0-8402-8053-X.

In the first chapter the author describes both basic and optional equipment used by the candlemaker. Chapter two offers the reader information about various materials used in candlemaking: paraffin wax, steric acid, polyethylene, microcrystalline, beeswax, wicks, dyes, molds, and others. Approximate prices of equipment and materials are included with their descriptions, where appropriate. Chapter three details the procedure for making one's first candle; the text is accompanied by step-by-step drawings. The last part of this chapter describes various methods of decorating the first attempt—including short descriptions of appliques, carving, wax crayon decorating, painting, whipped wax, and cutouts. The author describes other types of candles: striped, mottled, marbled, colorburst, chunk, ice, and many others. The final chapter suggests a variety of containers and holders for candles, some of which are intimate parts of the candle itself—ice cream sundae, beer, and coke candles. A glossary and a list of suppliers are appended. Although there are drawings, there are no photographs, so the final product is left up to the reader's imagination. The information here is sufficiently detailed for the beginner, and the range is wide enough to provide suggestions for those already involved with candles. Recommended.

94. Koeppel, Gary. **Sculptured Sandcast Candles**. Philadelphia, Chilton, 1972. 124p. illus. index. $9.95; $4.95pa. ISBN 0-8019-5748-6.

Written by the man who originated the idea of sandcast candles, this book describes in detail the techniques that the author uses to make these original creations. Chapters 1 through 6 describe the equipment and supplies needed for the home studio, telling how to make the mold, cast the wax, prepare the cast, and sculpt the candles. Chapters 7 through 9 give instructions for making and sculpting specific sandcasts: sandcast driftwood, and sandcast shell candles. Chapters 10 and 11 discuss the candle refills that will make these candles permanent, and tell how to care for the candles so that they last. Types of candleholders are illustrated, and the final chapter gives a list of suppliers. The black and white photos throughout the book show techniques that the author uses, and there are a number of color photos of the finished product. An excellent book on a deceptively simple craft. The author's hints will help the do-it-yourself enthusiast avoid many pitfalls.

95. Leinwoll, Stanley. **Candles and Candlecrafting**. New York, Scribner's, 1973. 144p. illus. $8.95; $4.95pa. LC 72-11143. ISBN 0-684-13187-0.

Leading the beginner as far as he can go as an amateur candlemaker, this new book discusses how to make dipped, rolled, and molded candles. Decoration of candles is also included.

96. Monroe, Ruth. **Kitchen Candlecrafting**. New York, A. S. Barnes, 1970. 172p. illus. index. $6.95. LC 72-85193. ISBN 0-498-06853-6.

The author gives the essential information on molds and materials and proceeds to a step-by-step description of the candlemaking process. This is followed by an accounting of various decorating techniques that make distinctive candles. Three sections of instructions for specific types of candles are entitled "Any-Time Candles," "Special Occasion Candles," and "Holiday Candles." The final chapter is devoted to two success stories about people who have become professional candlemakers. A list of suppliers is appended, and there is a description of the candlemakers' organization, the International Guild of Candle Artisans. A rather good adult treatment of the subject. Ms. Monroe's newest candle book was scheduled for September 1973 publication: *Candle Decorating* (A. S. Barnes, $8.95).

97. Newman, Thelma R. **Creative Candlemaking**. New York, Crown, 1972. 212p. illus. bibliog. index. $7.95; $3.95pa. LC 77-185071.

Like the author's other crafts books, this one has become a required classic for its area. Besides detailed and sound instructions—which will be helpful at all levels of candlemaking—Ms. Newman has included a history of the art, a list of suppliers, and a special section that deals with problems and solutions.

98. Newsome, Arden J. **Candles: A Step-by-Step Guide to Creative Candlemaking**. New York, Lancer Books, 1972. 160p. illus. $1.95pa.

This paperback offers a fairly comprehensive introduction to the candlemaker's craft. Beginning with a chapter on materials and supplies, the author provides valuable up-to-date information on the various additives, colors, scents, and molds that have become available to the home candlemaker in the past few years. Following this is a detailed, 16-step outline. Succeeding chapters give instructions for making novelty candles and holiday candles, with details on how to decorate them. There is a separate chapter on container candles (such as sandcast, shellcast, balloon cast), plus one that deals with holders and bases. The author indicates the possibilities of producing candles on a profitable basis. A list of suppliers of equipment and materials is appended. Line drawings illustrating methods are copious, and a color section gives examples of what can be accomplished. Recommended as a basic text for those interested in the whole range of this craft.

99. Olsen, Don, and Ray Olsen. **Modern Art of Candle Creating**. New York, A. S. Barnes, 1965. 152p. illus. $7.50. ISBN 0-498-06280-5.

The Olsen brothers' book on candlemaking has been recommended by the *Last Whole Earth Catalogue* in terms that amount to saying that it is the least bad among the bad. It is laid out like most candle books: supplies and molding materials come first, with information on wax, wicks, and scent. Part two discusses methods of securing the wick cones, and part three deals with molding of four basic candles (cylinders, square, cone, and irregular), with information on decorating techniques and achieving unusual effects. Part four gives examples of and directions for making candles with a seasonal or occasional theme for holidays and special events throughout the year. A section is devoted to beeswax candles and special ways of forming these to achieve unusual effects. Though it does not include developments since 1965, it offers techniques and information as good as the information found in most books. When it first appeared, it was the only book on the subject.

100. Schutz, Walter E. **Getting Started in Candlemaking**. New York, Macmillan, 1972. 95p. illus. $2.95pa. LC 70-183410.

Another useful beginner's book, this one covers the expected ground, with especially good material on molds. It will need to be supplemented soon by a more comprehensive text, however, since there is little information about types of paraffin or about additives.

101. Shaw, Ray. **Candle Art: A Gallery of Candle Designs and How to Make Them**. New York, Morrow, 1973. 160p. illus. $8.95. LC 73-5324.

The "gallery" of the subtitle consists of 16 color plates and 56 black and white photographs of candles, with instructions for making them. Notable for suggesting the variety of designs possible in the medium of wax, this book also includes basic instructions for the tyro. A list of mail-order suppliers is appended, and there is a glossary.

102. Unger, Joan Ann. **Creative Candlecraft**. New York, Grosset and Dunlap, 1972. 94p. illus. index. $1.95pa. ISBN 0-448-01556-0.

Though not so detailed as some of the books in this section, Ms. Unger's little volume on candlecrafting basically covers the usual territory. Instruction and illustrations are sufficient for the beginner, and the information and precautions advised are well worth noting. A useful addition is the detailed description of beeswax candles, a subject which is often rather cursorily treated. Another helpful section contains questions and answers, in an attempt to catalog the various problems one can run into in candlemaking. Additional suggestions for candles and found molds make this volume a worthwhile supplement to the crafts collection.

103. Webster, William E., with Claire McMullen. **The Complete Book of Candlemaking**. Garden City, N.Y., Doubleday, 1973. 160p. illus. $8.95. LC 72-84974. ISBN 0-385-01930-0.

Highly recommended for beginners, this expansion of *Contemporary Candlemaking* was prepared by a professor of design at the Philadelphia College of Art, with the help of the staff of *Farm Journal*. Directions are easy to follow, with photographs of the various stages of production. Chapters cover ice and sand candles; molds (improvised, metal, rubber, and plaster); hurricane candles; decorated, hanging, and floating candles; and "water fantasies." The final chapters discuss marketing your wax wares and candlemaking mistakes and how to avoid them. Excellent primer for adult beginners. A new work scheduled for October 1973 publication is Eugenia (Deannie) Broun's *Candlemaking for Profit* (A. S. Barnes, $6.95).

104. Webster, William, with Claire McMullen. **Contemporary Candlemaking**. Garden City, N.Y., Doubleday, 1972. 79p. illus. $3.95. LC 72-84974. ISBN 0-385-00775-2.

In the introductory chapter the authors describe the basic materials used in candlemaking—wax and additives—and describe the standard steps in melting and preparing to pour. Subsequent chapters give instructions for making different types of candles, including ice candles and sandcast candles. Chapter four describes various improvised molds for candles, and the method of whipping wax to achieve a foam effect. Molds described here include mugs, bottles, kitchen molds, and the ubiquitous milk carton. Metal molds are described in chapter five. Other chapters describe how to make rubber molds (which enormously widens the possiblities for the craftsman) and plaster molds. Unusual possibilities using hurricane candles are described in chapter eight, and decorated candles in chapter nine. A note on supplies is appended, along with a short list of suppliers. Black and white photos illustrate the basic processes, while color photos of finished candles show beautiful and simple creations far above the usual candle book quality. These pictures may be even more valuable to the candlecrafter than are the instructions provided. Recommended for a basic collection on crafts.

DECOUPAGE

105. Harrower, Dorothy. **Decoupage: A Limitless World in Decoration**. New York, Barrow, 1958. 191p. illus. index.

Ms. Harrower was one of the first of the modern practitioners of decoupage to publish a complete description of the craft in book form. The first part of her work defines decoupage, collage, and montage; provides a history of the craft; and discusses the traditions in various cultures. In addition, she points out the basic elements of design in relation to a decoupage project, and the basic operations of cutting and pasting up. Part two, entitled "Projects in Decoupage," consists of four chapters that treat the problems related to specific objects. One chapter deals with small household accessories (trays, boxes, lamp shades, etc.), a second with furniture (chests, tables, screens), a third with pictures (in relief as well as flat), and the fourth with Easter eggs, Valentines, Christmas cards, and scrapbooks. Many of the projects here described are unique, such as the subsections on tinsel pictures and pinprick pictures. In part three the author discusses materials and where they can be found and describes the layout of the workroom. She deals with the finishing process, discussing the relative advantages or disadvantages of paints, varnishes, and lacquer and the methods of applying them. The final chapter discusses special projects on glass, as well as preparation of old and new surfaces for decoupage, bleaching, and the application of gold leaf and marbling paper. Unusual formulas and methods for achieving special colors are a unique feature of this chapter. A final distinct addition is the description of quillwork, the use of tiny strips of gold-leafed paper formed into spirals, volutes, and scrolls. A glossary of terms and a list of sources of supply are appended.

The influence of Ms. Harrower's book is evident in several of the later works on decoupage. Although the later works have surpassed her in detailed descriptions of processes and techniques, certain features remain unique in Ms. Harrower's book, and it is still recommended as a valuable and useful text. The edition published by Barrow seems to be no longer available, but an edition by the same title is available from Bonanza Press (published in 1968). It is still recommended for public libraries, especially since the number of works on decoupage is quite limited. An announced new work is Eve Harlow's *Decoupage* (Drake, 1973. $7.95), which, according to the publishers, will cover "every aspect of the subject."

106. Manning, Hiram. **Manning on Decoupage**. New York, Hearthside, 1969. 254p. illus. index. $10.00. LC 76-76154.

This book was written by a man who is acknowledged in many circles to be the master of decoupage in this country. In it the author attempts to teach the amateur what he has taught in his Boston studio and his workshops throughout the country. In his introductory chapter, Mr. Manning tells what decoupage is and how he became interested in what was becoming a lost art; and he discusses the various styles. In subsequent chapters he gives marvellously detailed instructions and hints on choosing prints, preparing surfaces, color palettes, techniques for coloring prints, sealers, cutting, gluing, varnishing, and sanding and polishing.

Additional chapters are devoted to various special forms of the art, and Mr. Manning provides solutions to problems that the decoupeur will encounter. These include chapters on covering and lining boxes, ornamentation and special effects (marbleizing surfaces, applying mother-of-pearl, gold braid, etc.), decoupage on silk, mirrors, and porcelain, and decoupage under glass. There is a chapter on gesso and the application of gold and metal leaf, and a separate chapter is devoted to papier mâché collages and their use. An especially good feature of this book is the chapter entitled "Pitfalls, Disasters and Their Cures," which both beginning and experienced decoupeurs will constantly refer to. A glossary of terms is appended, as well as a list of suppliers (which, unfortunately, consists mainly of Mr. Manning's studio). Unfortunate also is Mr. Manning's reticence with regard to naming specific products that he uses, leaving the inexperienced to either trial and error (although admittedly there is sufficient precautionary advice) or to ordering a great deal from the Manning Studio. Mr. Manning's style, however, is informal and charmingly revealing of his own personality. There are numerous photographs (both color and black and white) of beautiful articles done by the author, his mother, and his students. A sophisticated treatment for a sophisticated audience.

107. Newman, Thelma R. **Contemporary Decoupage: New Plastic Materials, New and Traditional Processes**. New York, Crown, 1972. 214p. illus. index. $7.95; $3.95pa. LC 72-84321.

The author of this book on decoupage has written several excellent books on crafts (including plastics, paper, and candlemaking). Unlike other writers on decoupage, she does not have her own decoupage studio and is not attempting to promote her own products.

Contemporary decoupage, according to the author's definition, is the combination of traditional decoupage, collage, and montage. The author would encourage a freer approach to the traditional craft/art, with emphasis definitely on the art. After a short description and definition of decoupage, the reader is enjoined to widen his concept of the art and is then instructed in the elements of design and color. In chapter three the author describes the traditional decoupage process, providing instruction in selecting the decoupage object, coloring prints, sealing, preparation of the object (including application of gesso), cutting, gluing, hand painting, and varnishing. This chapter concludes with a list of "maladies" and their remedies, a list of basic decoupage materials, a chart of varnish finishes, their components and characteristics, and a gallery of illustrations of traditional decoupage objects done by contemporary decoupeurs. Subsequent chapters provide instruction on covering and lining boxes, designing oriental and contemporary themes, decoupage on glass and acrylics (with numerous photographs of excellent finished pieces), decoupage on ceramic, metal, cork, and papier mâché, and decoupage in relief. All the above chapters provide not only illustrations of finished processes but excellent step-by-step sequential photos of basic processes. One of the unique features of this book is the chapter devoted to cut paper decoupage, with excellent photographs. A final chapter brings us to the more "exotic" forms of the decoupeur's art, with trompe l'oeil, the use of acrylics as both adhesive and coating, and polyester embodiments. An excellent bibliography is appended, along with a list of supply sources that is unequalled in any of the other books on decoupage.

This text is the most comprehensive available in terms of the techniques, processes, and materials employed. For traditionalists, however, Hiram Manning's work or Patricia Nimocks' text will be more appealing, and for the beginner either Frances Wing's or Elyse Sommer's book might be more appropriate. Ms. Harrower's book also remains an excellent sourcebook for serious decoupeurs. For the experimental artist, however, this book by Thelma Newman is highly recommended. Few fields are so fortunate as to have such a plethora of excellent books.

108. Nimocks, Patricia. **Decoupage**. New York, Scribner's, 1968. 176p. illus. index. $9.95. LC 68-11372.

The five sections of Ms. Nimock's book provide the reader with information on the history of the craft, the materials used, the preparatory work necessary, decoupage procedures, and a number of projects. In each of the sections after the history, the reader is introduced to the various aspects of the craft. The section on materials discusses adhesives, sealers, paints, scissors and knives, tweezers, brushes, and other materials and tools, with each treated under a separate subheading. The section of preparing furniture for decoupage contains divisions on woodfilling, shellac and its application, painting on a variety of surfaces (including raw wood, varnished wood, painted wood, metal surfaces, gesso, plaster, marble, stone, leather, and bisque ware). The section dealing with decoupage procedure provides information on planning, coloring prints (including information on various palettes, sealing the print, cutting, pasting, varnishing, waxing, and using special or unusual techniques—mother-of-pearl, gold and metal leaf, tortoise shell, marquetry, trompe l'oeil, and others). The final section presents a series of projects, with instructions and step-by-step drawings. These projects are arranged in order of difficulty and include a metal tray, a basket purse, a shadowbox picture, a lamp and lamp shade, panels and screen (the last two are not provided with step-by-step instructions and illustrations). In all sections except the last the author has inserted questions and answers dealing with the subject under discussion; these provide considerable information that will be handy both to beginners and to experienced decoupeurs. A list of suppliers (primarily in the Midwest and South) is appended along with a glossary of terms used in the text and a bibliography of books and articles on the subject. Many black and white photographs of excellent antique and modern pieces are used throughout. There are five color plates.

Although there are points of contention in Ms. Nimocks' book, it is an extremely workable text, written matter-of-factly, with occasional forays into history. The beginner will be able to use the text, but because of the wide scope it will be equally useful to advanced students. An interesting divergence in approach apparent between this and Mr. Manning's text make the two supplementary, though Mr. Manning's style and personal touch are sometimes preferable to Ms. Nomocks' drier text. Highly recommended.

An abbreviated edition of Ms. Nimocks' book is now available in paperback (*The Craft of Decoupage*, New York, Scribner's, 1972. 128p. $2.95pa.).

109. Nussbaumer, Henny. **Lacquer and Crackle**. New York, Sterling, 1972. 48p. illus. index. (Little Craft Book Series). $2.99. LC 72-80664. ISBN 0-8069-5200-8.

This little book will be of interest to those decoupage enthusiasts who wish to attempt a crackle surface on their cut-out, paste-up works. The author tells in simple language with ample illustrative material how to achieve this cracked lacquered surface. The text is supplemented by a number of projects for decorating wastepaper baskets, lampshades, bookends, and a variety of other objects.

110. Sommer, Elyse. **Decoupage Old and New**. New York, Watson-Guptill, 1971. 175p. illus. index. $9.95; Lancer Books, 288p. $1.95pa.

The author explores the whole range of decoupage activities. Her chapter on techniques gives instructions on coloring, thinning (of paper for gluing purposes), cutting, gluing, varnishing, sanding, and rubbing. In subsequent chapters she discusses various projects, beginning with small-scale ones such as pins, pendants, and small boxes. A separate chapter is devoted to the techniques as applied to rock decoupage. The book also contains chapters on papier mâché decoupage, three-dimensional decoupage, mosaic decoupage, ceramic decoupage, decoupage under glass, and decoupage on eggs and egg shapes. There are also chapters on larger projects, on special effects, and on decoupage and the crafts teacher. A list of sources and suppliers is provided in the appendix, and there is a bibliography of books on decoupage and related subjects. The author employs a number of auxiliary materials and methods not usually discussed in books on decoupage—there is information here on ceramics and papier mâché. Whereas more specific details may be found in such books as Ms. Wing's or Ms. Nimocks', the projects found here are extremely practical for the beginning decoupeur who may lack confidence. A practical book with simple but comprehensive instructions for the beginner. Another book available in paperback is Leslie Linsley's *Decoupage: A New Look at an Old Craft* (Doubelday, 1972. $3.95pa.).

111. Sommer, Elyse. **Designing with Cutouts: The Art of Decoupage**. New York, Lothrop, Lee and Shepard, 1973. 96p. illus. $4.25.

In this book, Ms. Sommer adapts decoupage to the skills and interests of children in grades 5 through 9. The 48 projects decorate eggshells and pop bottles, among other items, with wallpaper, stamps, gift-wrapping paper, pebbles, shells, and pressed flowers. Bibliography.

112. Wing, Frances S. **The Complete Book of Decoupage**. Rev. ed. New York, Coward-McCann, 1970. 205p. $5.95. ISBN 0-698-10071-9.

Ms. Wing is a charming writer whose classic work on decoupage gives the beginner hope and encouragement. She begins with a short history of decoupage and a number of comments on the revival of the craft in this country. Subsequent chapters treat preparatory work, coloring background and prints, cutting, designing, varnishing, and working on and under glass. In each of these chapters, Ms. Wing describes and explains basic processes and indicates her own preferences for certain materials and methods while indicating other processes as well. Her directions are explicit and detailed, imbuing the beginner with confidence from the very start.

Numerous asides on the history of various aspects of this craft are informative and interesting, while the personal comments and anecdotes strewn throughout make the text a delight to read. Though not necessarily for the beginner only, Ms. Wing's book is well designed for an introduction. Black and white photos illustrate excellent finished objects, and some line drawings demonstrate techniques. Her final chapter provides short sketches of contemporary decoupeurs. A glossary of terms and a bibliography of books and articles on decoupage and related fields are appended. There is no list of suppliers, but the text includes constant reference to products, and that should be sufficient guidance. An excellent text, highly recommended for beginners.

EGG DECORATING

113. Disney, Rosemary. **The Splendid Art of Decorating Eggs**. Great Neck, N.Y., Hearthside, 1972. 192p. illus. index. $10.00.

This book is a guide to decorating eggs in the Fabergé tradition, as well as in numerous folk traditions. It provides step-by-step directions and diagrams for cutting doors and windows, for applying hinges and latches, for inserting drawers and platforms, and for adding linings, trimming, braid, figurines, and music box movements. A number of decorating methods are explained: applique, batik, the folk method of pysanky, collage, decoupage, etching, gold leafing, painting, and lacquering. In addition, new ways to dye eggs are explained in detail. The approximately 100 projects described include a jewel box, lacquered eggs in varying cuts, gift eggs, holiday eggs, a golden egg doll, and many others. Sources of supplies are listed. The beautiful color photographs show excellent examples of egg work, including some of Fabergé's works. Highly recommended for the fastidious craftsman who wants a challenge.

Another work aimed at an adult audience is Evelyn Coskey's *Easter Eggs for Everyone*. (Nashville, Abingdon Press, 1973. 191p. illus. $6.95). It begins with Easter egg legends and customs from Europe, the Near East, and the United States. Instructions are for traditional eggs, but simplified adaptations are also suggested. After a general discussion of techniques, materials, and dyes, step-by-step directions are given, accompanied by drawings and photographs. There are suggestions for children's Easter games, and a bibliography is appended.

114. Lang, Nancy M. **Getting Started in Egg Decoration**. New York, Bruce, 1971. 86p. illus. index. $2.95. LC 78-160383.

Though it is not as comprehensive as Ms. Disney's book on egg decorating, this inexpensive text will show the novice the basic operations involved in creating decorated eggs in a variety of traditions. The first chapter provides information on tools and equipment and gives pointers on sources of eggs, on cleaning, cutting and hardening, and on protective finishes. There are also suggestions concerning hanging eggs and findings to be used as pedestals. The chapter dealing with painted eggs provides numerous ideas for paints and for achieving special effects (marble finish, porcelain finish, etc.). In this chapter also are directions for making Ukrainian pysanky eggs. The chapter on covered and jewelled eggs provides ideas for jewelry and decorative attachments, including collage and decoupage effects. Three chapters treat the creation of decorated eggs in the Fabergé tradition with elaborate decorations, filigree work, windows, and internal scenes. Ms. Lang's directions are sometimes specific, sometimes general, but this does not seem to injure the practicality of the book. It is suitable for beginners as well as advanced egg decorators, though advanced amateurs might be better served by Ms. Disney's book. Lists of suppliers are included. Nice photos in black and white and color. A newer work is Louise Riotte's *Egg Decorating* (Drake, 1973. 192p. $9.95. LC 72-10494), which emphasizes unusual decorations and innovative techniques.

115. Newall, Venetia. **An Egg at Easter: A Folklore Study**. Bloomington, Indiana University Press, 1971. 423p. illus. index. $15.00. LC 72-146724. ISBN 0-253-31942-0.

Not a crafts book, but certainly an essential work for serious egg decorators, this is a study of the history of Easter egg decorating. The photographs (most of which are in color) depict eggs of all sorts, from Fabergé's jewelled creations to the scratched and dyed eggs from the kitchen. The bibliography is impressive.

116. Newsome, Arden J. **Egg Craft**. New York, Lothrop, Lee and Shepard, 1973. 128p. illus. $4.50.

Children in grades 5 through 9 will learn how to decorate eggs with the help of the latest of Ms. Newsome's contributions to handicrafts. Basic techniques (blowing, cutting, hanging, and coloring) are presented first, with the rest of the book devoted to progressively more difficult projects. Directions are detailed, step by step, with drawings for further clarification. Ms. Newsome also displays her crafty talents in *Egg Decoration: Plain and Fancy* (Crown, 1973. Arts and Crafts Series. $2.95pa.).

GLASS

GENERAL GLASSCRAFTING

117. Anderson, Harriette. **Kiln-Fired Glass**. Philadelphia, Chilton, 1970. 185p. illus. index. (Arts and Crafts Series). $12.50. LC 77-116917. ISBN 0-8019-5540-8.

Kiln-fired glass is a comparatively new method of glassworking for the home craftsman. It is essentially the application of the potter's practices to the firing of glass blanks, which may be treated by various methods to achieve a finished, decorated piece. Ms. Anderson's book describes various techniques of molding and laminating glass to achieve new objects. There are chapters on applying colorants to the glass using techniques known to the potter for many years. There is also a chapter on silk-screen printing on glass, plus useful and essential chapters on working with glass, equipment used, and techniques of cutting. An added feature is a section on stained glass and the application of the above techniques to this special medium. Numerous photographs, some in color, accompany the text. A glossary of terms is included along with a list of suppliers and a short bibliography. This useful introduction to an interesting craft is particularly suitable for the beginner.

118. Burton, John. **Glass: Hand-Blown, Sculptured, Colored, Philosophy and Method**. Philadelphia, Chilton, 1967. 278p. illus. index. $10.00. LC 67-28894.

This book is intended for the craftsman already initiated into the mysteries of glass and for anyone who has an interest in glass, its methods, and the viewpoint of the sophisticated craftsman. The first part is primarily a memoir of a well-known glass craftsman who, through his personal reflections upon the craft, provides insight into the manner and techniques of the artisan. In the midst of his reminiscences of his life as a man with a consuming interest in glass, Mr. Burton tells the reader how things are made—an air-twist goblet or a millefiori paperweight. The second part, entitled "My Methods," describes equipment and techniques used by the writer in a variety of projects. Detailed, step-by-step instructions are given for working with the torch and blowpipe, and for making beads, goblets, cigarette holders, and other objects. Mr. Burton's personalized style will appeal to many people and the personality of the man does evolve from his writing—though his style occasionally becomes precious when he attempts to wax poetic. His manner of giving instructions, however, is "crystal clear." Like most Chilton books, this one is a welcome addition to the subject. The book is replete with photos (both black and white and color) and line drawings. Excellent examples from various periods of history are shown.

119. Eppens-Van Veen, J. H. **Colorful Glasscrafting**. New York, Sterling, 1973. 96p. illus. $6.96.

This new book shows how to use pieces of window glass and old bottles to make mosaics, lamps, mobiles, jewelry, and Christmas ornaments. Using innovative techniques, the author shows how to use color, to cut bottles, to combine materials, and to fire.

120. Kinney, Kay. **Glass Craft: Designing, Forming, Decorating**. Philadelphia, Chilton, 1962. 178p. illus. index. $7.50. LC 61-14025.

In this book Ms. Kinney examines the details and teaches the craft of working glass, as well as the kindred arts associated with it. There are chapters on tools and equipment, cutting, drilling, firing, laminating, and jeweling. The book includes sections devoted to stained glass, glazing, and enameling, and to the working of metals in conjunction with glazing. Additional information is given on such materials as bottle glass, chunk flint glass, and gold glass crushings, and there is a chapter on the various mishaps that may be encountered in working glass.

The author offers a great deal of information about glass and glassworking in all its forms, but much of the information is too brief to suffice for the beginning student. The range of treatment, however, should appeal to anyone who wants to know more about glass and to expand his range of activities. Appended are a glossary of terms and a list of suppliers. A good bibliography would have been a welcome addition for specific phases of glasscrafting.

121.   Norman, Barbara. **Engraving and Decorating Glass**. New York, McGraw-Hill, 1972. 197p. illus. index. $8.95. LC 72-1989. ISBN 0-07-047215-7.

After a short introduction on the development of glass, methods of glassmaking, and the different types of glass, the author discusses the means of embellishing glass and the criteria for choosing the proper glass to work on. She describes in detail the major techniques of engraving glass in diamond point, copper wheel, and by electric drill, and discusses the numerous ways of decorating glass—from glass pointing and gold engraving under glass to mosaics, glassforming, and glass fusing. In each installment she gives specific instructions that range from finding the subject and planning the design to polishing the finished work. She describes also the different effects that can be obtained by each method and the equipment needed. This is not a book for the awkward craftsman, since this is a craft that requires some finesse and grace with respect to both design and execution. An appendix of suppliers is included as well as a short bibliography.

A simpler method of decorating glass is described in *Painting Bottles and Glasses* (Herder and Herder, 1970. $1.25pa.), edited by Raymond German.

122.   Schuler, Frederic. **Flameworking: Glassmaking for the Craftsman**. Philadelphia, Chilton, 1968. 131p. illus. index. $12.50. LC 68-30863. ISBN 0-8019-5350-2.

In the introduction the author briefly discusses the unique qualities of glass, techniques applied in forming glass, the history of flameworking, and the properties of glass. In the following chapter, methods of forming by flameworking are described in detail, including shaping without blowing (and the various operations associated with this) and shaping by blowing. Chapter three describes the various tools and equipment and their use and includes a discussion of glass colors and the coloring of glass. Chapter four deals with design and the methods of achieving various effects—fractured surface, smooth surface, optical effects, and bubbles. The final chapter deals again with methods and techniques and the various functions of such tools as the "blowiron" and "punty," the marver, forming block, wood jack, shears, etc. The emphasis in this last chapter, however, is on the small "factory" or shop. Three appendixes deal with physical properties of glass, annealing procedures, furnaces, and suppliers of materials and tools. There are many marvelous pictures, some in color, that show the quality and appeal of the modern craftsman's products in glass. Some step-by-step photos of processes are also used. Many of the art photos, however, could have been sacrificed to allow more sequential photos showing techniques, and additional textual elaboration of techniques would have been useful. Admittedly, this is a handsome book, and it discusses many glassworking processes, however briefly. One would hesitate to suggest this book as a self-study course, without the aid of some experienced person close by, but as an authoritative text in a somewhat neglected field, it is recommended for all public libraries with applied arts collections.

Two other books that deal specifically with glassblowing are James E. Hammesfahr and Clair L. Stong's *Creative Glass Blowing* (San Francisco, W. H. Freeman, 1968. 196p. $9.00) and Harvey K. Littleton's *Art of Glass Blowing* (Van Nostrand Reinhold, 1971). The Hammesfahr and Stong book is recommended by the *Last Whole Earth Catalogue* as the best book on the subject of art glass blowing.

123.   Schuler, Frederic W., and Lilli Schuler. **Glassforming: Glassmaking for the Craftsman**. Philadelphia, Chilton, 1970. 151p. illus. index. $12.50. LC 71-335056. ISBN 0-8019-5558-0.

Mr. Schuler's second book, written in collaboration with his wife, concentrates "on those glassforming methods which involve heating and softening of the glass" but excludes flameworking and glass blowing, topics that were treated in *Flameworking* (entry 122). Beginning with an introductory chapter that describes briefly the techniques used in glassforming and the history of this ancient craft, the author informs us that he wishes to describe those techniques that the craftsman will use working alone. Subsequently Part Two, as indicated, excludes glass blowing and flameworking and concentrates on other forms of manipulating glass—i.e., by sagging, laminating, enameling, fusing, and casting. Part Three describes various pieces of equipment for firing and grinding and describes coloring agents and acid etching methods. Part Four deals with design and describes the various possibilities for design expression using the techniques described earlier. The final part is a technical discussion of glass and the process of manufacture. The fine appendixes include a description of glass properties (somewhat expanded over the description in Mr. Schuler's earlier work), a description of the annealing process, a list of references, a much expanded list of suppliers, and a bibliography. There are good photos of excellent examples of work made by the methods described in this book, including an especially nice color section. The "padding" with art pictures so evident in the earlier work is less noticeable here, and sequential photos of processes are well integrated. On the whole, this is a commendable second performance. Highly recommended for applied arts sections of public libraries.

STAINED GLASS

124. Bernstein, Jack W. **Stained-Glass Craft**. New York, Macmillan, 1973. 118p. illus. $9.95. LC 72-91258.

Introduced by Leon G. Miller's historical survey of the art of stained glass, this beginner's book proceeds to discuss the equipment and materials needed. The text is amplified by photographs (a few in color) and diagrams. Techniques are presented for making lamps, mosaics, and windows (with hints on using copper foil instead of lead). A list of suppliers is appended, and there is a short bibliography. A work announced for November 1973 publication is Claude Lips's *Art and Stained Glass* (Doubleday).

125. Divine, J. A. F., and G. Blachford. **Stained Glass Craft**. New York, Dover, 1973. (Reprint of 1940 ed.) 115p. illus. $1.50pa. ISBN 0-486-22812-6.

This reprint covers all aspects of working with stained glass: tools, cutting eccentric shapes, pulling lead, fitting glass, soldering, and cementing. Projects that utilize the techniques discussed include mobiles, pendants, panels, and pictorial windows. There are ideas for projects that children can implement, which makes the book useful for art teachers and crafts teachers as well as for the amateur craftsman.

126. Duval, Jean-Jacques. **Working with Stained Glass: Fundamental Techniques and Applications**. New York, T. Y. Crowell, 1972. 132p. illus. index. $8.95. LC 74-184975. ISBN 0-690-89706-5.

The emphasis of Mr. Duval's book is on the fundamentals of various forms of construction in leaded or traditional glass, laminated glass, slab and faceted glass, and copper foil. He deals almost exclusively with technique, not with design. After a short introduction in which he discusses the nature of stained glass work and the various types of glass, the author describes the tools and materials of the craft. Each succeeding chapter is devoted to a simple project designed to illustrate the techniques of working with a particular form or material. The longest section deals with leaded glass construction, but laminated glass and slab glass are also treated in separate chapters. The "Tiffany" or copperfoil method is described in detail. A list of major suppliers of equipment and glass is appended. For the beginner, Mr. Duval's book is both simple and complete, providing over 175 black and white photographs and sketches for step-by-step reference. As he progresses, the novice may wish to consult the Isenbergs' books for pointers on design and refinements; but this book is far more basic as an introduction.

127. Isenberg, Anita, and Seymour Isenberg. **How to Work in Stained Glass**. Philadelphia, Chilton, 1972. 237p. illus. index. $12.50. LC 70-184138. ISBN 0-8019-5638-2.

Starting with the basic question, "What is stained glass?" the authors discuss the various aspects of the material and describe the types of lead came (leading) used to hold stained glass projects together. Important information and suggestions concerning solder are provided, and the authors describe the use of glass jewels in the craft. The second part of the book is devoted to procedures, including chapters on how to cut glass and how to design a project. Part Three describes such projects as making a stained glass window, stained glass lampshades, and free-form objects. There is a section on using scrap material and a section on the copperfoil ("Tiffany") method of construction. Additional sections are devoted to painting on glass (using both fired and unfired paints), and there is a chapter on the use of stained glass as jewelry. A final chapter advises the craftsman on how to display and sell his wares and concludes with information on repair and restoration of stained glass windows. A useful bibliography is appended.

Although this is not a simple text, the beginning artisan in stained glass will benefit from a careful study of this book. There are beautiful color photos of the authors' own works as well as works by other professionals. A basic book on stained glass covering more than adequately the whole range of possible activities. The Isenbergs have also prepared *Stained Glass Lamps: Construction and Design* (scheduled for November 1973, Chilton. $12.50; $5.95pa.).

128. Judson, Walter W. **Introduction to Stained Glass: A Step-by-Step Guide**. Los Angeles, Nash, 1972. 138p. illus. index. $2.45pa. LC 72-81852. ISBN 0-8402-8051-3.

Mr. Judson represents the fourth generation of Judsons to manufacture stained glass in Los Angeles since 1897. He has delivered lectures on stained glass throughout the country, and his studio trains apprentices for work in stained glass. Beginning with a chapter on the history of stained glass, the author then introduces the traditional elements of stained glass design, while cautioning the reader about designs to be avoided. Additional chapters deal with cartooning and layout, cut and color, painting and etching, and glazing and installation of a finished window. There is also a chapter on faceted glass and one on stained glass variations (applique on stained glass and mosaics). There are project sections for making an art nouveau lampshade, a shadow box for the window, and there is a short section on baking crystal ornaments. Mr. Judson's book is authoritative, but since it is intended for the beginner it must be pointed out that it would benefit from the inclusion of more illustrations. The Duval book is actually more helpful to the beginner, but the price of Mr. Judson's book is certainly more attractive. Another paperback on the subject is John Harries' *Stained Glass* (International Publications Service, 1968. $1.00pa.).

129. Metcalf, Robert, and Gertrude Metcalf. **Making Stained Glass: A Handbook for the Amateur and the Professional**. New York, McGraw-Hill, 1972. 158p. illus. $12.95.

This comprehensive guide to the subject touches on all the processes involved in making stained glass, including material, methods, and techniques. In an introductory section the authors discuss the history and tradition of the art, as well as its contemporary applications. Well illustrated. A glossary, a list of suppliers, and a bibliography are appended. Polly Rothenberg, author of crafts books in several other areas, has prepared *Creative Stained Glass* (announced by Crown for 1973. $4.95; $2.95pa.).

130. Reyntiens, Patrick. **The Technique of Stained Glass**. New York, Watson-Guptill, 1967. 196p. illus. $15.00. ISBN 0-8230-5225-7.

This handbook covers stained glass techniques comprehensively, from planning the studio through painting, staining, plating, glazing, and fixing. It discusses the use of antique glass and commercial glass. In addition to the bibliography and index, there is also a list of suppliers.

131. Wood, Paul W. **Stained Glass Crafting**. Rev. ed. New York, Sterling, 1971. 96p. illus. $3.99. LC 67-27750. ISBN 0-8069-5094-3.

This inexpensive book introduces the craftsman to a variety of projects in stained glass, each of which will sharpen the techniques of the novice in a newly discovered medium. There are instructions for bonding stained glass panels to home windows, and for making mobiles of stained glass, a glass sandwich panel, a leaded panel for an entrance door, a room divider, a lighting fixture, etc. Each project takes the student farther into the intricacies of the craft, with step-by-step instructions. There are also chapters on faceted glass, on fused glass, and on painting and firing stained glass in various ways, as well as a section on etching flashed glass. Considering the length of the book, the coverage of the subject is fairly comprehensive, although the student may, after an initial taste, wish to consult other books for more detailed information. For the price, however, this is a good introduction to a fascinating craft.

Mr. Wood has also written *Starting with Stained Glass* for Sterling's Little Craft Book Series (1973. 48p. $2.95). There are instructions for hanging ornaments, a mobile, a leaded window medallion, a lighting fixture, a leaded glass piano, and a Tiffany-style lampshade. Preliminary material discusses tools and techniques, and there are also a brief index and a list of 15 suppliers. Brief but good introduction.

JEWELRY

132. Baxter, William T. **Jewelry, Gem Cutting, and Metalcraft**. 3rd ed. rev. and enl. New York, McGraw-Hill, 1950. 334p. illus. index. $7.95. LC 50-7176.

This is the fourteenth printing of the third edition of this popular standard text, first published in 1938. The section on metalcraft details the basic methods of working with metals and gives information on the different metals used by the craftsman. The projects described include trays, bowls, etc.

The jewelry section, closely allied to the metalcraft section, describes further metalworking processes that are applicable to the construction of jewelry items. The author discusses tools and equipment, hard soldering, stone setting, and lost wax casting. The text gives instructions for grinding, sanding, polishing, and sawing, and provides tables of gold and silver weights and hardness, of sheet metal gauges and wire sizes, and of abrasive grit sizes. In the section on stone and gem cutting, information is provided on where to find material, hardness of minerals, diamond saw cutting, cameo and intaglio stone cutting, facet cutting, polishing, and optical properties of gems. The last section provides information on methods of testing, identifying, and evaluting gems. Lists of dealers, magazines devoted to minerals and gem cutting, and books of interest are appended. A standard text on three separate but closely related crafts. Written for beginners.

133. Boulay, R. **Make Your Own Elegant Jewelry**. New York, Sterling, 1970. 48p. illus. index. (Little Craft Book Series). $2.69.

A well-illustrated little book that teaches the elementary processes needed for making jewelry. Projects require a minimum of equipment and, as the title says, some of them are rather elegant. Two works announced by Sterling for 1973 publication are Elsie B. Ginnett's *Make Your Own Rings and Things* and Carson I. Ritchie's *Organic Jewelry You Can Make* ($2.95).

134. Brynner, Irena. **Modern Jewelry: Design and Techniques**. New York, Van Nostrand Reinhold, 1968. 95p. illus. $7.95. LC 68-16023.

In the introduction the author discloses to the reader her own artistic development, using some of her own works as illustrations. The body of the text provides instruction in several techniques used by the author in making jewelry. There are sections on constructed and forged jewelry, wax modeling, working with sheet wax, texturing, building a ring, and working with wax wires. A final section shows some of the small sculptures made by the author. Step-by-step photographs of the various processes are supplemented by instructions for making various pieces of jewelry. Illustrations of other pieces of jewelry using the same techniques accompany each section. Although the illustrations are from the studio of a professional, the instructions are simple enough for the beginning student to follow. The number of techniques needed is limited, and no expensive tools are required.

135. Choate, Sharr. **Creative Gold and Silversmithing: Jewelry, Decorative Metalcraft**. New York, Crown, 1970. 298p. illus. index. $8.95.

A reasonable price for this basic handbook. Unlike most jewelry texts, this one has only one short section of photographs of finished jewelry pieces. The rest of the work is devoted to explanations and illustrations of basic operations of the jewelry craft. The author describes the whole range of operations concerned with the working of silver and gold. Photos and drawings are all well integrated with the text, and tools and all operations are described in greatest detail. The 28 chapters describe all the basic hand processes such as texturing, annealing and pickling, sawing, shaping, flat metal soldering, buffing and polishing, and more modern techniques such as electroplating and electroforming. There is an appendix of technical information as well as a bibliography of books on enamelwork, jewelry work, and metalwork. An excellent text that should be in any basic craft collection.

Another valuable text by Sharr Choate is *Creative Casting: Jewelry, Silverware, Sculpture* (Crown, 1966. 213p. illus. $6.95), which covers the basic methods of casting used by artisans in various craft areas. Especially full details pertain to casting of jewelry. The types of casting included are lost wax, replica, hollow core, sand, cuttlefish bone, and rubber mold methods. Very specific instructions make the book of particular interest to the beginner.

136. Clegg, Helen, and Mary Larom. **Jewelry Making for Fun and Profit**. New York, McKay, 1951. 162p. illus. $4.50.

An older but still interesting book on designing and making all sorts of jewelry from gold, silver, brass, and wire.

137. Davidson, Ian. **Ideas for Jewelry**. London, Batsford; New York, Watson-Guptill, 1973. 96p. illus. index. $7.95. LC 71-190511.

This book presents a number of ideas for jewelry design and construction. The author suggests using ideas from natural and man-made objects as design sources (such as bricks, rock strata, stone walls, and random line patterns). He illustrates the translation of these into three-dimensional models by using cardboard, macaroni, and other simple materials. The techniques needed to make simple jewelry such as earrings and necklaces from wire, metal rods, and tubes are illustrated, as well as those used in making more complicated sculptural forms from bar and sheet metal. Refining, texturing, and finishing jewelry are also discussed. The second part of the book covers materials and their specifications. Sources of supply are listed, and techniques such as riveting and soldering are described. A bibliography is appended. Black and white photos illustrate various techniques. Useful for the beginner.

138. Franke, Lois E., and William L. Udell. **Handwrought Jewelry**. Bloomington, Ill., McKnight and McKnight, 1962. 222p. illus. index. $9.96.

A standard text on this ancient craft. Practical information on the various aspects and techniques of the craft is provided by the informative text and the numerous photos and line drawings. There is a glossary at the beginning of the text, then three chapters are devoted to materials, supplies, and tools. Technical data are provided in tables of weight, gauges, and melting points. Numerous photos of tools help eliminate confusion. Chapter 4 discusses design aspects of jewelry making and the methods of transferring design to metals. Chapters 5 through 11 provide instructions on the techniques needed. Under cutting operations, the student learns to saw, file, and cut with pliers and snips. Under "Soldering and Annealing," he also learns to "unsolder." Other chapters in this section deal with bending and forming metals, forging, rolling and drawing, surface texturing, and polishing. The final four chapters deal with specific problems of the jeweler, such as making chains and screw fasteners, the use of stones and stone settings, and making hinges. Although it is not comprehensive (casting is not covered), this book offers excellent instructions for the mature beginning student.

139. Garrison, William E., and Merle E. Dowd. **Handcrafting Jewelry**: **Designs and Techniques**. Chicago, Regnery, 1973. 204p. illus. $12.95.

Although experienced craftsmen will be able to utilize the design ideas illustrated in the photographs of finished projects, the novice and middling craftsmen will appreciate the step-by-step directions. Basic techniques are presented through specific projects, which are of graduated complexity.

140. Gentille, Thomas. **Step-by-Step Jewelry**: **A Complete Introduction to the Craft of Jewelry**. Racine, Wisc., Western, 1968. 96p. illus. $2.50pa. LC 67-21708.

This is basically a project book that introduces the student to jewelry making. Divided into four sections, the book covers, first, types of jewelry, tools and materials, and hints on safety and the workshop. The second section deals with processes—sawing, filing, soldering, buffing, oxidizing, surface treatment, and the elements of design. The third section gives details for making 10 projects of graduated difficulty and illustrates the various techniques described earlier. The fourth section introduces the student to advanced techniques of the jeweler's craft—forging, enamelling, casting, electroforming—and gives information on allied areas that are relevant to the jeweler, such as lapidary and found objects. A glossary, a list of suppliers, a bibliography, and a list of schools offering craft courses are appended. Some color photographs are included among the many black and white ones. Line drawings amply illustrate the techniques under discussion. The basic projects are suitable to the beginner, though the presentation of advanced techniques is sketchy and hardly does more than acknowledge that further techniques exist. Recommended, however, as a good introductory how-to book.

141. Grando, Michael D. **Jewelry**: **Form and Technique**. New York, Van Nostrand Reinhold, 1969. 80p. illus. index. $5.95.

This small, handsome book illustrates the jewelry works of the author in excellent black and white photographs. Written in essay form, the book provides the experienced jewelry maker with hints and discussions on various aspects of the craft. Four chapters discuss form, materials, methods, and finishing. In each an informal discussion of these various aspects of the craft provides information on materials, tools, and techniques. Although it is certainly not a how-to text, the reader will find a great deal of authoritative information that he can apply to his own work. An additional chapter provides a discussion of the future of jewelry as an art form (the most convincing evidence for which is Mr. Grando's own work illustrated here). A final section provides a list of suppliers of tools, stones, and metals.

142. Hardy, R. Allen, and John J. Bowman. **The Jewelry Repair Manual**. 2nd
ed. New York, Van Nostrand Reinhold, 1967. 253p. illus. index.
$6.95. LC 67-18068.

Although this is a jewelry repair handbook, the processes described here
would be equally useful in jewelry making. Basic processes are described in
thorough detail so that even the beginner should be able to benefit from the
text. Soldering, sawing, filing, buffing, and polishing are described, along with
specific tasks involving these processes. Chapters in addition to these are ring
sizing, chain and link repair, spectacle frame repair, hinge work, plating, and
stone setting, repairing, and mounting. The final two chapters discuss
solutions and formulae for the jeweler and the purchase of findings and
supplies. The instructions are detailed yet relatively simple so that most
people could follow the authors' instructions.

143. Hughes, Graham. **The Art of Jewelry**. New York, Viking, 1972. illus.
$25.00. LC 70-186743. ISBN 0-670-13480-5.

This is a history of jewelry, copiously illustrated by photographs (many
of which are in color). Jewelry from all eras is covered—from primitive stone
necklaces and ancient treasures through today's masterpieces.

144. Lewes, Klares. **Jewelry Making for the Amateur**. New York, Van
Nostrand Reinhold, 1965. 164p. illus. $8.00.

Another good text for the beginner, this one provides basic information
on materials and procedures of jewelry making. Emphasis is on contemporary
design. A selected bibliography is appended.

145. Morton, Philip G. **Contemporary Jewelry: A Studio Handbook**. New
York, Holt Rinehart and Winston, 1970. 308p. illus. index.
$9.95. LC 69-16080.

Written for artists, students, and other interested readers, this book
attempts to consolidate in a single source the history, design principles,
materials, and processes of twentieth century jewelry making. It is organized
topically according to the major processes of the craft. The subject is
presented through text and illustrations that provide step-by-step guidance to
such procedures as fusing and soldering, cutting, hammering, casting, stone
setting, and finishing. There are also chapters on gems, semiprecious stones,
toolmaking, marketing, and production. Three excellent chapters are devoted
to design, and there is a section on craft associations. Appendixes offer a
record of major exhibitions in the historical development of contemporary
jewelry, a list of the tools illustrated throughout the book, information about
findings and supplies, and technical data. More than 450 procedural diagrams

and 16 pages of color photos are provided. An excellent bibliography on design, journals, history and techniques is also appended. This is one of the most comprehensive and practical texts available on jewelry making. A basic handbook for students as well as for practicing jewelers, it is highly recommended for applied arts collections in public, school, and university libraries.

146. Pack, Greta. **Jewelry Making by the Lost Wax Process**. New York, Van Nostrand Reinhold, 1968. 113p. illus. index. $6.95.

In this book Ms. Pack describes the up-to-date method of casting jewelry by centrifugal force in a mold of dental investment formed from a wax pattern. The material is presented in five parts. The first two discuss in detail tools and equipment needed, the different waxes and their uses, and the methods employed to form the pattern and the mold in which the articles are to be cast. Part Two offers 14 projects and gives detailed instructions for making brooches, pendants, bola tie slides, and other types of jewelry. The third part describes the process of stone setting and wire working, and the final section describes finishing processes such as texturing, sawing, filing, soldering, cleaning, coloring, and polishing. The appendixes give technical data and sources of supply; a glossary of terms is provided. Numerous drawings provide ideas and supplement the instructions, while the good, clear text makes a complicated process seem simple.

Another book on the lost wax process is Murry Bovin's *Centrifugal or Lost Wax Jewelry Casting for Schools, Tradesmen, Craftsmen* (published by the author, 1971. $7.50; $5.00pa.).

147. Pack, Greta. **Jewelry Making for the Beginning Craftsman**. New York, Van Nostrand Reinhold, 1957. 68p. illus. index. $4.75. LC 57-8146.

The first part of this book introduces the various metals (copper, brass, silver, iron, and tin) and describes and illustrates the tools of the craft. Correct methods of sawing, piercing, filing, soldering, and finishing are described and fundamental decorative processes—twisting wire, shaping coils and chains—are demonstrated. Projects are then grouped not in order of difficulty, but in order of fundamental processes employed. All the projects are handsome and instructions for making them are fully detailed. The book is excellently illustrated by half-tone drawings. Highly recommended as an elementary text.

A more comprehensive text by the same author is *Jewelry and Enameling* (3rd ed., Van Nostrand Reinhold, 1961. 396p. $6.75). Basically a work manual, this book provides information on jewelry processes and ideas for design. A bibliography is appended.

148. Quick, Lelande, and Hugh Leiper. **Gemcraft: How to Cut and Polish Gemstones**. Philadelphia, Chilton, 1959. 189p. illus. index. $7.50. LC 59-13626. ISBN 0-8019-0430-7.

After a description of the properties and physical characteristics of gems, the authors tell the beginner how to get started, with details on the equipment needed and on techniques of sawing, grinding, lapping, sanding, and polishing. Included are descriptions of the grinding and polishing of cabochons, the cutting and polishing of faceted stones, and a special section on lapping, carving, and sculpturing gemstones, mosaics, and intarsia. They also treat special polishing problems of gemstones and discuss such gemstone novelties as bookends, clocks, lamps, ashtrays, etc. An additional section deals with where and how to collect gemstones. Step-by-step series of photographs illustrate basic techniques involved in gemwork. A bibliography of books current at the time of publication is appended. Despite its age, this is a basic text on lapidary work, telling in clear concise language everything that the beginner needs to know in order to get started. An excellent text.

A more recent text is Helen Hutton's *Practical Gemstone Craft* (Viking, 1972. $8.95). This is a workable text although it is not as complete as the Quick and Leiper book.

149. Rose, Augustus F., and Antonio Cirino. **Jewelry Making and Design**. 4th ed. New York, Davis Press, 1949; rev. and repr. New York, Dover, 1967. 306p. illus. index. $2.75. LC 66-29501. ISBN 0-486-21750-7.

A reprint of the third edition, with material restored from the second edition. In the first chapter, the authors survey the materials and methods, and in the second they simply list the techniques that are to be illustrated in the text. With the third chapter the student is introduced to the problem of making a pierced brooch. He learns to affix a tracing of the design to the metal, and to handle a center punch, saw frame and saw, needle file and half-round file, and emery cloth. This project is fully illustrated, and suggestions for similar projects are given. Subsequent problems teach the student to make brooches, wire pendants, rings, chains, and cuff links. Techniques covered include using a gas jet and blow pipe, making a plain and shouldered bezel, annealing, enameling, making a mold for casting, etc.

Following the section on making jewelry, the author discusses the aesthetics of jewelry design, suggesting sources in nature and in art for ideas and motifs. A bibliography of books has been newly compiled for the Dover edition. The illustrations, all black and white, show processes as well as various examples of the type of jewelry being discussed. Although many of the designs seem to be old-fashioned, this may provide an added appeal for some people. The techniques are still sound.

150. Sanford, William R. **Jewelry: Queen of Crafts**. New York, Bruce, 1970. 196p. illus. index. $8.95. LC 77-116783.

This introductory text provides sufficient information to satisfy the most curious beginning student. The author's introductory essay on design is followed by a description of materials and tools. Techniques are treated in the main chapter under separate rubrics, alphabetically arranged; these include annealing, applique, bending, carving, casting, coloring, finding, granulation, etc. In addition, separate chapters are devoted to jewelry without solder, jewelry using solder, cast jewelry, gems, and simple lapidary. There is an appendix of technical data, a glossary of terms, and a good bibliography. This is not a project book; the information here is more in the nature of a handbook, which should help the student to comprehend and master the various techniques of the craft. The beginning student should find it extremely helpful, and there is sufficient information to suggest possibilities to the more advanced student. Black and white photographs and illustrations are well integrated with the text.

151. Seitz, Marianne. **Creating Silver Jewelry with Beads**. New York, Sterling, 1971. 48p. illus. index. (Little Craft Book Series). $2.69.

This small book tells how to form silver jewelry using nothing more than a pair of pliers. Handsome ornamental jewelry results from the combination of silver wire with beads. There are clear instructions for making pins, earrings, bracelets, cuff links, mirror decorations, wall plaques, and a lampshade. Each project includes a list of materials and a photograph of the finished item. Line drawings demonstrate techniques.

152. Shoenfelt, Joseph F. **Designing and Making Handwrought Jewelry**. New York, McGraw-Hill, 1960. 168p. illus. $1.95pa. LC 60-10613. ISBN 0-07-057004-3.

This book provides simple instructions accompanied by drawings and step-by-step photographs of the basic jewelry-making processes. Progressing from the simple to the more difficult, the author introduces the reader to the basic techniques of jewelry making. Chapters cover annealing, soldering, pickling, cutting, drilling and piercing sheet metals, shaping, hanging and planishing (sheet metals), and decorating techniques. Others discuss stones and stone setting and how to combine materials and techniques. There is a chapter on jewelry design, and appendixes give information on problems, tools, and suppliers. A good handbook for the beginner as well as for the advanced amateur.

153. Sinkankas, John. **Gem Cutting: A Lapidary's Manual**. 2nd ed. New York, Van Nostrand Reinhold, 1962. 297p. illus. index. $12.95.

This practical and extremely worthwhile handbook provides the most comprehensive treatment available of the gem cutter's craft. The author gives the uninitiated basic information on gemstones, on how to get started, on amateur clubs and societies, and on equipment (including how to save money on its purchase). Sections three through nine treat various essential processes—sawing, grinding, lapping, sanding, polishing, and drilling—with discussion of the equipment associated with each procedure and its proper use. Chapter eight discusses the all-purpose unit. Chapters 10 through 18 introduce types of gems, their forms and treatments—the cabochons, faceted gems, spheres and beads, and stones. Directions are given for working each of these (how to cut cabochon, how to cut faceted stones, etc.). Additional chapters deal with tumbling, carving and engraving, and mosaic and inlay work. The author's aim is to make it possible for the reader to teach himself all aspects of gem cutting without having to attend a class. To facilitate this, the author points out various pitfalls along the way and uses photos and line drawings to illustrate processes and techniques. Though it is written for the beginning student, the book progresses to techniques that will challenge the experienced amateur. Directions are clear throughout. This basic text should be in any collection on gem cutting.

For the advanced craftsman, a supplementary text on the subject of gem testing is Basil William Anderson's *Gem Testing* (8th ed. New York, Van Nostrand Reinhold, 1971. 384p. illus. bibliog. $19.50).

154. Solberg, Ramona. **Inventive Jewelry-Making**. New York, Van Nostrand Reinhold, 1972. 128p. illus. $8.95. LC 79-184822. ISBN 0-442-27874-6.

As the title implies, this manual emphasizes unique applications of jewelry-making techniques, with the aim of achieving new artistic goals.

155. Villiard, Paul. **A First Book of Jewelrymaking**. New York, Funk and Wagnalls, 1969. 148p. illus. index. $4.95. LC 68-56462.

A practical book for the beginner on the basic operations involved in making jewelry. It covers tools, materials, and methods and gives step-by-step instructions for the fashioning of pins and brooches, gem settings, bracelets, and other types of jewelry. Although the text is clearly written, the beginning student would benefit from more and clearer illustrations covering the basic operations. Without such illustrations, it is sometimes difficult to envision the techniques and equipment that Mr. Villiard describes. For the most part, however, the text itself is quite informative, and the beginner should be able to profit from a careful reading of it.

156. Villiard, Paul. **Jewelrymaking**. Garden City, N.Y., Doubleday, 1973. 96p. illus. (Crafts for Children Series). $4.95.

The photographs of techniques and of finished items are better than those in Mr. Villiard's earlier work (entry 155). Projects include jewelry made from all sorts of materials—from macaroni to enamel on silver. Supplementary matter discusses tools and equipment, jewelrymaking kits, etc. Designed for a younger audience than the previous book.

157. Von Neumann, Robert. **The Design and Creation of Jewelry**. Rev. ed. Philadelphia, Chilton, 1972. 271p. illus. index. $12.50. LC 72-1500. ISBN 0-8019-5671-4.

A revision of a standard work on jewelry making, this book deals with the basic procedures of sound craftsmanship, giving exact and explicit information, supplemented by necessary photographs and descriptive drawings. Useful to the sophisticated beginner—though primarily suitable as a handbook for one already practicing the craft—this work offers a full treatment of the jeweler's craft.

The introductory chapter catalogs the various metals and alloys and gives information on the workability and melting point of the pure metal and its alloys. It also provides information on materials besides metals (including enamels, gems, plastics, and woods). Notes on tools conclude the chapter. Chapters two through six give extensive treatment to the techniques of the craft. Basic techniques are supplemented by a chapter dealing with forging, repousse and chasing, annealing, casting, fusing, etc. Another chapter deals with surface decorations, including engraving, etching, filigree, and inlaying. Japanese processes and techniques are treated, as well as the contemporary techniques of electroforming, photo-etching, and reticulation. The chapters on the elements of design concentrate on the possibilities and limitations that the material imposes on the creation of different types of jewelry. The final chapter treats design as an abstract principle and offers a gallery of photos of natural objects that might be creatively adapted to the jeweler's craft. A fine bibliography of books and articles is appended, as well as a list of supply sources and a section of technical data. A highly useful book for the advanced craftsman, though less so for the beginner. Nevertheless, as a supplementary text to more elementary treatments, it would be a valuable aid in deepening the beginner's understanding of the materials and processes of his craft.

158. Von Socher, Millie. **Jewelry to Make Yourself**. New York, Taplinger, 1967. 95p. illus. $2.95. LC 67-11516.

A well-illustrated guide for the novice craftsman interested in costume jewelry. The author deals with bead, woven, raffia, leather, fur, ceramic, wire, and enamel jewelry. There are illustrations of finished pieces, and integrated series of photos demonstrate the manner by which the jewelry is made. Projects range in difficulty from elementary undertakings to those that will appeal to the advanced craftsman.

159. Walter, Martin. **Gem Cutting Is Easy**. New York, Crown, 1972. 95p. illus. $4.95; $1.98pa.

Primarily for beginners, although new techniques are also included for more experienced lapidaries. All the basics are covered: equipment; cutting, sawing, sanding, and polishing; faceting the standard oval cut; etc. Instructions are step by step, complemented by 144 illustrations and 20 color plates.

160. Wiener, Louis. **Hand Made Jewelry: A Manual of Techniques with a Section on Metal Enameling**. 2nd ed. New York, Van Nostrand Reinhold, 1960. 221p. illus. $4.95.

Long a basic manual on the subject (first edition was published in 1948). Detailed instructions are given for a variety of projects, through which the beginning jewelrymaker will acquire the necessary techniques of the craft.

161. Willcox, Donald J. **New Design in Jewelry**. New York, Van Nostrand Reinhold, 1970. 120p. illus. $7.50. LC 79-126870.

This is a photo album of avant-garde jewelry design as practiced in Scandinavia. The author is an enthusiast of the first order, and his somewhat pretentious introduction may or may not interest the reader. Also, the examples he has selected do not always fit the author's own criteria. Some examples of folk jewelry are interspersed with the new. A few beautiful color photos are included, although the majority are in black and white.

162. Ziek, Nona. **Making Silver Jewelry**. New York, Lancer Books, 1973. 237p. illus. $1.95pa.

This paperback book is intended for the beginning jewelrysmith who must work in a minimum of space and with few tools. The author describes the basic materials of the craft, their use, the tools and the basic operations performed by each, and their use and misuse. The body of the book is devoted to an elaboration of techniques and step-by-step instructions for making different types of jewelry or performing various operations fundamental to the jeweler's craft. Bent-wire jewelry has its own chapter, as do stamped patterns, sawed shapes, twisted wire, chains, etc. In addition, there are chapters on soldering, forging, and fusing. Directions in each case are accompanied by line drawings integrated with the text. A few photos of finished pieces are also provided. Reference lists at the end provide information on gem stones, metal gauges, solders, craft organizations, and sources of supplies. A glossary of jewelers' terms is appended, plus a short bibliography. Although it is not as well illustrated as it might be, this is a practical book for the beginning student with no previous knowledge of the craft.

LEATHER

163. Cherry, Raymond. **General Leathercraft**. 4th ed. Bloomington, Ill., McKnight and McKnight, 1955. 144p. index. $2.64pa.

A basic how-to text for the home craftsman, this book is intended for the beginner. The four sections deal with the following subjects: 1) tools and basic information on leather, its properties and preservation; 2) fundamental operations of leatherwork, including laying out, preparation, tooling, carving, forming, folding, lacing, attaching, and finishing; 3) standard projects that demonstrate the fundamental techniques described in section two; and 4) illustrations of designs that students may wish to imitate. The illustrations throughout are numerous and helpful. A list of suggested tools and supplies for classroom use is appended, as well as a short bibliography. A useful and well-organized text. Because of its price, it will be well suited for classroom use in vocational schools; it is also recommended for a home collection for the beginning craftsman.

164. Grant, Bruce. **Encyclopedia of Rawhide and Leather Braiding**. Cambridge, Md., Cornell Maritime Press, 1972. 528p. illus. index. $10.00. LC 72-10407. ISBN 0-87033-161-2.

Emphasizing Western leather products (riding crops, reins, etc.), this encyclopedia is not designed for the beginner attracted by the current popularity of leatherworking. It presents in detail alternative curing processes for rawhide, and gives instructions for various braids: twist, slit, round, crocodile ridge, etc. Definitely essential for the serious and experienced leatherworker who is ready to appreciate the traditional aspects of his craft. A list of suppliers is appended.

165. Groneman, Chris H. **Leathercraft**. Peoria, Ill., Bennett, 1963. 160p.
    illus. index. $6.48 text ed. LC 58-5509.

A standard how-to-do-it book on leathercraft, this work aims to
acquaint the beginning student with the essential details of this ancient art.
Chapters include essential information on leather types and descriptions of
the basic tools of leatherwork, with notes on their care. Further chapters deal
with the preparation of the leather for working, and descriptions of the
techniques involved in making useful and decorative objects. The methods
described include all the usual methods employed, including cutting, carving,
braiding, designing and transfer, tooling and modelling, stippling, stamping,
and embossing. Each short chapter is accompanied by numerous photographs
of work in progress so that the student may observe not only the method
being illustrated but also the possibilities that that method offers. Several
chapters deal with the various methods of attaching pieces of leather, such as
sewing, braiding, splicing, and lacing. A number of project plans for objects of
somewhat dubious utility are included for the purpose of getting the student
started. Other chapters provide information on the history of leather, the
process of making leather, and information on some of its industrial uses. On
the whole, this is a useful book that should suffice for the needs of the
beginning craftsman. A short bibliography is appended.

166. Hanauer, Elsie. **Creating with Leather**. New York, A. S. Barnes, 1970.
    135p. illus. $6.95. LC 73-107115. ISBN 0-498-07620-2.

Hand-lettered and illustrated by the author, this book provides
instructions for making 38 articles from leather. Most of the projects are
simple and many are useful, though there are numbers of cute little things
that may or may not be appealing even to the young reader. Instructions are,
however, simple and very specific so that with care (and perhaps the aid of an
older brother or sister) a child of eight should be able to make most of the
projects.

167. Hayes, M. Vincent. **Making It in Leather**. New York, Drake, 1972.
    104p. illus. bibliog. $5.95. ISBN 0-87749-257-3.

This is primarily a book of techniques rather than a book of projects.
Early chapters cover the history and making of leather, buying leather, tools,
and the work center. Succeeding chapters deal with specific techniques such
as treating the edges, punching holes and slits, lacing, tooling, use of findings,
etc. Although no projects are detailed, there are suggestions and tips
(illustrated) for making leather clothes and footwear, bookbinding, etc. This
will serve as an essential supplement to some of the less detailed books of
projects. Anyone interested in a professional-looking product will benefit
from its hints.

168. Hills, Pat, with Joan Wiener. **The Leathercraft Book**. New York, Random House, 1973. 132p. illus. $8.95; $3.95pa. LC 73-163948.

After a preliminary discussion of cuts, grades, and weights of leather, and an explanation of tools and basic techniques, the author provides patterns and step-by-step instructions for projects. These projects are weighted somewhat heavily toward belts (over 20 are suggested), but there are patterns for purses and sandals as well. Line drawings illustrate the instructions. Another new work is *Leather as Art and Craft*, by Thelma Newman, who is well known for her basic texts in other crafts areas (Crown, 1973. $8.95; $4.95pa.).

169. Meilach, Dona. **Contemporary Leather**. Chicago, Regnery, 1971. 186p. illus. index. $10.00. LC 79-163266.

After a brief survey of the historical use of leather and a description of its contemporary use, this book describes where to find leather and how to buy it, how hides differ, and the terminology used when shopping for and discussing leather. Step-by-step instructions for treating and handling leather also illustrate the proper use of tools for cutting and stripping, punching, thonging, stitching and looping, finishing and coloring. Following the discussion of techniques and tools, the author explains how to make modern weed pots and boxes, collages and constructions, sculpture, sandals, clothes, and furniture. The potpourri section shows how to use leather for macrame, knitting, crocheting, and applique.

This is not a collection of the usual tooled leatherwork projects. The ideas here are for novices as well as experienced workers, but many of the objects illustrated are aesthetically quite pleasing. An excellent collection of photographs and ideas for unusual designs using leather.

170. Parker, Xenia Ley. **Working with Leather**. New York, Scribner's, 1972. 159p. illus. index. $8.95. LC 77-37227. ISBN 0-684-12760-1.

After a short history of leather crafts, the author introduces the material itself, listing the types of leathers available and how and where to buy them. Included here is a chart of various suedes and leathers and their characteristics. Tools are illustrated and their functions are described. Succeeding chapters explain how to use patterns, how to attach various findings to leather (snaps, eyelets, grommets, rivets, buckles, appliques, cutouts, fringes, tassels, with a description of braiding and incised laces), how to tool and carve leather (stamping, embossing), how to paint, dye, and finish. After the description of the techniques involved in the above operations, the author provides 12 projects ranging from a very simple change purse to a relatively complicated suede jacket. In between are plans and directions for making a pillow, a checkbook holder, a passport case, belts, suede sack, pocket book, vest, and skirt. The directions are relatively simple and clear for each of the projects. Line drawings augment the description of basic operations. A good text for the beginner.

171. Patton, Mary. **Designing with Leather and Fur**. New York, Hearthside Press, 1972. 254p. illus. index. $8.95. LC 70-185809.

Despite the title, this work emphasizes leather. Chapters are "Leather Now," "Leather How," "Leather Fashions," "Leather Designs for the Home," "Fur Fashions," and "Creativity in Leather." The preliminary chapters cover materials, tools, and techniques (fake leather and fur are also covered), illustrated by the author's numerous line drawings. Besides the standard techniques that one would expect, there are also sections on working with scraps; designs and decorations; dyeing, finishing, and painting (including batik). Projects—all of which are copiously illustrated with black and white photographs and with line drawings—range from a "suede choker" to an appliqued tablecloth. The author's fine sense of contemporary design is evident in almost all the projects. Certainly a necessary book for today's craftsman.

172. Petersen, Grete. **Creative Leathercraft**. New York, Sterling, 1960. $3.95.

Basically a project book, *Creative Leathercraft* begins with a description of the materials, tools, and techniques to be used in the "creation" of the various items described in the body of this book. The emphasis is not on those more traditional projects that allow the beginner to practice his newly discovered techniques of tooling, stippling, molding, etc., but upon simple and useful objects with a minimum of fancy leather work. The inevitable key-case is here again, but without frills, and this is followed by plans for a number of attractive plain purses. Plans for objects trimmed in leather are also given, as well as patterns for jackets, a pair of suede pants, sandals, and a stuffed toy. In addition to scaled-down patterns, detailed instructions for making each item are provided. For the most part, any of the articles could be made by anyone who can sew.

173. Petersen, Grete. **Leathercrafting**. New York, Sterling, 1973. 48p. illus. index. (Little Craft Book Series). $2.95. LC 72-95205. ISBN 0-8069-5236-9.

Sterling's Little Craft Book Series, which now consists of some 50 titles, provides compact and reliable information on every currently popular craft. This one is a translation from the Danish. After introductory chapters that discuss general techniques, tools, and materials, the book presents directions for specific items that use various methods of leatherworking: braided and woven headbands and belts; tote bags; hats; vests and trousers; and sandals. Heavily illustrated, like the other books of the series, with photographs, patterns, and line drawings. A list of 20 suppliers is appended, but only half of these are in the United States.

174. Shaw, G. J. **Leathercraft**. Leicester, England, Dryad Handicraft, 1925; repr. Kentfield, Calif., Newton K. Gregg, 1971. 62p. illus. $2.95pa. ISBN 0-912318-09-0.

This reprint of an English work is basically a project book outlining instructions for making a number of leather articles. There are short sections on types of leathers and methods of working and finishing. The major portion of the book, however, is devoted to detailed instructions for making simple leather objects beginning with a lined gusset and progressing to more complicated projects: a comb case, a cigarette case, a tobacco pouch, a purse, etc. Instructions show only the finished projects, thus indicating what the reader is aiming for but not how to achieve it. Each project introduces the reader to a different technique. If the craftsman works through the book, he will be able to do most of the basic operations necessary to leatherwork. It is difficult to see how a rank beginner would be able to do this, however, without the aid of a supplementary text. And since the projects are intended for beginners, it seems obvious that a more detailed text should be recommended—either the Cherry or the Zimmerman text is better.

175. Sunset Books and Sunset Magazine, editors. **Things to Make with Leather: Techniques and Projects**. Menlo Park, Calif., Lane Books, 1973. 80p. illus. $1.95pa. LC 72-92511.

Illustrated instructions for about 40 projects form the bulk of this Sunset Book. Items to make range from belts and wallets to sandals, pillows, aprons, and leather-covered objects. Some patterns are included. Directions vary in detail; often they consist simply of leather-working suggestions for adapting a standard pattern (e.g., the teddy-bear). Beginning sections cover how to choose skins, and tools and techniques.

176. Villiard, Paul. **A First Book of Leather Working**. New York, Abelard-Schuman, 1972. 126p. illus. index. $7.95; $3.95pa. LC 74-141557. ISBN 0-200-71774-4.

This book, written for the beginning student, describes the essential operations of the leather craftsman. The emphasis is on the way to work leather rather than on how to make things out of leather. The initial chapter deals with the various types of leather, and it is followed by a chapter devoted to the tools necessary for working leather. In the third chapter the author defines briefly the various methods used by the craftsman and the effect that each method is intended to achieve. Succeeding chapters then give instructions concerning the details of each of these methods—including stitching and lacing, tooling, modelling, incising, carving, stencilling, etc. A unique feature of this book is the description of the almost exclusively European technique known as the Venetian lacquer method. Photographs are well integrated in the text, though it would be helpful if there were more of them. Although it is a useful supplementary text, other better illustrated and more detailed books would be recommended for the beginner.

177. Waterer, John W. **A Guide to the Conservation and Restoration of Objects Made Wholly or in Part of Leather.** New York, Drake, 1972. 500p. illus. $11.95. LC 70-180136. ISBN 0-87749-180-1.

This hefty work is a thorough treatment of the subject. It covers the different kinds of fungi that attack leather and provides treatment information incorporating the most recent developments in the area.

178. Waterer, John W. **Leather Craftsmanship**. New York, Praeger, 1968. 121p. illus. index. $11.00.

Though it is not a how-to book, this text should be useful and instructive for those who take their work in leathercraft seriously. The book is divided into two sections. In the first the author discusses leather, how it is made, its nature, its uses, and the tools used for working it. A glossary of terms is also provided in the first section. The second section deals with the techniques used in working leather. Both traditional methods and modern innovations are described, and the various methods employed for specific tasks are discussed under the headings of the objects made. Chapters in the second part are divided according to processes. Thus, there are chapters on molding, lamination, covering, and ornamentation. The author's approach is historical and emphasizes the continuity of traditional approaches to leather. Illustrations are basically of museum pieces and emphasize the craftsmanship of the pieces shown. Although this is not a practical teaching text, a well-rounded collection of books on leathercraft would be improved by its addition. The author, who is a designer and producer of luggage and a founding member of the Museum of Leathercraft in London, has also written *Spanish Leather* (Watson-Guptill, 1973. $34.50. ISBN 0-8230-4882-9).

179. Willcox, Donald. **Modern Leather Design**. New York, Watson-Guptill, 1969. 160p. illus. index. $12.50. LC 69-17667.

This work provides a thorough approach to the subject. In addition to the standard discussion of tools, techniques, and types of leather, and the usual presentation of projects that utilize the various techniques, this book appends a bibliography and a list of suppliers. Specific topics that are not treated in depth are augmented by citations to specialized works on the subject. The illustrations and the detailed index contribute to the general excellence. Worth the price.

180. Willcox, Donald J., and James Scott Manning. **Leather**. Chicago, Regnery, 1973. 229p. illus. $14.95. LC 72-11202.

Another solid text by Mr. Willcox on all aspects of working with leather. This newer work is well illustrated and, like *Modern Leather Design*, includes bibliographical references.

181. Williams, Guy R. **Working with Leather**. New York, Emerson Books, 1967. 128p. illus. $4.95.

This basic handbook for the beginner offers a collection of simple projects intended to introduce the reader to leatherwork and to develop his skill in a number of areas. The projects suggested are designed to make use of various skills and include such objects as a bookmark, a simple purse, a folding purse, wallet, briefcase, handbags, travelling case, gloves, and simple bookbinding. Diagrams and dimensions for cutting are enclosed with each process, and basic techniques are illustrated by line drawings. Although it is not an inspiring book, the reader should be able to master a number of basic techniques by working his way through the projects.

182. Yount, John T. **Leathercraft Handbook**. San Angelo, Texas, Educator Books, 1971. 96p. $6.95. LC 78-180260. ISBN 0-912092-43-2.

This handbook was compiled, according to the author, to assist anyone, "irregardless [sic] of experience," in developing the skills necessary for leatherwork for either "pleasure or profit." It is organized into five chapters, the first of which gives a short history of leather and a description of certain industrial uses and processes involving leather. The next two describe the various types of leather and the tools of the trade. The main body deals with the techniques used by the craftsman and covers all the usual methods found in leatherworking manuals in more or less adequate detail. The subsections of this chapter discuss patterns, cutting, tooling and embossing, carving, filigree work, and attachments. The last chapter covers the various types of sewing and lacing techniques and ends with a note on projects for the purpose of illustrating how the craftsman must proceed. The illustrations, consisting of poorly executed drawings, are barely adequate, though if carefully studied they may be of some use to the student.

183. Zimmerman, Fred W. **Leathercraft**. South Holland, Ill., Goodheart-Willcox, 1969. 96p. illus. index. $3.00.

One of the Goodheart-Willcox "Build-a-Course" series, Mr. Zimmerman's text is intended for instruction in high school or junior high craft courses. It acquaints the student with the materials, tools, terms, and procedures of carving and stamping leather, then proceeds to a number of projects that provide, in graduated stages, step-by-step instructions for using these procedures. There are chapters on preparation of leather; finishing, measuring, and grading leather; shaping, carving, and decorating; and a final section on tool sharpening and maintenance. Overall, the book is well designed for a craft course, and the ample illustrations, well integrated with the text, make this also a useful instructional aid to the do-it-yourself enthusiast. There are quizzes after each chapter, and the teacher is provided with an instructor's guide and answer key.

METAL AND WIRE

METALWORKING

184. Baldwin, John. **Contemporary Sculpture Techniques: Welded Metal and Fiberglass.** New York, Van Nostrand Reinhold, 1967. 120p. illus. index. $10.00. LC 67-14152.

The introduction discusses the techniques and history of sculpture and its modern innovations. Part two, a handbook on welding, is directed to the sculptor. The author describes the various types of equipment and their operation. Metals and the welding techniques used for joining are discussed in detail, and there is a handbook on the use of the oxygen and acetylene torch as well as the electric arc. Special effects achieved by the artist with the use of these instruments are described. Part three provides instructions in the use of reinforced fiberglass in sculpture and the materials and techniques used by the artist in this material. Various types of plastics are described, with directions for use. The section on welded metal is quite good from a technical point of view. However, the section on plastics is less comprehensive, and the student would be well advised to consult the text by Nicholas Roukes, *Sculpture in Plastics* (entry 316). The Baldwin work is nevertheless recommended for the discussion on metal welding.

185. Bollinger, J. W. **Fun with Metalwork**. Milwaukee, Wisc., Bruce, 1958. 184p. illus.

Although it is now out of print, this basic text is available in many libraries. The first section, consisting of 15 pages, provides an outline of such fundamental procedures as transferring and cutting silhouette patterns, instructions on the selection of metals, and a discussion of the various methods of shaping, strengthening, and finishing. The subsequent sections present a wide selection of projects, all of which apply these basic skills. Well over 100 projects are detailed and specifications are given in diagram form. Although many of them use silhouettes, a wide range of different types of projects are illustrated. A good elementary text recommended because of the large number of projects suitable for high school and camp craft classes.

186. Daniele, Joseph William. **Early American Metal Projects**. Bloomington, Ill., McKnight and McKnight, 1971. 145p. illus. $7.96. LC 75-130495. ISBN 0-87345-142-2.

The 34 different items in this project book are all true to the colonial tradition. They include such items as sconces, fire tools, andirons, pistols, miniature cannon, weather vane, bells, and many others. Complete project plans, a list of materials, and instructions accompany each project. Some projects are simple and suitable for the beginner, while others will require more skill and the aid of fairly sophisticated tools (the cannon is an example of a more complicated project). Illustrations show variations of some of the basic items, and techniques are explained. Prior knowledge of metalworking techniques is needed for some of the items. Excellent.

187. Feirer, John L. **General Metals**. 3rd ed. New York, McGraw-Hill, 1967. 470p. illus. index. $8.48 text ed. ISBN 0-07-020365-2.

Although it is not a book on art metalwork, this widely used high school text can be very useful to the interested metal craftsman. Chapters that specifically relate to the home craftsman are those on bench and wrought metal, sheet metal, and art metal and jewelry, plus the section on "projects." Basic processes for working metal are described, with accompanying photos. The remainder of the book, intended for the industrial arts shop, requires equipment not usually available to the home craftsman. Descriptions of tools and a discussion of design and planning will also be of some interest to the craftsman.

Similar in scope is a book by the same author in collaboration with John R. Lindbeck, *Metalwork* (2nd ed., Bennett, 1970. 248p. $6.60. LC 65-18200). The craftsman may wish to consult the chapters on drilling, filing, cutting, cleaning, annealing, and overlaying, as well as those on soldering and welding. The overall emphasis, however, is on mass production.

188. Glass, F. J. **Metal Craft**. London, University of London Press, 1928; repr. Kentfield, Calif., Newton K. Gregg, 1971. 70p. illus. $2.95pa.

The author describes a number of copper articles that can be cut and decorated by children. Various processes are described for making finger plates, hinges, paper knives, name plates, escutcheons, napkin rings, lanterns, candlesticks, plaques, fire screens, etc. Processes described include raising, riveting, interlocking joints, tube marking, etc. Surface decoration includes work with various stamps for repoussage work. A small compact book with nice line drawings. Although the projects are suitable for children, most will appeal to adults as well. The designs are slightly dated but are nevertheless very handsome.

189. Granström, K. E. **Creating with Metal**. New York, Van Nostrand Reinhold, 1968. 92p. $4.95.

Specifically directed toward the hobbyist, this book requires only that the reader have the minimum of tools and materials described in the first section, "Workshop Techniques and Materials." The author instructs the student in the basic processes for constructing handmade objects of metals—soldered, riveted, and screw joints; surface treatment of metals (polishing, cleaning, etching, enamelling, etc.). Part two gives a series of working drawings for easy items such as a pencil holder, a paperweight, an ink blotter, etc. Section three offers working drawings for more difficult models—letter opener, napkin rings, and bracelets. Part four, which deals with smithing and forging, requires more complicated instruments as well as use of the forge itself. Projects for the forge include fireplace pokers, candlesticks, wall sconces, and a small sculptured piece. Good photos. The relatively simple techniques needed make this a useful book for the beginner.

190. Gruber, Elmar. **Metal and Wire Sculpture**. New York, Sterling, 1973. 48p. illus. index. (Little Craft Book Series). $3.50. LC 73-168399.

This book guides the reader, with step-by-step instruction, through the creation of art objects from sheet metal (brass and copper) and wire. Techniques of cutting, bending, and soldering are described, as are the tools necessary for these operations. Projects illustrated include wall decorations, candleholders, baskets, flower pots, ash trays, etc. The projects, handsome for the most part, are simple enough for even the most maladroit craftsman. Recommended for 12-year-olds to adults.

191. Gruber, Elmar. **Nail Sculpture**. New York, Sterling, 1967. 47p. illus. index. (Little Craft Book Series). $2.95. LC 68-8768. ISBN 0-8069-5106-0.

With a soldering iron, a vise, a couple of pliers, a heat-resistant base, and, of course, nails (lots of nails of all types and shapes), you can create sculpture. Here's the book that proves it. Not so much a how-to as a what-to book, this little volume shows some of the things that can be wrought from nails. Instruction on supplies and techniques is short but sufficient, and there are pictures of nail "sculpture," some of which is rather interesting. Recommended for anyone who can use a soldering iron and who has the strength to bend a nail (with the help of a vise and pliers, of course).

192. Hawkins, Leslie V. **Art Metal and Enameling**. Peoria, Ill., Bennett, 1967. 234p. illus. index. $5.85 text ed. LC 67-10594.

This text, designed for a high school craft class, begins with a description of art metal, its history, and its place in American industry and domestic life. After a few comments on safety and work habits, the author presents chapters on design—elements and principles of design, aids for design, and free-form design. These chapters are followed by chapters on drawing, sketches, how to develop a drawing into a design, enlarging sketches, and transferring a design to a mold. The chapters that deal with tools and materials are accompanied by hints on use and care, precautionary advice, and information on various metals used in art metal work. Chapters 28 through 41 treat the various processes used in working metals, including raising, etching, decorating, fluting, surface ornamentation, cleaning, enameling, and firing. Step-by-step photos accompany the text in the chapters describing the various processes, and a multitude of other photos illustrate tools, industrial processes, and finished articles, some of the latter in color plates. The book emphasizes the handicraft aspect in the chapters on processes, but it also points out the relationship to industrial processes used in the production of metals and finished metal articles. It is a good introductory text, however, that is suitable for self-instruction.

193. Howard, Sylvia W. **Tin-Can Crafting**. Rev. ed. New York, Sterling, 1971 (c.1964). 64p. illus. index. $3.95. LC 64-24689. ISBN 0-8069-5032-3.

After a discussion of various techniques, tools, and equipment, the author gives detailed instructions (with line drawings, patterns, and photographs) for about 40 projects. These range from wall hangings (sunbursts are prevalent) and decorated mirrors to earrings, sconces, and Christmas decorations. The explicitness of the instructions makes this an excellent work for beginners, but the variety of the projects will appeal to more advanced tin-snippers as well.

Hearthside Press has announced the November 1973 publication of Helen Hornberger's *The Art of Making Tole Flowers and Ornaments*

($10.00). This specialized text discusses cutting, gluing, assembling, painting, and antiquing flowers and ornaments from painted tin.

194. Kauffman, Henry J. **The Colonial Silversmith: His Techniques and His Products**. Camden, N.J., Thomas Nelson, 1969. 176p. illus. index. $15.00. LC 71-101526.

This book explains the tools and techniques used by colonial craftsmen in fashioning a wide variety of silver objects. Photographs of the finished product and illustrations of the step-by-step fabrication of individual items supplement the text. The author explains the silversmith's transformation of a block of metal into a finished object. Starting with the simplest (forks and spoons), he progresses to the more complex techniques used to fashion plates, cups, beakers, and teapots and coffeepots—as well as other household utensils and decorative objects of the colonial period. Many of the techniques are the same as those used today. The book should deepen the modern craftsman's feeling of identity with his historic co-worker. Of interest to collectors as well as metalworkers.

195. Kramer, Karl Robert, and Nora Kramer. **Coppercraft and Silver Made at Home**. New York, Greenberg Publishers, 1957; repr. New York, Dover, 1971. 175p. $3.00pa. LC 70-178088. ISBN 0-486-22790-1.

A project book describing in detail 14 simple but handsome projects, with step-by-step instructions and sequential photos and drawings. Processes are described in the text accompanying the project. The projects, designed so they may be done in one's kitchen, include a napkin ring, name plate, bracelet, bib clasps, earrings, tea tray, and others. Suitable for the Sunday craftsman and for camp craft groups.

196. Kronquist, Emil F. **Metal for Craftsmen: A Step-by-Step Guide with 55 Projects**. New York, Dover, 1972. 202p. illus. index. $2.50pa. ISBN 0-486-22789-8.

Projects are in pewter, copper, brass, silver, and aluminum. Directions, lists of materials and tools needed, sources, and suggested modifications for each project are on one page, faced by drawings of the finished product and of the working process. Among the projects are coasters, candlesticks, platters, a reading lamp, etc. This is a reprint of the work originally titled *Art Metalwork*; it was reprinted by Peter Smith as well as Dover.

197. Lidstone, John. **Building with Wire**. New York, Van Nostrand Reinhold, 1972. 95p. illus. $6.95. LC 70-149258.

Teachers and amateur craftsmen will find ideas here for jewelry, mobiles, and abstract pieces of sculpture. Directions are clear and are further amplified by photographs. There are sections on how to find supplies and on basic wire-working techniques. No index.

198. Lynch, John. **Metal Sculpture: New Forms, New Techniques**. New York, Viking, 1957. 153p. illus. (A Studio Book). $4.95.

In the first chapter the author discusses the developments in modern metal sculpture and the influences that have contributed to its development. In the five chapters following this the student is acquainted with various aspects of this modern art. There are chapters on wire and light metals, soldering, silver soldering constructions (including mobiles, stabiles, and kinetic sculpture), and welded sculpture. Each chapter discusses tools and craftsmanship techniques used as well as artistic objectives of modern sculpture. An excellent introduction for both the student and the professional.

199. Maryon, Herbert. **Metalwork and Enameling**. 5th rev. ed. London, Chapman and Hall, 1959; repr. New York, Dover, 1971. 335p. illus. index. $3.50pa. LC 76-1308811. ISBN 0-486-22702-2.

This standard handbook should be of use to the professional as well as the amateur craftsman. The author, who was responsible for reconstruction work on the Sutton Hoo treasure in the British Museum, treats all aspects of the craft, from basic tools to casting and enamelling. After discussing materials and tools, he provides an extensive treatment of soldering in rare metals. He continues into filigree work, the setting of stones, raising and shaping, spinning, repousse work, wire, twisting, hinges and joints, inlaying and overlaying, niello, alloys and stratified fabrics, enamelling (including cloisonné, plique-à-jour, champlevé, bassetaille, encrusted and painted enamels), metal casting, construction, setting out, polishing and coloring, design, and essaying and hallmarking. When possible, he analyzes examples of fine craftsmanship, ancient and modern, to illustrate practical aspects of the process he is explaining. Helpful hints are included on shop safety. There are some 30 figures and photographs to amplify the discussion of tools, materials, and construction.

200. Mattson, E. B. **Creative Metalwork**. Milwaukee, Wisc., Bruce, 1960. 121p. illus. index.

Although it is now out of print, this book is nevertheless still available in libraries. It is divided into two sections; the first provides instructions in the basic processes and uses of equipment, and the second suggests a series of metal projects. The first section details such operations as drilling, metal cutting, forming and shaping, fastening, and finishing, and also discusses project design and layout. The second section provides detailed descriptions and directions for 36 projects. Plans and specifications for each are provided, as well as a list of materials and instructions. The handsome projects, which are challenging for the beginning student, include such objects as a fire set, various decorative pieces, candleholders, tray, salt and pepper shakers, and many others. Various metals are used. Especially suitable for elementary classes in metalworking and for the home craftsman looking for specific projects.

201. Meriel-Bussy, Yves. **Repoussage: The Embossing of Metal**. New York, Sterling, 1971. 48p. illus. (Little Craft Book Series). $2.95. LC 70-115445. ISBN 0-8069-5148-6.

This little volume treats the art of embossing thin metals with simple tools. Basic techniques are described at the beginning, and then these techniques are used to construct decorative boxes, copper jewelry, a weather vane, mobiles, stabiles, and various other objects. A separate section at the end discusses special techniques such as patina, hammering, stamping, intaglio, crushed metal, and coloring. Each of these, however, is described very briefly, leaving application to the reader.

202. Sargent, Lucy. **Tincraft for Christmas**. New York, William Morrow, 1969. 190p. illus. index. $7.95. LC 68-56413.

The author gives complete directions for making beautiful Christmas decorations out of tin. The section on tools, materials, and techniques lists implements for working tin and provides information on glue and paints that adhere to tin. The author explains easy techniques that apply even to seemingly intricate designs, starting with how to take tin cans apart. The project sections include "Trifles for the Tree," "Treasures for the House," and "Trinkets for Gifts." What Ms. Sargent manages to do with tin cans can be appreciated only by examining the intricate decorative objects in this book. Few tools are necessary, and everyone has tin cans. Highly recommended for everyone as a beautiful solution to part of the pollution problem.

203. Thomas, Richard. **Metal Smithing for the Artist-Craftsman**. Philadelphia, Chilton, 1960. 173p. illus. index. $7.50. LC 60-14633. ISBN 0-8019-0465-X.

The specific metalworking skills discussed in this text fall into three major categories: raising and forming, joining, and surface treatment. Within each group the significant means are defined by text, sequential photographs, and drawings. In addition, there are sections dealing with selection and maintenance of tools, proper purpose of machine tools, use, preparation, and safety factors of chemical agents, abrasive agents, shop facilities, sources of supply, etc. The author's purpose is to discuss the major techniques and to suggest alternatives to and combinations of these for fulfilling the workman's project. For example, he suggests nine ways of making a hemispheric vessel with any reasonably malleable metal. The book is directed to the craftsman whose object is to make individualized objects. The excellent photographs throughout are augmented by a series at the end illustrating what craftsmen have accomplished in metal. Not a project book. Bibliography appended.

ENAMELLING

204. **AMACO Metal Enameling.** Indianapolis, American Art Clay Company, 1972. 23p. illus. (Booklet No. 7). $0.75.

A clear and concise little booklet on methods of enamelling on metals. Drawings and text indicate basic operations such as cutting copper shapes, cleaning copper, washing enamels, dusting, counter-enamelling, stencil, and other methods of applying the enamel. Also covered is enamelling on gold and silver, and there is a page on special effects (crackle and metal foil). The back section (pages 16 to 23) is a catalog of AMACO products relevant to metal.

205. Ball, Fred. **Experimental Techniques in Enameling.** New York, Van Nostrand Reinhold, 1972. 144p. illus. index. bibliog. $9.95. LC 72-184823.

As the title implies, this work emphasizes not standard but experimental techniques in enamelling, such as unusual inlays and overlays, incorporating fire scale into the design, etc. Illustrations supplement the clear instructions.

206. Ceramics Monthly Staff. **A CM Handbook on Copper Enameling.** Columbus, Ohio, Professional Publications, 1956. 64p. illus. index.

Although it is an older work that is now out of print, this booklet, available in libraries, is an excellent introduction for the beginner. It presents the basic operations of enamelling, with a description of equipment and tools and a discussion of the properties and nature of enamels. Various methods and materials used in enameling are discussed in separate sections—the sift and stencil method, wet inlay method, gold and silver foil, and special effects. A separate section also deals with defects, their causes and cures. Additional sections consider possibilities of designing with bits of foil, cloisonné, copperwire accents, necklaces, wireless cloisonné, earrings, etc. Step-by-step photographic sequences follow the text. Information on where to obtain supplies is included in the text, but this information is, of course, quite dated.

207. Newble, Brian. **Practical Enamelling and Jewelry Work**. New York, Viking, 1967. 94p. illus. index. $6.95.

The author describes and illustrates basic tools and equipment, their function, and metals used in enamel and jewelry work. A simple project employs the basic processes used in enamelwork, and a separate chapter describes the various processes—annealing, pickling, soldering, setting enamels, drawing wire, sharpening tools, polishing, etc. Selection and preparation of enamel is discussed, and cloisonné, champlevé, bassetaille, mosaics, and enamels are all treated separately. A method of estimating the cost of a particular work is described and a short discussion of design is included. A technical appendix provides charts showing metal gauges, weights and melting points as well as information on solders, hallmarks, and hydrofluoric acid. A list of suppliers in the United States and England is provided, along with a glossary of terms and a short bibliography. Photos, some in color, show processes as well as finished projects. Though it is not a how-to book in the usual sense, the beginner as well as the advanced craftsman may gain basic information from this book. Recommended as a supplemental text in basic craft collections of public libraries.

208. Seeler, Margaret E. **The Art of Enameling**. New York, Van Nostrand Reinhold, 1969. 128p. illus. index. $14.95. LC 69-55891.

Intended as an introduction to the art of enamelling, this text is also of interest to the amateur and even to the professional. Beginning with the basic layout of work space and the tools necessary for enamelling and art metalworking, the author proceeds to a discussion of enamels. She assumes little previous knowledge on the part of the reader.

209. Untracht, Oppi. **Enameling on Metal**. New York, Greenberg Publishers, 1957. 191p. illus. index. $7.50; $3.95pa. LC 57-11904.

This standard text on enamelling describes what enamel is and what materials and tools are essential. In addition to basic information on how to prepare for enamelling on metal, instructions are also given for making a sampler. Traditional techniques such as cloisonné, plique-à-jour, and champlevé are described in a separate chapter, and techniques for achieving special effects—sgraffito, oxidation, incising, etc.—are described in another. In addition, there are chapters devoted to stencil transfer and silkscreen designs and to enamelling defects (and how to avoid or correct them). The final chapter suggests a number of projects with innumerable photos of various objects for inspiration. The appendix provides technical information in chart form on melting points of metals, metal gauges, metal alloy compositions, plus information on sources of tools and materials. A bibliography is also appended, and a list of names and addresses of enamellists. A good suggestive text for the enamellist already acquainted with the medium, though it includes material useful for the beginner as well. Pieces illustrated (in black and white) are of high artistic merit.

210. Winter, Edward. **Enamel Painting Techniques**. New York, Praeger, 1970. 86p. illus. index. $14.95.

The high price of this text is somewhat justified in view of the 116 full-page photographic plates added to the basic, 86-page text. In addition, a great deal of information is provided in succinct note form. Thus, the chapter on "glassforming materials" briefly lists the basic elements and their characteristics. The section on glass enamels does the same. This is a book about enamel painting, and the author discusses the various resins, thinners, brushes, and tools to be used. In addition, he provides practical rules to aid the enamel painter. There are chapters on drawing, using the airbrush, and using the palette knife, as well as sections on sculptural forms, on copper, and on steel. Additional chapters discuss enamel and architecture, professional enamelling, and the history of the craft. Color oxides are treated in a separate section under the various colors to be achieved. A final chapter provides questions and answers on various problems of the enameller's craft. The numerous photographs, a few of which are in color, illustrate techniques and processes as well as finished pieces.

MISCELLANEOUS CRAFTS

211. Adkins, Jan. **The Art and Industry of Sandcastles.** New York, Walker, 1971. 29p. illus. $4.50. LC 76-141615. ISBN 0-8027-0336-4.

An irresistibly charming, handlettered book for anyone who loves to play in sand. Not a crafts book, really, since the last page of the book shows the afternoon's work destroyed by the tide—an ephemeral craft, at best. Lots of castle lore (remember the oubliette?), along with authentic construction details. Mr. Adkins is the author of a number of equally delightful books with the same general format: *How a House Happens*, *The Craft of Making Wine*, *The Craft of Sail*, and *Toolchest* (all published by Walker).

212. Albaum, Charlet. **Ojo de Dios: Eye of God.** New York, Grosset and Dunlap, 1972. 87p. illus. $1.50pa. ISBN 0-448-01149-2.

After explaining what the Ojo de Dios is and describing its origin and function, the author proceeds to describe the various materials necessary for making these colorful decorative objects and the basic weaves used in their construction. The many geometric forms are then described in detail, including variations on the basic weaves. Black and white illustrations of basic shapes and step-by-step illustrations of basic techniques are included.

213. Bressard, M. J. **Creating with Burlap.** Tr. from the French by Rhea Rollin. New York, Sterling, 1970. 48p. illus. index. (Little Craft Book Series). $2.95.

The author tells how to make things from burlap (lampshades, teapot covers, toys) and how to embroider, paint, and otherwise decorate this crude but appealing material. There are also suggestions for using burlap as a background for weaving. Black and white illustrations suggest imaginative uses.

214. Fischman, Walter Ian. **101 Projects for Bottle Cutters**. New York, Crowell, 1972. 132p. illus. $4.95. LC 72-82851. ISBN 0-690-59717-7.

Considering the number of people who, in the interests of ecology, have talked themselves into blowing ten dollars on a bottle-cutting kit, there must be a ready-made audience for this book. One household can use only so many sets of glasses made from Michelob bottles. Mr. Fischman gives information on tools, materials, and safety precautions, and he suggests, as the title indicates, 101 projects to keep the bottle-cutter busy. Instructions for projects are clear and are supplemented by illustrations.

215. Goldman, Phyllis W. **Make It from Felt**. New York, T. Y. Crowell, 1971. 133p. illus. $6.95.

After some preliminary hints on felt, work space, and working techniques, the author divides her book into chapters according to the type of object to be made—bean bags, hand puppets, hangers and mobiles, bookmarks, clipboards, and a chapter on miscellaneous objects. Numerous projects are included, each accompanied by a list of materials, directions, and a diagram for cutting. A final chapter is a personal anecdote telling why you should not go into business making felt toys. A project book for all ages. Recommended for school and public libraries. Ms. Goldman has prepared another Crowell book on felt, titled *Decorate with Felt* (scheduled for September 1973. $4.95).

216. Iida, Miyuki, and Tomoko Iida. **The Art of Handmade Flowers**. Palo Alto, Calif., Kodansha International, 1971. 124p. illus. $10.00. LC 77-128687.

The emphasis in this handsome book is on the "art," though the craft is fully described. The first two pages consist of step-by-step sequential color photos showing how to make a rose. The details of this procedure apply to all the other flowers described in the book. Following this is a section of full-page color photos of arrangements of all the flowers described in the instructions section. The instructions section describes materials and tools, then provides step-by-step illustrations for making each of the flowers illustrated in the previous photo sections. A final section provides full-size, traceable patterns for each of these flowers. All flowers are made from fabrics and are extremely life-like, with the added interest of texture which the fabrics lend to the construction. Directions are specific enough so that all the reader needs is patience and a degree of manual dexterity. One of the best books on the subject of handmade flowers. Excellent photos, all in color, of completed arrangements of the authors' own flowers. Some are hard to distinguish from the real. Highly recommended.

217. Jayne, Caroline F. **String Figures and How to Make Them**. New York, Dover, 1962. (Reprint of the 1906 ed.). 407p. illus. $2.50pa. LC 62-57880.

After an ethnological introduction by Alfred C. Haddon, this book presents clearly illustrated instructions for making 107 string figures. The figures suggested come from all over the world.

218. Kreischer, Lois. **Symmography: Three Dimensional Creative Designs with Yarn without Knotting or Knitting**. New York, Crown, 1971. illus. index. $4.95; $1.98pa. LC 78-167759.

Symmography is perhaps more of a mathematical puzzle than a craft, though few would deny that many of the results have artistic merit. Symmography projects are often available in kit form—those boards studded with nails about which yarn is wound, stretched, and woven in intricate mathematical patterns. The author of this book instructs the reader in how this is done, providing information on tools, preparation, weaving, and framing. For the most part, the photographs and drawings are sufficient for the beginner. Realistic (though stylized) representations of plants and animals are depicted, as well as geometric and abstract designs. Apparently there are no other books on this subject. Recommended for public and school libraries.

219. Newsome, Arden J. **Spoolcraft**. New York, Lothrop, Lee and Shepard, 1970. 158p. illus. index. $4.95. LC 70 101476.

How long wooden spools will be with us is a moot point. Possibly plastic spools can be substituted for wooden in some of the projects suggested here, but not in all of them. The author provides directions for making over 60 different objects from spools. The appeal of the objects produced is limited to small children, though some of the projects require sawing and cutting, which will have to be done by older children and parents. Parents will recognize many of the projects as things they made as children—but without the aid of a book. Recommended for children's crafts collections.

220. Roberts, Patricia Easterbrook. **How to Make Flower Decorations**. New York, Studio Publications, in association with T. Y. Crowell, 1958. 100p. illus. index. LC 58-5669.

In eight short chapters, the author describes how to make and arrange artificial flowers. Chapters are organized by materials used: paper, wax, beads, foil, tin, and wrought iron. The chapters on plastic and bead flowers simply give pointers on arranging the purchased products. Other chapters provide instructions for making the flowers themselves. Numerous illustrations provide ideas for arrangements. Sequential how-to photographs would have been helpful; still, the directions are specific and lists of materials are provided. Two pages provide outline forms of specific flowers for tracing. Recommended because of the variety of materials used, though the Iidas' book is far more helpful for making fabric flowers.

221. Sommer, Elyse. **Make It with Burlap**. New York, Lothrop, Lee and Shepard, 1973. illus. $4.50. LC 73-4954. ISBN 0-688-41559-8.

Projects include burlap sculpture, burlap flowers, and games made from burlap, among others. Step-by-step instructions are easy for children to follow.

MOBILES AND COLLAGES

222. Borja, Corinne, and Robert Borja. **Making Collages**. Chicago, Albert Whitman, 1972. 39p. illus. $3.75. LC 78-188427.

Collage is not an easily definable art—or perhaps "containable" would be a better term. This little book suggests what a collage is and then leaves it to the reader to create his own. Colorfully illustrated. Recommended for pre-teens and older. An announced new work is Mary Webb and Mary Jane Mayer's *New Ways in Collage* (Van Nostrand Reinhold, November 1973. $10.95).

223. Meilach, Dona Z., and Elvie Ten Hoor. **Collage and Assemblage: Trends and Techniques**. New York, Crown, 1973. illus. (Crown Arts and Crafts Series). $7.95.

Everything the novice should know about making collages. All materials are covered (paper, fabric, acrylic, combinations, etc.).

224. Schegger, T. M. **Make Your Own Mobiles**. New York, Sterling, 1965. 96p. illus. index. $2.95. LC 64-24683. ISBN 0-8069-5066-8.

The author discusses the principle of balance that applies to the mobile structure, describes the various materials that may be used in the construction of the individual units, and provides suggested themes for interpretation in a number of materials. Step-by-step instructions for making a number of mobiles are included. All are simple structures that could easily be managed even by those with no previous acquaintance with craft work.

225. Vanderbilt, Gloria, with Alfred Allen Lewis. **Gloria Vanderbilt Book of Collage**. New York, Van Nostrand Reinhold, 1970. 111p. illus. index. $12.95. LC 78-103625.

Definitely not a how-to book, but one that is filled with imaginative ways to use collage as a decorative and an artistic medium.

226. Williams, Guy R. **Making Mobiles**. New York, Emerson, 1969. illus. $4.95. ISBN 0-87523-167-5.

Even the least experienced of craftsmen will find a mobile at his level. Beginning with very simple and inexpensive mobiles, this book progresses to much more complicated structures of metal. In addition to the step-by-step directions, there are drawings of techniques and photographs (for inspiration) of mobiles by artists such as Calder.

MOSAICS

227. Arvois, Edmond. **Making Mosaics**. New York, Sterling, 1971. 88p. illus. index. $3.99. LC 64-15109. ISBN 0-8069-5060-9.

Beginning with a description of various mosaic stones and adhesives, the author introduces the reader to a number of simple projects designed to provide familiarity with the medium, the tools necessary for cutting, and the materials used in finishing the mosaics. Examples are shown of difficult works by professionals as well as unusual works that the reader may hope to emulate in a short time. Suggestions for projects are made to help the reader launch out on his own. The author suggests appropriate uses for mosaics and gives instructions on laying out and developing a design. Various methods of treating background are illustrated. The final chapter gives a short history of mosaic development. Recommended as an elementary text for self-instruction.

228. Berry, John. **Making Mosaics**. New York, Watson-Guptill, 1967 (c.1966). 104p. illus. $1.95pa. LC 67-10437.

This basic book provides the reader with a short history of mosaics and gives information on how mosaic tiles (tesserae) are made. Tools used in working with mosaics are described, along with such basic operations as cutting and layout. Design possibilities are suggested by the author, including ways of using mosaics in coffee tables, lamp bases, and patios. A short bibliography is appended.

229. Hendrickson, Edwin. **Mosaics: Hobby and Art**. New York, Hill and Wang, 1957. 111p. illus. $3.75. LC 57-8589.

The first section of this book describes how to make 12 basic projects—a trivet, a small table-top, a shelf with a mosaic edge, a hot plate, a lamp base, a brass tray, an end table, coffee tables, book ends, ash trays, and a round table top. Part two deals with materials and methods. The author describes different types of tiles (and how to cut and shape them), backings, edgings and hardware, adhesives, cements, and dyes. The remainder of the second section discusses how to design a mosaic and gives the requirements for wall mosaics and panels, mosaic floors, and mosaic walkways. Part three provides descriptions and photographs of a number of mosaic designs that can be copied or adapted. Instructions throughout the book are simple and easy to follow. There are lists of equipment and materials needed for each of the 12 projects, as well as numbered sequential instruction. The author, who has worked in ceramics for years, is responsible for developing and merchandising the first do-it-yourself mosaic kit. Recommended for public libraries as a beginning text.

230. Hendrickson, Edwin. **Mosaic Patterns**. New York, Farrar, Straus, and Giroux, 1958. 95p. illus index. $2.45pa. LC 58-14158.

There are 72 black and white diagrams for mosaics and four color plate diagrams in this book of designs. The diagrams are arranged in order of the complexity of the figure and background. The introduction provides information on mosaic materials (tesserae, in this case), backing, adhesives, methods of application, and background techniques. The ideas here laid out for the hobbyist will tax his imagination only in the use of color, though nothing forbids his using these diagrams simply as a point of departure. In spite of its age, this design book can be of essential help to anyone interested in mosaics. The designs were prepared by mosaic artists, hobbyists, and mosaic dealers. Appended are credits for the designs and suggestions for size and use.

231. Hutton, Helen. **Mosaic Making**. New York, Van Nostrand Reinhold, 1966. 136p. illus. $7.95. LC 66-22688.

A unique feature of this book is the inclusion of a section on stained glass mosaics and other unusual forms. In addition, of course, there are the expected chapters on design, equipment, materials, cutting, treatment of surfaces, etc. Appended are a bibliography, a glossary of terms, and a list of suppliers.

232. Jenkins, Louisa, and Barbara Mills. **The Art of Making Mosaics**. New York, Van Nostrand Reinhold, 1957. 132p. illus. $5.95. LC 57-11592.

The purpose of this book is to present basic techniques for making mosaics so that teachers, artists, and amateurs "may know what tools and materials are necessary." To accomplish this, the authors describe the workshop and the materials used in construction, including how to make one's own tiles, the wood base, concrete base, how to cut and prepare materials, the use of mortars, and the description of various methods of laying the mosaic (direct method, reverse method, Italian method). Besides the information on tile mosaics, there is also a separate chapter on pebble mosaics. Additional chapters discuss mosaic creation in the classroom, mosaic design, and church art and graphic symbols. A final chapter displays various works by artists and gives some biographical information on individual artists. A bibliography of symbolism, mosaic history, and design is appended. Twelve projects are included, and the reader is given step-by-step instruction for each. Recommended for public and high school libraries with craft collections, in spite of its age.

233. Lewis, Beatrice, and Leslie McGuire. **Making Mosaics.** New York, Drake, 1973. 192p. illus. $7.95. LC 72-10519. ISBN 0-87749-420-7.

This comprehensive guide to making mosaics discusses tools and materials, adhesives, and designs. In addition to the step-by-step instructions, there are also about 80 pages of color illustrations.

234. Lovoos, Janice, and Felice Paramore. **Modern Mosaic Techniques.** New York, Watson-Guptill, 1967. 169p. illus. $9.95. LC 67-13744. ISBN 0-8230-3120-9.

Advanced and innovative use of materials is the unique feature of this work. The authors emphasize modern techniques, including step-by-step demonstrations of direct and indirect methods, sandcasting, collage, sculpture, and mosaics from found materials. Appended are a bibliography and a list of suppliers. Highly recommended.

235. Luchner, Adolf. **Crystal-Glass Mosaic.** New York, Drake, 1971. 80p. illus. index. $3.95. ISBN 0-87749-094-5.

This specialized book describes the techniques used in making mosaics from translucent glass. The basic principles, of course, can also be applied to mosaics in more traditional materials. Illustrated with photographs, line drawings, and 10 color plates.

236. Seidelman, James E., and Grace Mintonye. **Creating Mosaics.** New York, Macmillan, 1967. 56p. $4.50.

The authors of this work, which is aimed at a young audience, encourage an inventive and experimental approach to mosaics. Explanations are given of the proper way to use materials, but the children are then left on their own to create projects and designs.

237. Stribling, Mary Lou. **Mosaic Techniques: New Aspects of Fragmented Design**. New York, Crown, 1966. 244p. illus. $7.95. LC 66-15121.

This work describes materials, techniques, and tools, then gives instructions for a number of decorative and useful objects. Because Ms. Stribling encourages inventiveness and experimentation (in both materials and design), the work will have appeal to advanced amateurs and professional craftsmen as well as to beginners.

238. Tanner, June. **Let's Make a Mosaic**. New York, Franklin Watts, 1969. 54p. illus. $3.95. LC 69-10885.

The object of this book is "to give practical advice about the process involved in making different kinds of mosaic art forms." The author also provides a brief history of mosaics and indicates how the forms used in the past may be adapted to present-day designs. The main sections deal with paper, seed, wood, tile, and pebble mosaics. The author provides hints and instructions for working with each of these materials and suggests objects that may be used as a mosaic base—lamps, table tops, game boards, etc. Instructions are clear and simple. Illustrations provide ideas and instruction. Recommended for beginners.

239. Timmons, Virginia Gayheart. **Designing and Making Mosaics**. Worcester, Mass., Davis Publications, 1971. 112p. illus. $8.95. LC 77-163725. ISBN 0-87192-042-5.

The aim of the author is to encourage art teachers and others who work with young people to include mosaics in their plans for art activities. But this is an instructive text for anyone interested in mosaics. The author believes that mosaics offer a "uniquely appropriate" experience for the student, for he is intimately involved with "choices relating to materials, color, textures, shapes, values and how to use them in his own creative expression." The historical introduction is illustrated with fine mosaic works of the past and present. A section on design, which provides suggestions for sources and methods, is followed by a section on tools, equipment, and materials. Here the author describes not only traditional material but found and made materials to be incorporated into mosaic designs. There is also information on modern plastics and adhesives. Processes and techniques are detailed in the chapter on methods, where casting, lamination, and fusing are also treated.

The final chapter deals with the classroom and the accumulation of materials for classroom instruction and activities. The book is well illustrated throughout with excellent examples of mosaics of many types, using a large variety of materials. Some excellent full-color plates are included. Recommended to teachers of art as well as to anyone who wants ideas for materials and designs in mosaics.

240. Young, Joseph L. **Course in Making Mosaics**. New York, Van Nostrand Reinhold, 1957. 60p. illus. LC 57-9557.

This older book is out of print, but it is still available in many libraries. The author describes the materials and tools of the craft and provides the student with a description of the processes involved in making a mosaic. Suggestions on adhesives, tiles, and other equipment are scattered throughout. Methods are accompanied by photographs illustrating the techniques under discussion. Various types of mosaics are discussed, including wall panels, table tops, and mosaic sculpture. Black and white illustrations show numerous examples of mosaic art—from wall panels to Juan O'Gorman's library at the University of Mexico. Although it is not a project book, it will provide the amateur with practical information and advice while illustrating the scope of the craft.

PAPER

GENERAL

241. Alkema, Chester Jay. **Creative Paper Crafts**. New York, Sterling, 1970. 179p. illus. index. $7.89. LC 67-27751. ISBN 0-8069-5086-2.

Mr. Alkema offers numerous suggestions for children's creative activities using paper. Providing basic instructions in making both two- and three-dimensional objects, the author instructs the child in the basic techniques of pasting, weaving, folding, and cutting, and then gives him freedom to create something original. He does this through numerous photos (in both color and black and white) that show the possibilities open to the child. However, even adults may be fascinated by the handsome objects here illustrated. The author has had a great deal of experience teaching art courses to children. School and public libraries should have this one.

242. Ask, Gunvor, and Harriet Ask. **Simple Paper Craft**. Newton Centre, Mass., Branford, 1971. 125p. illus. $4.95. LC 72-131435.

Translated from the Danish, this work provides directions for Danish holiday decorations as well as for more prosaic projects (lamp shades, masks, etc.). Instructions are easy to follow, and they are supplemented by patterns, line drawings, and photographs.

243. **Card and Cardboard**. New York, Franklin Watts, 1971. 175p. illus. index. $5.95. LC 71-158980. ISBN 0-531-02002-9.

How-to instructions for making 61 different projects from cardboard, color coded for difficulty from grades 1 to 4. Projects range from a cardboard mouse made from a tube to a Bugatti roadster. All materials are easily accessible. The book has a large format for easy display in the classroom. Recommended for elementary school libraries.

244. Fabri, Ralph. **Sculpture in Paper**. New York, Watson-Guptill, 1966. 165p. illus. index. $8.50. LC 66-19734.

Using construction paper and a number of simple tools, the author shows the reader in detailed step-by-step drawings how sculpture may be created from this humble material. After a note on design and the necessity for stylization, he tells how to make the basic shapes and how to combine them in the creation of sculptured forms—i.e., three-dimensional forms. Subsequent sections describe the forming and attaching of various parts of the body (torso, arms, head and neck, legs) followed by ways of detailing each of these to achieve realistic effects. Noses, ears, mouths, eyes, moustaches, heads, hands, and feet are all treated in order. Following chapters deal with specific building projects—a clown, a figure in uniform, an angel, a queen, figures in motion, four-legged animals, winged animals, insects, sea creatures, imaginary creatures, mobiles and several others. Along with the text, detailed drawings and diagrams provide the necessary instructions. Each section is accompanied by photos of finished projects of the type described in that section. A final chapter discusses commercial possibilities in paper sculpture. The text is simply written, with excellent selections of projects, which should both challenge and excite anyone with an eye for witty ingenuity. Excellent. Recommended for people with an inventive flair and for public libraries with such patrons.

A work on the subject scheduled for September 1973 publication is *Paper Sculpture*, by George Borchard (Taplinger. $6.50). This work progresses from the simplest principles of working with paper to advanced designs for Christmas decorations, lampshades, and an elaborate rendering of St. George and the dragon.

245. Glass, F. J. **Paper Craft**. London, University of London Press, 1927; repr. Kentfield, Calif., Newton K. Gregg, 1971. 76p. illus. $2.95pa. LC 73-163531. ISBN 0-91238-03-1.

This reprint may perhaps suffer because of its age, but the basic principles still remain sound. Recent developments in papier mâché, however, create a more durable form than the flour and water paste used here. The author gives instructions for making lampshades and for piercing paper for decorative effect. The section dealing with lacquer and its application to papier mâché objects is excellent. Few illustrations, but the text is clear. Recommended especially for the chapter on lacquer.

246. Granit, Inga. **Cardboard Crafting: How to Make Things out of Cardboard**. New York, Sterling, 1964. 96p. illus. index. $3.99. LC 64-15108. ISBN 0-8069-5054-4.

Using only a few simple tools, the author instructs the reader in how to make a number of practical articles—memo pads, loose leaf binders, covers for books, desk caddies, paper baskets, closet storage boxes, sewing booklets, jewel boxes, etc. Step-by-step instructions show how to use materials available in practically every home. For all ages, though projects seem to appeal more to an adult audience.

247. Grater, Michael. **Make It in Paper: A Simple Introduction to Paper Sculpture for Children**. London, Mills and Boon; New York, Taplinger, 1962. 88p. illus. $5.95.

The paper sculpture projects in this book are intended strictly for children, though the text is definitely for their elders. The first chapter is devoted to the basic techniques—straight and curved score, center cut, the "return," curling, etc. Projects are suggested through the numerous photos and drawings that accompany the text. The second section deals with three-dimensional modelling of paper and includes mobiles and three-dimensional representations of fish, birds, and other creatures. Basic shapes and their manipulation are treated in a separate section that is directed to the teacher. All of Mr. Grater's books are of exceptional merit and this one, being earlier, perhaps set the mold. It should be of value especially to teachers of elementary grades, but parents who like working with their children will also be interested. Recommended for elementary school and public libraries.

248. Grater, Michael. **Paper People**. New York, Taplinger, 1969. 192p. illus. $6.95. LC 77-99308. ISBN 0-8008-6255-4.

In this book on paper craft, Mr. Grater explores ways in which human figures can be cut, folded, or molded by using sheets of construction paper, wrapping paper, newspaper, or aluminum foil. Included among the human menagerie are clowns, acrobats, witches, housewives, kings, Santas, and others, in both two and three dimensions. Included also are marionettes, flat articulated figures, and jack-in-the-boxes. All are highly imaginative and delightful. Full instructions for making various figures are given, along with photographs of the author's own creations, and diagrams for easy copying. The figures range from the very simple to quite complex, and there is little duplication with Mr. Grater's *Paper Faces* (entry 428). Those that children are not able to make they will be delighted to play with. An excellent book recommended for all school and public libraries. Most recently Mr. Grater has published *Paper Play* (Taplinger, 1973. $9.95).

249. Grol, Lini. **Scissorscraft**. New York, Sterling, 1970. 48p. illus. index. (Little Craft Book Series). $2.95. LC 70-126849. ISBN 0-8069-5160-5.

A book on cutting paper for silhouette as well as detailed internal forms. Illustrated with cutouts that range in difficulty from very simple to complex. Recommended for children. A newly announced work on the subject is Brigitte Stoddart's *Papercutting* (Taplinger, 1973. $6.50).

250. Hollander, Annette. **Decorative Papers and Fabrics**. New York, Van Nostrand Reinhold, 1971. 119p. illus. $8.95. LC 73-149256.

Beautifully illustrated, this book describes several methods of decorating paper and fabrics. Marbled paper, fold and dye, wax resist, sewing machine stitchery, potato printing, and starch paper are illustrated, and the techniques used by the author to achieve unusual effects are described. Many black and white photos show designs and a few beautiful color prints indicate the author's artistry. Beautiful holiday wrappings can be made by following the instructions here, and some pieces are worthy of framing. An excellent book recommended highly for all public libraries and for hobbyists with a flair for the unusual and colorful.

251. Johnson, Pauline. **Creating with Paper: Basic Forms and Variations**. Seattle, University of Washington Press, 1966. 207p. illus. $8.95. LC 58-6007.

In this now-standard work on paper craft, the author explores a wide range of techniques and activities in paper. After a listing of tools and materials, there is a description of some of the properties of paper, and basic shapes are illustrated. Succeeding sections provide graphic displays of methods for forming paper into various shapes by cutting and expanding, one-fold cutting, multiple fold cutting, symmetrical cutting, cutouts, surface treatment, curling, bending, folding, and scoring. She describes how to make window cutouts, screen models, geometric solids, three-dimensional forms, cages and blocks, vehicles, moving forms (mobiles), and plane sculptural forms. The section on basic shapes deals with rectangles, squares, circles, and cylinders, and describes how to use these in forming various objects. Several sections treat holiday decorations, while others deal with birds, masks, etc. There are numerous projects for children. This is a basic text that should be available in elementary school libraries, although the range of projects will appeal to a wide group. A mature approach, moreover, precludes its use by children alone, in spite of the fact that the forms, in most cases, are simple. It should be an excellent aid to teachers. Recommended for all school and public libraries.

252. Kampmann, Lothar. **Creating with Colored Paper**. New York, Van Nostrand Reinhold, 1968. illus. index. (Art Media Series). $5.95. LC 68-26804.

This series includes a number of titles by Mr. Kampmann: *Creating with... Crayons* (1968), *Poster Paints* (1968), *Colored Ink* (1969), and *Printing Material* (1969). Although they represent varying degrees of success, in general they will provide teachers with a guide to the possibilities inherent in each of the media. The illustrations (often of children's work) are excellent. Those who need fresh approaches to crafts for children will find this series useful.

253. Laliberte, Norman, and Alex Mogelon. **Silhouettes, Shadows and Cutouts: History and Modern Use**. New York, Van Nostrand Reinhold, 1968. 112p. $8.95. LC 68-16021.

Providing a history of the cutout in all eras, the authors illustrate their text with beautiful examples of the art culled from many sources, including shopsigns, trademarks, and advertisements. In addition, Mr. Laliberte's own cutout work is displayed. Directions for cutting are brief, however, and the how-to intention of the book has been neglected. German, British, Polish, and American cutouts are represented, though Oriental work is underrepresented. As a sourcebook for inspiration to the modern enthusiast, however, this work provides ample material. Recommended for public libraries with do-it-yourself patrons.

254. Munson, Don, and Allianora Rosse. **The Paper Book: 187 Things to Make**. New York, Scribner's, 1970. 176p. illus. $8.95.

The authors provide a list of necessary supplies in their preface, and then plunge into step-by-step descriptions of 187 projects made of paper. Chapters divide the projects into areas of interest. The first chapter deals with paper planes, kites, and books; the second with dollhouses, furniture and villages; chapter three with lanterns, lampshades, and window pictures. Subsequent chapters describe how to make costumes and masks, boxes, baskets, gift wrapping, dolls, animals, birds, dust jackets, greeting cards, fans, and other objects. Two separate chapters are devoted to more complicated scientific and artistic creations—the chapter on origami, and the chapter on pictures and collages. A final chapter treats holiday creations. Since the book is intended to make working with paper seem easy, it is therefore suitable for children and their teachers. The wide variety of items presented will appeal to anyone seeking ideas for projects.

255. Newman, Thelma R., Jay Hartley Newman, and Lee Scott Newman. **Paper as Art and Craft: The Complete Book of the History and Processes of the Paper Arts**. New York, Crown, 1973. 308p. illus. bibliog. index. $9.95. LC 72-96648. ISBN 0-517-503700.

A "complete" book of anything awakens one's suspicions. But it is hard to imagine another book on paper that encompasses so many aspects of the subject. Copiously illustrated with the authors' photographs (color as well as black and white) and line drawings, the book is divided into nine chapters. The first presents not only the history of paper but the processes of making paper by hand and by machine, types of paper, and watermarks. The chapter on "paper vocabulary" presents the creative possibilities of paper: bending, crumpling, wadding, folding, etc., through a total of 15 ways of creating with paper. Remaining chapters cover two-dimensional uses of paper, paper in relief, sculptural and architectural forms, collage, decoupage and papier mâché, decorative paper and bookbinding, and "useful and decorative forms." Among the latter are crepe paper; paper flowers; weaving, knitting, and macrame with paper twine; paper beads and quilling; boxes; and lampshades. An essential, basic work for the crafts collection of any public or school library. Crafts teachers and art teachers will find it a treasure trove of information.

256. Ody, Kenneth. **Paper Folding and Paper Sculpture**. New York, Emerson, 1965. 174p. illus. $6.95. LC 65-20776. ISBN 0-87523-155-1.

The author's intention is to explore the basic methods and principles of working with paper and "to provide a summary of techniques that can be drawn upon to create original designs." Beginning with simple forms, the author describes the basic ways of manipulating paper—folding, origami, paper cuts, animals and figure cutouts, curling, waving, weaving, geometric solids, paper sculpture, relief, and in the round. He includes directions (with text and line drawings) for making dozens of items. The projects range in difficulty from simple lanterns for kindergarten pupils to complicated sculptural forms. Excellent clear drawings and explanatory text. Plates at the end provide a large number of excellent examples of what can be accomplished. Though not as comprehensive as Pauline Johnson's text or the Newmans' work, it is nevertheless quite impressive.

257. Rainey, Sarita, and Arnel Pattemore. **Ways with Paper**. Worcester, Mass., Davis. 36p. illus. (Basic Concept Series). $1.95pa. LC 79-185460. ISBN 0-87192-046-8.

Designed for beginners, this little book concentrates on colored paper and its creative possibilities. The aim of the series is to present only basic fundamentals of various crafts.

258. Röttger, Ernst. **Creative Paper Design**. New York, Van Nostrand Reinhold, 1961. 95p. illus. $5.95. LC 60-16591.

The author treats the manipulation of paper as a serious creative task that is nevertheless fun. He describes various ways of treating paper, and provides numerous designs and forms intended to stimulate creativity in the child. Excellent illustrations and beautiful imaginative designs with descriptions of how they are made.

259. Rubi, Christian. **Cut Paper, Silhouettes, and Stencils: An Instruction Book**. New York, Van Nostrand Reinhold, 1972. 177p. illus. $8.50. LC 73-150728. ISBN 0-7182-0793-9.

Published in Switzerland in 1970 and here translated by Alba Lorman, this book presents the craft of papercutting from the traditional Swiss viewpoint. The designs include those suitable for the beginner as well as for the advanced papercutter.

260. Sadler, Arthur. **An Introduction to Paper Sculpture**. Newton Centre, Mass., Branford, 1966. $3.75.

Mr. Sadler treats paper sculpture as an entertaining as well as artistic hobby that can offer at little expense a great deal of pleasure to its practitioners. The tools are simple, the materials readily available, and here is Mr. Sadler to provide the would-be artist with basic techniques and a number of projects created as a point of departure for the reader's inspiration. The projects are simple but appealing, and in the process the novice paper sculptor may find himself hooked. Highly recommended. A recent title on the subject is Alan Allport's *Paper Sculpture* (Drake, 1971. $5.95), which discusses modelling in cardboard and wood as well as paper.

261. Sperling, Walter. **How to Make Things Out of Paper**. New York, Sterling, 1971. 124p. illus. index. $2.95. LC 60-14331. ISBN 0-8069-5044-7.

This book provides instruction for making 48 objects from paper. Many involve simple origami folding techniques; others use paste and glue to make kites, boxes, and decorations. Suitable for elementary school children.

262. Strose, Susanne. **Making Paper Flowers**. New York, Sterling, 1972. 48p. illus. index. (Little Craft Book Series). $2.95. LC 69-19490. ISBN 0-8069-5130-3.

With step-by-step directions and illustrations, the author shows how to create flowers of tissue and crepe paper by means of folding and cutting. Included are iris, carnation, daisy, bluebell, lily, tulip, peony, lilac, and zinnia. In addition there is a section on creating floral fantasies of metal foil. Instructions are clear and precise, and color photos show some of the finished products individually and in arrangements. A small book with considerable information.

Taplinger has announced a work on this topic for publication in November 1973: *Making Paper Flowers*, by Suzy Ives ($6.95). This work provides directions for flowers from crepe paper, cartridge paper, and tissue paper. The many suggestions for using the flowers range from arrangements in combination with dried grasses to Christmas decorations and necklaces.

263. Strose, Susanne. **Coloring Paper**. New York, Sterling, 1969. 48p. illus. index. (Little Craft Book Series). $2.95. LC 68-8762. ISBN 0-8069-5102-8.

The author gives brief instructions (including lists of materials and tools) for decorating paper in many different ways. The techniques used here are far more numerous than those suggested by Annette Hollander in her *Decorative Papers and Fabrics* (entry 250), but instructions and suggestions—which may make the difference between success and failure—are not as detailed or as good. As an inventory of various methods of decorating paper, however, this supplements Ms. Hollander's book and may be more appealing to those who simply need the initial push and then want to be left on their own.

264. **Tissue Paper Activities**. Worcester, Mass., Davis, 1971. 34p. illus. (Basic Concept Series). $1.95. LC 76-166219. ISBN 0-87192-037-9.

Useful as a classroom guide or as a source of ideas for interesting colorful creations to make at home, this book contains sections on tissue collages, three-dimensional constructions, drawing on tissue, rubbings, "tissue-mâché," simulated stained glass, and other inventive ways of working with a colorful medium. Instructions are ample. Black and white as well as color photographs illustrate various ways to use tissue. Recommended for elementary school teachers and others who may wish to have additional ideas for exploring paper.

A more comprehensive and advanced work on the subject is *Creating with Tissue Paper*, by Barbara Stephan (Crown, 1973. $7.95).

265. Van Voorst, Dick. **Corrugated Carton Crafting**. New York, Sterling, 1968. 48p. illus. index. (Little Craft Book Series). $2.95. LC 71-90803. ISBN 0-8069-5138-9.

Taking advantage of the structural peculiarities of corrugated paper cartons, the author provides instruction for working with this material and suggests projects that can be made from it. Many are quite complicated structures that should appeal to the pre-teenage group. Along the way other possibilities will suggest themselves to the inventive mind. Recommended for school and public libraries. *Nomadic Furniture* (see entry 459) includes a number of furniture projects that use corrugated cardboard.

266. Wood, Louise, and Orvelo Wood. **Make It with Paper**. New York, David McKay, 1970. 247p. illus. $5.95. LC 73-135583.

The projects in this book are primarily intended to interest children and are simple enough in execution to serve as a handbook for teachers whose charges are involved in an inexpensive "art experience." The first three chapters describe materials and techniques, cutouts, and basic forms. Subsequent chapters provide instructions for building forms in a number of categories—animals, masks, mats, baskets, ornaments, flowers, jewelry, wheeled vehicles, and wind-blown constructions (kites, pinwheels). The final chapter deals with more artistic uses of paper (mosaics, collages, mobiles, etc.). Many of the projects are at the same time imaginative and simple, and they should be extremely attractive to children. There are black and white photos of the finished items, with cutting diagrams for some of the more complicated ones. Recommended for teachers of the primary grades, and for parents who enjoy helping their children.

267. **Working with Paper**. New York, Franklin Watts, 1971. 191p. illus. index. $5.95. LC 73-158978.

Colorful illustrations of how to make about 90 objects from paper. Intended for the lower grades of the elementary schools, the various projects are color-coded for difficulty. Each project is preceded by a list of materials needed, all of which are easily obtainable. Projects include Christmas cards, snakes, trains, stars, mobiles, Chinese lanterns, etc. Large format makes the book convenient for classroom use.

268. Yamada, Sadami, and Kiyotada Ito. **New Dimensions in Paper Craft**. San Francisco, Japan Publications Trading Company, 1966. 263p. illus. $12.00.

The authors of this authoritative text rarely venture beyond projects that will appeal to children (though, admittedly, sophisticated children). The book, however, is intended not for children but for their teachers, parents, and would-be instructors who may lack a feeling for this inexpensive but creative medium. All the basic techniques are treated (tearing and cutting, folding, scoring and bending) and all the basic shapes (cylinders, cones, pyramids). Also discussed are piercing, wrinkling, curling, cutouts, surface treatment, origami, layer folding, papier mâché, joining, and dying. Toward the end of the text projects are pictured and diagrammed. As indicated above, all the projects are intended to appeal to children. The photographic work is really exceptionally clear; in many cases the photographs furnish sufficient explanation of the process involved in construction. The written text is authoritative, informative, and clearly written. Though all the processes can certainly be used in making more sophisticated forms and constructions, the book is intended for those who wish to introduce the techniques to children. For this purpose, the organization, layout, and illustrations of this text are quite exceptional.

ORIGAMI

269. Adachi, Katsuyuki. **Kayaragusa: Volume 8**. Washington, D.C., Pine Cone Press, 1961.

This is a nineteenth century manuscript reproduced with translation and commentary by Julia and Marlin Brossman. Origami enthusiasts will consider this a document of historical significance. Instructions are given for more than 30 models. Recommended for serious origami collections.

270. Araki, Chiyo. **Origami in the Classroom, Book I: Activities for Autumn through Christmas**. Rutland, Vt., Tuttle, 1965. 40p. illus. $3.60. LC 65-13412. ISBN 0-8048-0452-4.

271. Araki, Chiyo. **Origami in the Classroom, Book II: Activities for Winter through Summer**. Rutland, Vt., Tuttle, 1968. 40p. illus. $3.75. LC 65-13412. ISBN 0-8048-0453-2.

The author's aim is to introduce American children to the "unique" Japanese origami by adapting the methods and forms used in Japan to the annual events and holidays of American children. Thus, the models in the first book are appropriate to the first half of the school year (a ship for Columbus Day; a cat, a bat, and a jack-o-lantern for Halloween; and a Santa for Christmas). The second book continues the themes of the school year with a penguin for winter, a horse and rider for Washington's Birthday, etc. Most of the models are relatively simple; they are graduated in difficulty for children in grades 1 to 6. Both books are nicely illustrated and directions are clear. Recommended for teachers of primary grades and for parents of children in this age group.

272. Arnstein, Bennett. **Origami Polyhedra**. New York, Exposition Press, 1968. 112p. illus. $5.00. LC 67-26388. ISBN 0-682-46771-5.

This book explains how to make three-dimensional geometric models by combining folded pieces of paper. Most of the numerous figures use only three basic origami folds, and combining these forms requires only cellophane tape. There are 95 diagrams that illustrate the foldings, and 154 photographs that show how the folded bases fit together. A unique book on the mathematical aspects of origami.

273. Cerceda, Adolfo. **Folding Money**. Chicago, Ireland Magic Company, 1963. 36p.

This 36-page booklet, illustrated with 100 drawings, is a little novelty item devoted exclusively to figures folded from dollar bills. This may be the only aspect of the dollar to remain unaffected by devaluation.

274. Harbin, Robert. **New Adventures in Origami**. New York, Funk and Wagnalls, 1971. 186p. illus. $1.25pa.

Prefacing this volume with a table of standard symbols, the author illustrates through diagrams 58 different figures and folds. Most of the folds are traditional, but a few new ones are introduced. Since this is a book for beginners, it should be worked progressively from the first section, so that basic folds can be mastered first. No text, only diagrams. Excellent once you catch on to the code and the basic folds. A bibliography is appended.

275. Harbin, Robert. **Origami: The Art of Paper Folding**. New York, Funk and Wagnalls, 1969. illus. $1.25pa.

This book, a reprint of an older work, offers a comprehensive collection of folds from all over the world. Step-by-step instructions are included. Models range from simple to complex. Like Mr. Harbin's other books, it is an excellent standard text on paperfolding, in spite of its age.

276. Harbin, Robert. **Paper Magic**. London, Oldbourne Press, 1956; repr. Newton Centre, Mass., Branford, 1957. 103p. illus. index.

An excellent standard text with over 100 models. The book is arranged to be especially helpful to beginners. All procedures are graphically displayed with step-by-step instructions provided by line drawings. Highly recommended, but apparently out of print.

277. Harbin, Robert. **Secrets of Origami**. London, Oldbourne Press, 1963.

One hundred and fifty models are explained by 1,400 drawings and 70 photographs. The standard line and arrow code is used. The leading paperfolders of the world contributed original models to this wonderful anthology, which contains, in addition, a large section of traditional folds.

278. Honda, Isao. **Living Origami**. Rutland, Vt., Tuttle, 1962. 25p. illus. $2.95.

Using patterned papers that are provided in a folder at the back of the book, the reader can make two of each of the 16 objects illustrated. Step-by-step instructions are provided for each. Some of the models, already folded, have been tipped in. Recommended for teachers of primary grades. Other children's books by Isao Honda are *Origami Folding Fun: Kangaroo Book* ($1.50); *Origami Folding Fun: Pony Book* ($1.50); *Origami Festival* ($1.75); and *Origami Holiday* ($2.75pa.). All are published by Japan Publications in Tokyo and are distributed by Japan Publications Trading Company in San Francisco. All are recommended by the publisher for grades 1 to 6.

279. Honda, Isao. **The World of Origami**. San Francisco, Japan Publications Trading Company. 264p. illus. $12.00.

Contains 160 models, over 2,000 explanatory charts, and 150 photographs of completed figures. The author leads the student from traditional to modern works and from copying to original origami creation. One of the most complete treatments available. Large format, boxed. Highly recommended for adult enthusiasts. The same author has edited *All About Origami* (Toto Bunka Company, 1960), which suggests 130 origami figures and which serves as a sort of summary of his previous compilations.

280. Jones, Madeline. **The Mysterious Flexagon: An Introduction to a Fascinating New Concept in Paper Folding**. New York, Crown, 1966. 48p. illus. $1.95.

This cutout book introduces the reader to the "flexagon," a figure that "reveals any number of faces from three to infinity." Simple directions are given for making simple to complex figures. Many are extremely attractive, with colorful designs. Recommended for elementary school teachers.

281. Kasahara, Kunihiko. **Creative Origami**. Tokyo, Japan Publications; distr. San Francisco, Japan Publications Trading Company, 1967. 175p. illus. $9.95.

Each of the first four chapters is devoted to a single fold and to step-by-step directions for building 25 different models using that basic fold. In all, then, there are 100 models—many traditional, some new. The final chapter deals with creating original models. Large format with some color photos of origami displays. An excellent text for beginner or expert.

282. Massoglia, Elinor Tripato, and George Rhoads. **Fun-Time Paper Folding**. Chicago, Children's Press, 1959. 31p. illus. $2.75.

Using traditional folds, the authors give instructions and illustrations for making 13 different models, from a sailboat to a butterfly. Recommended for grades 3 to 6.

283. Murray, William D., and Francis J. Rigney. **Paper Folding for Beginners**. New York, Dover. 94p. illus. $1.00pa. ISBN 0-486-20713-7.

The original title of this work was *Introduction to Paperfolding*. Using basic techniques, the authors illustrate how to make 42 different models, from a simple boat to a Japanese lantern. Each model builds upon the preceding ones, so the student is forced to work from the beginning. For the most part, models are simple. Recommended for children from first grade on up. An illustrated story, in which a single piece of paper is folded and refolded to form a number of objects, concludes the book.

284. **My Origami Animals and Fishes**. New York, Crown. illus. $1.00.

The companion volumes to this one are *My Origami Flowers* and *My Origami Birds* ($1.00 each). All three of the books present easy-to-follow instructions for making an assortment of models. Color photos of models are included, and a packet of origami paper is enclosed in each book. Recommended for grades 4 to 8.

285. Phillips, Jo. **Right Angles: Paper-Folding Geometry**. New York, T. Y. Crowell, 1972. 40p. illus. $3.75. LC 72-171007. ISBN 0-690-60916-7.

Although it is not an origami book, this work uses the principles of folding to introduce the young student to geometric concepts. Through paper folding the author introduces the young student to the right angle, the rectangle, the square, congruence, similarity, and quadrilaterals. The simple-to-understand text is augmented by drawings. Recommended for grades 3 to 5.

286. Randlett, Samuel. **The Art of Origami: Paper Folding, Traditional and Modern**. New York, Dutton, 1961. $7.95.

This book provides 57 models, many of them by the author, with over 500 line drawings and 41 photographs. The format, organization, and conventions of illustration are the same as for the author's *The Best of Origami*. Text includes essays on origami history, teaching, and creation. Excellent for both beginners and experts. Traditional and original folds. The author uses an analytical approach that is especially helpful to beginner and expert. Highly recommended.

287. Randlett, Samuel. **The Best of Origami: New Models by Contemporary Folders**. New York, Dutton, 1963. 185p. illus. $6.95.

In this book each of the "traditional" basic folds has a chapter to itself, and within each chapter the models are presented in order of difficulty—from elementary figures to very complex. The book is thus suited to the beginner as well as the virtuoso. Figures are folded from triangles, rectangles, diamond shapes, or hexagons. Many of the 76 figures appear here for the first time. Conventional diagrams provide how-to instructions by line drawings. Excellent and essential for a basic collection. A bibliography and a directory of contributors are included.

288. Sakade, Florence, and Kazuhiko Sono. **Fold-and-Paste Origami Storybook**. Rutland, Vt., Tuttle, 1964. 32p. illus. $2.50. LC 64-22899. ISBN 0-8048-0189-4.

Using five short stories as a framework, the authors provide illustrated instructions for folding 14 different characters taken from the stories. The illustrations for the stories provide blank spaces for pasting in the folded project. A packet of multi-colored origami paper is provided with the book. Projects (with full instructions for folding) include a turtle, fish, crab, water bird, swallow, flower, frog, flying bird, pagoda, and others. Good for capturing a child's interest. Another work by Ms. Sakade is *Origami: Japanese Paper Folding* (3v., Tuttle. $1.25pa.ea.vol.).

289. Sarasas, Claude. **The ABC's of Origami: Paper Folding for Children**. Rutland, Vt., Tuttle. 55p. illus. $3.25. LC 64-17160. ISBN 0-8048-0000-6

With captions in English, French, and Japanese, the step-by-step illustrations show how to make a whole alphabet of origami creatures, from albatross to zebra. Nicely illustrated.

290. Soong, Maying. **The Art of Chinese Paper Folding: For Young and Old**. New York, Harcourt Brace, 1948. 132p. illus. $4.50.

The author describes approximately 30 especially charming models, including lighthouse, toys, furniture, and a pagoda bookmark. The beginner should have little trouble with the models, which are organized in progressive order of difficulty. Clearly illustrated for easy duplication.

291. Temko, Florence. **Paper Folding to Begin With**. Indianapolis, Bobbs-Merrill, 1968. 31p. illus. $4.50.

Directions are provided for making a number of play objects from several types of paper, including newspapers. Newspaper hats and paper airplanes are among the 25 projects described. All are made without glue or scissors. A brief history of paper folding is included.

PAPIER MACHE

292. Anderson, Mildred. **Original Creations with Papier Mâché**. New York, Sterling, 1967. 92p. illus. index. $3.95. LC 67-27751.

In this book Ms. Anderson develops the process of working with papier mâché somewhat more fully than in her first book (*Papier Mâché and How to Work with It*). Although the projects use the same techniques as those described in her other work, they are more ambitious. Black and white photos fail to convey the charm of many of her creations, so the color photos included here make a difference. A list of materials is included with each project. A recipe for paper mash (which she calls pulp) uses a blender to help with the initial steps. Somewhat more advanced than her earlier volume, but it is still for beginners.

293. Anderson, Mildred. **Papier Mâché and How to Use It**. New York, Sterling, 1971. 96p. illus. index. $3.95. LC 64-24685. ISBN 0-8069-5098-4.

This little book describes how to make simple things from papier mâché using strips of paper and the papier mâché mash. Strip techniques are put to use by the author in the construction of several projects—wastepaper baskets, lampshades, bowls, trays, hat boxes, beads, and even woven objects. The author then tells how to make similar objects using the mash. A short chapter gives information on and suggestions for drying, while other chapters describe methods of finishing. The author uses only the most ordinary of materials and molds, so the reader is not enticed into spending a lot of money. Photos, all black and white, unfortunately do not show the real character of what can be accomplished in papier mâché. For the beginner.

294. Betts, Victoria Bedford. **Exploring Papier Mâché**. Rev. ed. Worcester, Mass., Davis, 1966. 134p. illus. $6.50.

After an introductory chapter in which the author defines the nature of papier mâché and suggests many of its general applications, the reader is then introduced to the materials, equipment, and tools of the craft. Chapter three provides information on the basic construction techniques and gives hints on working with the basic material. Successive chapters deal with various suggested projects including paper bag creations, solid paper people, birds and animals, hand puppets and marionettes, masks, and gifts and displays (including jewelry). A final chapter provides suggestions for surface design and decoration. The basic elements of papier mâché are all treated by the author though, of course, more advanced techniques developed in recent years are missing. Still, Ms. Betts's work remains a basic text especially suitable for school and club purposes. Recommended as an elementary text for school and public libraries with craft collections.

295. Brock, Virginia. **Piñatas**. Nashville, Abingdon Press, 1966. 112p. illus. $3.00. LC 66-16567. ISBN 0-687-31436-4.

About half this book tells how to make piñatas. The remainder gives a short history, tells how to use the piñata, and provides three children's stories. The directions for making piñatas are simple; a child over 10 should be able to follow them. There are suggestions for about a dozen piñatas, both seasonal (Santa and a witch) as well as those for no special occasion. Recommended for school and public libraries.

296. Johnson, Lillian. **Papier-Mâché**. New York, David McKay, 1958. 88p. $4.95.

Ms. Johnson's figures offer little artistic inspiration, but she describes how to mold papier mâché figures using both positive and negative molds and then by construction on an armature of wire or pipe cleaners. Some elementary information on color is provided, and there are suggestions for various display uses of papier mâché figures. The age of this book works to its disadvantage. More appealing books with more up-to-date information on methods and finishing techniques are available. A beginner's book useful for those who work with children.

297. Kenny, Carla, and John B. Kenny. **The Art of Papier Mâché**. Philadelphia, Chilton, 1968. 143p. illus. index. $12.50. LC 68-26488.

The authors cover the methods of creating with papier mâché and other materials from the beginning of the process to its final finish. They instruct the student in making the mash and tell how to use it to make numerous articles—all of which, illustrated here in color and balck and white, are quite beautiful. After the chapter on the mash there are chapters on cylinders, domed shapes, pasting on a balloon, paper sculpture, pressing in molds and making molds. In other chapters the authors tell how to make jewelry, items of interior decor, and patio sculpture. A separate chapter deals with the use of papier mâché in the theatre, including the making of props, masks, and marionette heads. Step-by-step series of photographs show how to make various objects, and color photos illustrate artistic creations in this versatile medium. Even at its rather stiff price it is a good book for both the beginner and the craftsman experienced in the medium.

298. Kenny, Carla, and John B. Kenny. **Design in Papier Mâché**. Philadelphia, Chilton, 1971. 190p. illus. index. $12.50. LC 70-162978. ISBN 0-8019-5583-1.

Those who have graduated from the Kennys' first book on papier mâché and who haven't grown tired of the medium will want to continue through this sequel. Treating more advanced work in papier mâché, the authors tell how to make articles for home decoration—furniture, large pieces of sculpture, decorative wall plaques—as well as a large variety of small objects designed both to amuse and to serve utilitarian purposes. After a description of the basic techniques of construction in papier mâché and allied materials, they proceed to a discussion of design principles that should aid the reader in making his own work more exciting. Excellent for the already experienced craftsman.

299. Kuykendall, Karen. **Art and Design in Papier-Mâché**. New York, Hearthside Press, 1969. 191p. illus. index. $8.95.

In the first two chapters the author provides an introduction to papier mâché and a description of the tools, materials, and methods for working with this material. A number of projects are then suggested within the broad categories of the chapter headings, which include jewelry, cast-offs, furniture and clocks, Christmas ornaments, animals and insects, panels and plaques, sculptural figures. Within each chapter step-by-step instructions, accompanied by photographs, tell the reader how to make and decorate a number of projects. A section of color plates shows a few of the most handsome of the finished projects. Directions are very specific for anyone with an artistic flair and some experience. Numbers of design possibilities are provided. The author's insect creatures are especially unusual and attractive.

300. Lorrimar, Betty. **Creative Papier Mâché**. New York, Watson-Guptill, 1972. 104p. illus. index. bibliog. $7.95. LC 74-114196. ISBN 0-8230-1096-1.

An excellent introduction to the subject for teachers and students. In addition to diagrams, photographs, and instructions for using papier mâché in interesting and useful ways, there are also suggestions for decorating the results. A history of the art is included.

301. Meilach, Dona Z. **Papier-Mâché Artistry**. New York, Crown, 1971. 211p. illus. index. $7.95. LC 78-147334.

The author details the four basic procedures for making objects of papier mâché: the application of the papier mâché, sealing the surface, decoration of the surface, and finishing. These procedures are used with all three of the approaches described by the author: covering existing objects, applying over an armature, and molding. After detailing procedures, the author presents step-by-step instructions for making a number of projects. The 388 photographs and 18 color plates provide ample instructional guides and inspirational material for crafts enthusiasts, serious adults, home decorators, theatrical designers, and people who teach crafts to children. Instructions are clear and up to date with respect to new materials and techniques. Projects include many original ideas as well as the usual figures with a new twist. Highly recommended for those with some experience looking for challenging new ideas.

302. Shannon, Alice. **Decorative Treasures from Papier-Mâché**. New York, Hearthside Press, 1970. $6.95.

Ms. Shannon's book is intended for the beginning worker in papier mâché and requires little artistic flair or experience. Working primarily with extremely common basic materials, the author tells the reader how to make and decorate a number of attractive projects. These projects include such objects as matching bath accessories, boxes, bracelets (from bleach bottles), beads, trays, birds and simple figures, and Christmas ornaments. These are not overly ambitious projects, and most of them require no previous experience with the medium. Projects are arranged in order of difficulty. Ms. Shannon's intent is to provide an intermediary text between children's books and more advanced texts.

303. Sunset Editorial Staff, with William J. Shelley and Barbara Linse. **Papier Mâché**. Menlo Park, Calif., Lane Books, 1971. 79p. illus. $1.95pa.

Though not as thorough nor as artistically sophisticated as the Kennys' book, this Lane publication may have more appeal to the weekend and spare-time craftsman. The authors treat the basic elements of working with papier mâché, describing the materials and various ways of using the materials in a variety of projects on a variety of bases—balloons, newspapers, cardboard, cylindrical objects, wire, and such objects as oranges, lightbulbs, styrene balls, etc. There is also a short section on laminated papers. The numerous illustrations of papier mâché objects are accompanied by directions, and a few step-by-step series of photos describe the more complicated projects. Most of the projects fall into the category of "cute," though one could use one's imagination and create less cute adaptations. A good buy in an inexpensive text for the beginner.

PEBBLES
AND SHELLS

304. Conroy, Norma M. **Making Shell Flowers**. New York, Sterling, 1972. 48p. illus. index. (Little Craft Book Series). $2.95. LC 72-78587. ISBN 0-8096-5212-1.

The author tells and shows how to turn ordinary seashells into flowers by using glue, wire, and paint. She gives step-by-step instructions for fastening the shells together, and making several kinds of flowers—daisies, zinnias, violets, and others. Full instructions plus sequential photos of techniques and some full-color photos of finished flowers. A specialized book on shellcraft has been announced for November 1973 publication: Carson I. A. Ritchie's *Shell Carving: History and Techniques* (Barnes, 1973. $10.00).

305. Fletcher, Edward. **Pebble Collecting and Polishing**. New York, Sterling, 1973. 96p. illus. index. $3.95. LC 72-95210. ISBN 0-8069-3054-3.

Written for children, but designed to attract the whole family to the joys of pebble-collecting, this little book covers all beginning aspects of the hobby. The black and white photos are nondescript, but the colored ones are more detailed, thus more helpful. The line drawings are adequate. After a discussion of where to go to collect pebbles, chapters cover selection of the proper kind, tumbling and polishing machines, "perfect polishing," and jewelry making (covering basic equipment, findings, and how to work with them). Excellent starting point. Janet Barber's *Pebbles as a Hobby* is another fine work on the subject (Hippocrene Books, 1972. $6.95).

306. Pelosi, Frank, and Marjorie Pelosi. **The Book of Shellcraft Instruction.** St. Petersburg, Fla., Great Outdoors Publishing Company, 1959. 80p. illus. index. $1.75. ISBN 0-8200-0501-0.

Most of the projects here are designed to use commercially packaged shells (pikaki shells, chula shells, etc.). Instructions are clear, and there is a photograph of each finished project. Jewelry predominates, but handbags and wall plaques are well represented.

307. Sommer, Elyse. **Rock and Stone Craft.** New York, Crown, 1973. 96p. illus. index. $4.95; $2.95pa. LC 72-96661. ISBN 0-517-503530.

Chapters cover painting on stones, painting alternatives (decoupage, stencilling, "straw-blown ink designs," etc.), useful stones, assemblages, sculpture, mosaics, jewelry, holidays, and "owls and the rock artist." Copiously illustrated with black and white photographs. Projects are definitely for adults, not children, but even rank beginners will find something within their capabilities. Since the choice of rockcraft projects depends, to a great extent, on the rocks that are available, this book describes techniques and explores possibilities, rather than serving as a step-by-step guide to a particular finished product.

PLASTICS

308. Bunch, Clarence. **Acrylic for Sculpture and Design.** New York, Van Nostrand Reinhold, 1972. 144p. illus. index. $11.95. LC 75-149251.

This text deals with acrylic plastics only. Beginning with a discussion of acrylic and its special characteristics and nature, the author then discusses in two chapters the uses of this material in twentieth century sculpture and furniture. The works of individual artists are described and illustrated. In the final chapter the author discusses the various processes used in working with solid acrylic. Sawing, turning, bending, vacuum forming, bonding, finishing, cleaning, annealing, and other processes are described and, where necessary, illustrated. The text concludes with a note on plastics merchants and books on plastics. Although somewhat padded with handsome photographs of plastic objects, Mr. Bunch's book will serve as an inspirational and instructive guide to those who wish to know about acrylic forms and the techniques of working with this material.

309. Cherry, Raymond. **General Plastics: Projects and Procedures.** 4th ed. Bloomington, Ill., McKnight and McKnight, 1967. 318p. illus. index. $7.96 text ed. LC 65-19552.

A very practical handbook which details the basic operations involved in working with plastics. Part I offers an introduction to plastics, a description of most commonly used plastics, and basic information on how plastics are processed and fabricated. Information on plastic supplies, their storage and care is also provided. Part II deals in 22 chapters with the fundamental tool operations used in working plastics. This includes chapters on such basic procedures as squaring and cutting stock, filing, buffing and polishing, annealing acrylic, bonding, welding, thermoforming, laminating, embedding, casting, and many others. Part III deals with machine operations, treating such subjects as machine buffing and polishing, sawing, drill press operation, lathe work, shaping and routing, milling and planing. A final section deals with experimental techniques for further exploration of the medium. Each section is accompanied by various suggestions for projects. Step-by-step procedures are listed for some projects, and step-by-step photos accompany the text when basic operations are being described. A bibliography is appended.

This is a practical text for self-study as well as an excellent guide for high school courses in plastics. Illustrations and text are extremely clear. Recommended for the beginner because of its clear description of processes that can be used in the home shop. A glossary of terms appears at the beginning of the book.

310. Edwards, Lauton. **Industrial Arts Plastics**. Peoria, Ill., Charles A. Bennett, 1964. 280p. illus. index. $8.12 text ed. LC 64-14340.

Intended as an industrial arts text, Mr. Edward's book provides a general introduction to plastics, its properties and uses, and describes the operations used by the industrial arts shop in working with plastic materials. In the first half of the text chapters are divided according to the operations under discussion. Thus, there are chapters on measuring and marking, sawing with power tools, machine sanders, the buffing machine, drill press, carving tools, dyes and coloring, molds, gluing, engraving, and several other topics. Included here also is a chapter on fiberglass. In the second half one long chapter is devoted to projects of plastic. There are lists of materials and procedures as well as diagrams of projects. A separate chapter is devoted to projects in acrylics. Also covered are making signs from plastics, problems in the general shop, and plastics as a project material for camp and vacation shops. The text throughout is extremely specific and well illustrated with photos. Though not as well organized as Mr. Cherry's text, the book will be very useful to the beginning craftsman. Machine techniques are emphasized over hand techniques. A glossary of terms is located at the beginning. Suitable for the beginner in a home workshop with power tools, as well as for high school industrial arts classes.

311. Hollander, Harry B. **Plastics for Artists and Craftsmen**. Ed. by Margit Malmstrom. New York, Watson-Guptill, 1972. 224p. illus. index. $14.95. LC 77-177378. ISBN 0-8230-4025-9.

In addition to discussions of the various techniques of working with plastics, Mr. Hollander has a section on safety hints, a glossary, and a list of suppliers. The clearly written text is supplemented by illustrations, some of which are in color.

312. Newman, Jay Hartley, and Lee Scott Newman. **Plastics for the Craftsman: Basic Techniques for Working with Plastics**. New York, Crown, 1972. 214p. illus. index. (Arts and Craft Series). $7.95; $3.95pa. LC 75-185084.

This book explains the basic techniques for working with such materials as polyester resins, acrylics, fusible thermoplastics, and plastic foam. The authors explain what plastics are and differentiate between thermoplastics (rigid at normal temperature but becoming soft and moldable when heated) and thermosetting plastics (liquids requiring heat or some other catalyst to make them harder). They explain in detail five fundamental processes used in working with plastics: casting, fabrication, forming, cutting and pouring, and lamination. They offer numerous tips on working with acrylics, fusible thermoplastics, polyesters, epoxy resins, and rigid polystyrene and polyurethane, discussing such processes as coloring, polishing, sealing, finishing, etching and other printing techniques, drilling, and collage. Aided by this information the reader then may launch into the 45 different projects, aided by step-by-step photographs. Among the projects are window decorations, mobiles, jewelry, ornaments, mosaics, stained panels, table tops, etc. Some photographs are in color. A glossary and a list of suppliers are appended. Highly recommended as an introductory text.

313. Newman, Thelma R. **Plastics as a Design Form**. Philadelphia, Chilton, 1972. 348p. illus. index. bibliog. $17.95. LC 70-169585. ISBN 0-8019-5595-5.

Another example of Ms. Newman's ability to state technical material in layman's language, this is an excellent view of the field of plastics. Instructions, which are step-by-step and are illustrated with numerous photographs and line drawings, cover most plastics currently available. Additional information is provided in the appendixes.

314. Newman, Thelma R. **Plastics as an Art Form**. Rev. ed. Philadelphia, Chilton, 1969. 403p. illus. index. $12.50. LC 76-91122. ISBN 0-8019-5445-2.

According to the preface, "this is essentially a source book for artists, craftsmen, and art educators who desire a foundation in plastics as an art form." Thus, while indicating "potential directions for expression" in the plastic media, the basic thrust of the text is directed toward informing the artist of the properties and nature of plastics. After a short history of plastics the author acquaints the student with the basic terminology. General properties of the basic families of plastics are described as well as the specific properties of plastics with which the artist works. With step-by-step sequential photos and text, the author describes mold-making, laminating, embedding, and casting. Plastic as a painting vehicle is also discussed, and there is an expanded treatment of acrylics and vinyls. This is the most comprehensive treatment of plastics for the artist available today. The new revision brings the text up to date and makes it an invaluable encyclopedic handbook for the artist. Sources of supply are listed, and a bibliography and a glossary of terms are appended. Highly recommended for practicing artists and for libraries with artist patrons.

Another text of a general character is Robert S. Swanson's *Plastic Technology* (Bloomington, Ill., McKnight and McKnight, 1956). Although it is an older text, Mr. Swanson's book is a clearly written and well-illustrated guide to working with plastics.

315. Roukes, Nicholas. **Crafts in Plastics**. New York, Watson-Guptill, 1970. 176p. illus. index. $10.95. LC 70-117075.ISBN 0-8230-1000-7.

The 27 projects covered by the author range from extremely simple projects that need little equipment to complex ones that need sophisticated equipment. Numerous types of plastics are described and characterized with respect to their appropriateness to a specific task. Projects include relief panels, simulated stained glass, vases, jewelry, and many others. All projects are provided with step-by-step instructions and sequential photographs demonstrating the processes involved. The author is extremely well qualified for his undertaking. He is a professor of art and the winner of the Stanford Humanities Prize for his contributions in the field of experimental art. Highly recommended for schools and public libraries because of the wide range of the techniques and projects.

316. Roukes, Nichoas. **Sculpture in Plastics**. New York, Watson-Guptill, 1968. 175p. illus. index. $12.50. LC 68-12401. ISBN 0-8230-4700-8.

This is a basic text for the sculptor who wants to experiment with plastics. There are two kinds of chapters. In the first type the author describes a particular plastic medium, delineating its characteristics and behavior. Following this discussion of the medium are chapters in which a well-known artist illustrates, step by step, the creation of a piece of sculpture in this medium. The various types of plastics covered include polyester, epoxy resins, acrylics, and plastic foams. In addition, there are chapters on dyes, pigments, and coatings for plastics as well as sections on vacuum forming, using sprayable plastic and molding pellets. Highly detailed in its descriptions, this is a very practical text for the artist. There are excellent photos of numerous contemporary plastic pieces. Recommended for teachers, sculptors, students, and serious amateurs. A bibliography is appended.

317. Smale, Claude. **Creative Plastics Techniques**. New York, Van Nostrand Reinhold, 1973. 124p. illus. $6.95. LC 75-39888. ISBN 0-442-29952-4.

This new handbook describes the characteristics of different kinds of plastic materials and includes suggestions for methods of creating objects from plastic.

318. Zechlin, Katharina. **Setting in Clear Plastic**. New York, Taplinger, 1972. 72p. $4.95. ISBN 0-8008-7070-0.

This book provides the reader with a basic introduction to molding and casting in polyester resins. Various conventional projects are illustrated and instructions for using the resins are given in detail. Information on coloring is also provided. There are descriptions of tools and supplies, as well as tables of weights, measures, and temperatures. General directions are given for obtaining supplies.

POTTERY

AND CERAMICS

GENERAL

319. Ball, F. Carlton, and Janice Lovoos. **Making Pottery without a Wheel**. New York, Van Nostrand Reinhold, 1965. 160p. illus. index. $9.95. LC 65-12975.

Although the authors state that "this is not a beginning book on pottery," the beginning student will be able to learn a great deal about a limited area of ceramics by studying its photographs and carefully reading the text. Mr. Ball is a great believer in the "demonstration" method of teaching and his photographs offer step-by-step instructions in those pottery techniques that do not require the potter's wheel. In addition to demonstrating the basic techniques of slab, coil, and mold forming, he offers numerous suggestions and illustrations of ways by which these techniques are used in the construction of pottery ware. Surface textures and the means of achieving them are treated extensively, as well as simple but ingenious means of molding slabs into desirable shapes. There is a short but excellent chapter on preparation of pots for the kiln, followed by a chapter on glaze recipes. A final page describes the ancient method of finishing pottery called "terra sigillata." There is a short but adequate glossary at the end. The author states that a supplementary introductory text may be useful to the beginner. This is a highly useful text whose main virtue is that it treats comprehensively and maturely an area of ceramics that is often treated simplistically and without sophistication. Recommended for both beginners and those advanced students who wish to glean ideas from an experienced craftsman.

320. Bjørn, Arne. **Exploring Fire and Clay: Man, Fire and Clay Through the Ages**. New York, Van Nostrand Reinhold, 1969. 88p. illus. $4.50. LC 72-118559.

Though this is not specifically a book on ceramics, the ceramicist may well find the discussion of fire to be of interest and possibly also of some utility. Despite certain precautionary advice that we assume was meant primarily for children, the text is literate and interestingly written. The author's main interest is in primitive fire and primitive fire modes: the bonfire, the primitive hearth for cooking, and finally the primitive kiln and the primitive potter's techniques of firing. There are plans for all these types of fires, plus drawings of primitive kilns and the way they work. Many of the kilns have been reconstructed and photographed specifically for this book. The author's main interest is, of course, archaeological, though there is information here that will be of use to the practicing potter. Of course, the basic work on kilns, both primitive and modern, is still Daniel Rhodes's *Kilns: Design, Construction and Operation* (see entry 354).

321. Brennan, Thomas J. **Ceramics**. South Holland, Ill., Goodheart-Willcox, 1964. 96p. illus. index. $3.00. LC 64-12361. ISBN 0-87006-141-0.

Provided with an instructor's guide and an answer key to the quizzes, this text is primarily intended for school instruction; but it is simple enough for anyone who wants to begin working with clay. It contains units on clays and tools, modelling, coil and slab techniques, casting, wheel forming, firing and decoration. The instructions are accompanied by numerous photographs illustrating the techniques used. There is nothing aesthetically outstanding about the objects illustrated, so the student will have to go elsewhere for inspiration. But the text is clear and the instructions adequate. Recommended only as a beginning text.

322. Cardew, Michael. **Pioneer Pottery**. New York, St. Martin's Press, 1971. 327p. illus. index. $15.00. LC 74-141313.

This is a textbook that provides much more than information on techniques. The basic tenet of the book—no doubt a result of Mr. Cardew's years of teaching in West Africa and his preliminary study under Bernard Leach—concerns the importance of natural materials and local clays, and the unimportance of sophisticated equipment.

323. Christy, Judith, and Roy Christy. **Making Pottery**. Baltimore, Penguin, 1969. 138p. illus. index. $2.25pa.

This little book is intended for the beginning potter who starts at home. Because it emphasizes those methods and materials whose cost to the student is minimal, it concentrates on earthenware, whose availability and inexpensiveness especially recommend it to the beginner. Nevertheless, the authors introduce the novice to the whole range of techniques used by the potter. Illustrations consist only of a few line drawings integrated with the text. There are the usual descriptions of the basic potter's methods—coil, slab, modelling, throwing, etc.—with chapters on decorations, firing, and mold casting. There is a short appendix on glazes and one providing addresses of British suppliers of materials and equipment. There are two sections of photographs, the first illustrating various techniques, the second, examples of finished pottery. The cost makes this little book attractive to the beginner, and it does manage to introduce a wide range of activities.

324. Clark, Kenneth. **Pottery Throwing for Beginners**. New York, Watson-Guptill, 1970. 103p. illus. index. $2.50.

Anyone who has a wheel will be able to benefit from Mr. Clark's discussion of the art of throwing. The photographs that accompany the text give pointers on how to center and how to achieve various forms by manipulating the clay on the wheel; there are also informative photographs of cross-sections of thrown pottery. In addition to the basic instructions on throwing, there are sections on form, firing, decoration, and equipment (wheels, kilns, and turning tools). An excellent text for any basic collection on pottery making.

An older book on pottery throwing that is still of great utility to the beginner is a *Ceramics Monthly* handbook, *Throwing on the Potter's Wheel*, by Thomas Sellers (Columbus, Ohio, Professional Publications, 1960. 79p. illus. $4.00pa.). The author gives practical instructions in the basic techniques of using the wheel and includes instructions in related processes such as pulling and attaching handles. Excellent photographic sequences.

325. Clark, Kenneth. **Practical Pottery and Ceramics**. New York, Viking, 1972. 80p. illus. index. $3.25pa. LC 64-12382. ISBN 0-670-02024-9.

Written by a professional potter, designer, and lecturer, this book is an introduction for the beginner as well as a handbook for the experienced potter. Though it is not a how-to book, it provides an explanation of the full range of the ceramicist's art for the beginner. In addition, the experienced potter will find a great deal of information on clay forms and processes used, which will expand his own understanding of the craft. The author writes knowledgeably and with clarity; illustrations could be of better quality. Recommended as an informative source on the techniques and range of the potter's craft.

326. Colbeck, John. **Pottery: The Technique of Throwing**. New York, Watson-Guptill, 1969. 144p. illus. $10.00. ISBN 0-8230-4250-2.

Devoted, as the title indicates, to the techniques of throwing. The detailed, easy-to-follow explanations are further clarified by the 200 accompanying photographs. This book is intended for fairly experienced potters. Highly recommended in *The Last Whole Earth Catalogue*.

327. Conrad, John W. **Ceramic Formulas: The Complete Compendium**. New York, Macmillan, 1973. 309p. $10.95. LC 72-90282.

Intended for serious ceramicists and, incidentally, for the ceramic industry, this new book is an essential reference on the subject. It is a collection of over 700 formulas for clay, glaze, enamel, and glass. Each chapter begins with an introduction on the formulation, application, and testing process; the listings of the formulas give the chemicals (and percentages), firing temperatures, suggested use, firing results, color, and a color code number that refers to a color chart. Potters, glassblowers, and enamelists will need this. A similar work that is of narrower scope is the new edition of Kenneth Shaw's *Science for Craft Potters and Enamellers* (Drake, 1972. $7.95).

328. Counts, Charles. **Pottery Workshop: A Study in the Making of Pottery from Idea to Finished Form**. New York, Macmillan, 1973. 198p. illus. $8.95. LC 72-86029.

This work provides step-by-step guidance for the beginner. Directions are given for many kinds of objects. The student progresses, with the help of black and white photographs, from preliminary clay preparation through firing, glazing, and decorating. A list of supply sources and a bibliography complete the work.

329. Dodd, A. E. **Dictionary of Ceramics**. Totowa, N.J., Littlefield Adams, 1967. 327p. illus. $1.95pa.

The author is Information Officer for the British Ceramic Research Association. The dictionary contains approximately 3,000 entries on all phases of ceramic science and work. It contains common as well as technical terms and gives succinct definitions, with cross references where needed. Physical and chemical data are provided when appropriate. In addition to terms of ceramic science, art, and industry, the author provides definitions of terms from closely allied industries—glass, vitreous enamel, and cement.

Appendixes provide charts of sieve sizes, temperature equivalents of pyrometric cones, and a conversion table from Celsius to Fahrenheit. Particularly useful to students of ceramic science and those engaged in the ceramic industry. Comprehensive, easy-to-use, and inexpensive, it is a handy reference tool for the practicing potter and the amateur.

330. Drawbell, Marjorie. **Making Pottery Figures**. London and New York, Studio; also Levittown, N.Y., Transatlantic Arts, 1953. 96p. illus. $5.50; $2.45pa.

This essay on pottery figures describes the limitations placed on the craftsman in making figures for reproduction by means of plaster molds. There are notes on design, information on glazes and decoration, and lists and descriptions of materials and tools. The author describes how to make a two-piece mold, discusses clays and slips, and details the method of pouring. Finishing of the figure after molding is fully treated. Special problems involving multiple molds for single figures are investigated. The final chapters cover kilns (their packing and firing) and terracotta sculpture and its problems. A bibliography is appended. This brief treatment of a special form of ceramic activity is an extremely useful work for the experienced potter who wants an introduction to figure making. Photographs complement the descriptive text. Recommended for ceramic collections in small and large public libraries.

331. Engel, Gertrude. **How to Make Ceramics**. New York, Arco, 1968 (c.1957). 144p. illus. (The Do-It-Yourself Series). $3.50. LC 57-12452. ISBN 0-668-00607-2.

In addition to providing instructions on making a kiln and a pottery wheel, Ms. Engel discusses all sorts of ceramic work, including jewelry and ceramic sculpture. Heavily illustrated, with a glossary and a list of suppliers, this is a standard work for amateur and professional ceramicists. Another work with a do-it-yourself approach is Glen Pownall's *Pottery* (Drake, 1973. New ed. $3.95). The emphasis is on primitive methods, materials, and tools.

332. Fournier, Robert L. **Ceramic Creations**. New York, Sterling, 1971. 112p. illus. index. $6.95. LC 75-126845. ISBN 0-8069-5152-4.

According to the author, this book is for the potter who already has a working knowledge of clay and glazes and who wishes to expand upon and utilize his knowledge in new and creative ways. It is an attempt to reexamine pottery technique—pinch pots, slab building, coil building, pottery without molds, modelling, pulling, raku, and glazing. The author, a former teacher of pottery making, has not attempted a how-to book. Instead, he concentrates upon each method discussed and gives professional hints to the students.

Accompanying photos of good quality help the process along. His basic purpose is to urge the already initiated student to improve his techniques and to apply them in the creation of modern pottery. Basically, the book will be of interest to those who have only recently graduated from the beginning level (e.g., the section on how to build an electric kiln should appeal to this group).

333. Fournier, Robert. **Illustrated Dictionary of Practical Pottery**. N.Y., Van Nostrand Reinhold, 1973. 256p. illus. $12.50. LC 78-39886. ISBN 0-442-29950-8.

This new dictionary of practical pottery will be essential for any serious potter's library. Terms (omitting industrial and archaic terms) are listed in one alphabet. Definitions are clear and well written, and are illustrated with diagrams and with many excellent black and white photographs. Bibliographic references are provided at the end of many of the definitions. Includes formulas. Highly recommended for the potter's reference shelf.

334. Guilland, Harold F. **Early American Folk Pottery**. Philadelphia, Chilton, 1971. 322p. illus. index. $12.50. ISBN 0-8019-5436-3.

A good idea book. Folk pottery offers many useful and fanciful examples of the potter's craft that are unpretentious and simple in form and decoration. In his use of primitive methods and natural clays, the folk potter was often a very original fellow. An examination of the examples in this book provides a nostalgic look into our past and at the same time serves to put down some of our more pretentious modern ambitions. Numerous examples of American earthenware and stoneware from the seventeenth to the end of the nineteenth centuries are shown in both black and white and color, and there are details on glaze and size as well as the name of the potter, when available. Prefacing the section of plates are excellent essays on the stoneware and earthenware tradition, as well as a section on design.

335. Hartung, Rolf. **Exploring Clay: Hand Techniques**. New York, Van Nostrand Reinhold, 1971. 79p. illus. (Creative Craft Series). $4.95. LC 79-178699. ISBN 0-442-23176-8.

Since the emphasis of this book is on hand techniques, explanation of tools and their uses is kept to a minimum. Fabrication of vessels of all sorts is explored, and Mr. Hartung takes into account the influence of function upon form—and thus upon technique.

336. Hofsted, Jolyon. **Step-by-Step Ceramics: A Complete Introduction to the Craft of Ceramics**. New York, Golden Press, 1967. 95p. illus. index. $4.95; $2.50pa. from Western Publishers, Racine, Wisc.

In the first sections of this book the author describes briefly the basic techniques used in making pottery, the workshop and tools, and the preparation of the clay. Texturing, by hand and stamp, is discussed in some detail. The major portion of the book, however, is devoted to a series of portfolio projects divided according to the method of building or molding. There are sections on slab work, coil, press molding, slip casting, sand casting, and combined methods, with a final section devoted to projects in Egyptian paste jewelry. Also treated are the wheel (and projects for the wheel), glazing, firing, and decorating. Each of the project sections gives step-by-step directions with accompanying sequential photographs that illustrate the techniques used. Photographs of finished pieces, some in color, are distributed throughout the book, and there are directions for making a unique kiln. A good elementary text recommended for school and public libraries.

337. Hyman, Richard. **Ceramics Handbook**. New York, Arco, 1967 (c.1953). 112p. illus. $3.50. LC 59-13674. ISBN 0-668-00347-2.

An inexpensive work appropriate for the beginning student, this book describes basic techniques and gives directions for making a potter's wheel. The illustrations and the arrangement make this a convenient workshop companion.

338. Isenstein, Harald. **Creative Claywork**. New York, Sterling, 1972. 96p. illus. $3.99. ISBN 0-8069-5034-X.

Primarily intended as a do-it-yourself book for children in grades 4 to 8, this book may satisfy a child's curiosity about clay work. There are some objectionably simplistic features (such as referring to the coil method as the sausage technique) that should have been avoided. In addition, the text advances rather rapidly from an explanation of the slab techniques to the final chapter on figure sculpting, and the illustrations of relatively advanced work might inspire the child to initial attempts but might also discourage him from further attempts if he falls short on his first try. Still, the book does cover the techniques of working in clay without a wheel, and it would be of some value in initiating interest in the craft. Recommended as a supplement to the children's crafts collection.

Another children's book is *Creating with Clay*, by James Seidelman and Grace Mintonye (see entry 362).

339. Kampmann, Lothar. **Creating with Clay**. New York, Van Nostrand Reinhold, 1971. 75p. illus. $5.95. LC 78-142216.

Translated from the German, this book is intended principally for teachers and interested parents who wish to introduce children to expression in a plastic form. Assuming that the plastic medium is the most natural for children, the author illustrates (through color photographs) the appropriate types of figures and forms to develop skills for working clay, paper clay, and plasticine. The activities are suitable for children in grades 1 to 9, and an index indicates which pages are appropriate to which grade level. A technical appendix gives information on pottery, clay, its preparation and storage, sizes, firing, and glazing. There are examples of work done by children of various ages. Recommended for the teacher or parent who is unacquainted with clay but who wishes to introduce his charges to an expressive medium.

340. Kenny, John B. **The Complete Book of Pottery Making**. Philadelphia, Chilton, 1949. 242p. illus. index. $7.50. LC 72-187553.

Mr. Kenny treats the whole range of pottery making, beginning with a chapter on the rudiments of clay, its properties, nature and types, the tools necessary for the potter, and a description of the types of pottery. At the same time he introduces the initiate to his first project, a cup, which is intended to familiarize the student with the medium. In the second chapter he proceeds to the non-wheel techniques of the potter—coiling, slabbing, and surface decoration by means of scrubbing, pressing, and piercing. The third chapter introduces the student to throwing and the various techniques of the wheel. Successive chapters cover plaster and its properties and uses, the making of both drain and solid cast molds, slip casting, and jiggering, roughly equivalent to the lathe operation in woodworking. All these chapters are illustrated with copious photographs and line drawings that are so comprehensive as to render the text almost redundant. Additional chapters are devoted to more technical descriptions of clay, the kiln and fire, glazes and their mixing, and decoration. A final chapter is an anecdotal answer to the question of whether one can make a living as a potter.

As an introduction to the whole range of the potter's art, the Kenny book has not been superseded, although other books treat various aspects in far greater detail. The fundamental operation of simple and basic processes is treated in clear, step-by-step manner. The language is simple (sometimes cute but not offensively so), and terms are defined as they are introduced. A glossary might have been convenient, but it is not a necessity. Recommended especially for the beginning student and for those who wish to expand the range of their work.

341. Kenny, John B. **Ceramic Design**. Philadelphia, Chilton, 1963. 322p. illus. index. $9.95. LC 63-10419. ISBN 0-8019-0474-9.

This book by Mr. Kenny is both a how-to and a what-to-do book. Like his other books (the preceding entry plus entry 379, *Ceramic Sculpture*), it is suited to both the beginner and the experienced amateur. While dealing with the elements of design in ceramics and attempting to make the student aware of the elements of good design in ceramics, the author also manages to produce a basic text on ceramic techniques. There are chapters on form, sketching, coiling, rolling, slabbing, draping, twining, pressing, pouring, throwing, and combining, supplemented by others on carved design, shaping, coloring, glazing, firing, and drawing for the ceramic artist. There is a section devoted to glass in relation to the art of the ceramicist and others on decorating techniques. A final chapter introduces the reader to career opportunities in ceramics. An appendix gives technical data on clay and glazes, and there is a glossary of ceramic terms and a separate glossary of ceramic materials. All of Mr. Kenny's books are self-sufficient and will stand alone without aid from the others, an effect achieved at the cost of considerable redundancy, since each volume treats the same material as the others. But there is sufficient change of perspective and emphasis in each to repay the reader for a study of all three. And, although *Ceramic Design* would not necessarily be my first choice if I were to choose only one book for the beginner, as a supplemental text to his *Complete Book of Pottery Making* it is highly recommended.

342. Lauder, Ian. **The Home Potter**. New York, Universe Books, 1970. 143p. illus. index. $5.95. LC 71-130802. ISBN 0-87663-136-7.

Ian Lauder is a self-taught potter who here attempts to tutor those who also are learning pottery the hard way—i.e., by themselves. There is an introductory chapter on clay and pottery, after which the author tells the reader how to prepare one's own clay bodies. Successive chapters deal with the techniques of slab and coil work, throwing and turning, decorating, biscuit firing, and glazing. There is a chapter on how to build an electric wheel, which the author feels the beginner would prefer, and a final chapter on building a simple kiln. All this is consistent with the author's belief that few courses offer the opportunity actually to try out the craft that is being taught. Hence, by building and utilizing the inexpensive and simple tools which the author recommends, the student will be able to experiment on his own. The book is popularly written, with many photographs and line drawings integrated with the text. It covers much the same territory as other beginning ceramics books, though many of the descriptions are brief. There are, however, many useful hints that should repay the student's reading. There are appendixes of temperatures of pyrometric cones, diagrams of motor and kiln connections, and a list of suppliers.

Another text of interest to those who wish to learn pottery techniques in the confines of their home is Kenneth Drake's *Simple Pottery* (Watson-Guptill, 1966. 96p. illus. $1.95. LC 66-13003), which demonstrates elements of pottery using ordinary equipment found around the house. The author's contention is that handsome pottery can be made without the wheel. Molded forms are included, however, as well as instructions for decorating, glazing, and firing.

343. Leach, Bernard. **A Potter's Book**. Levittown, N.Y., Transatlantic Arts, 1948. 294p. illus. $8.75. LC 48-6491.

Despite its age, this work remains the single most important book for professional and amateur potters. It is found on the bookshelves of potters everywhere. Mr. Leach studied pottery in Japan and England and is universally recognized for this outstanding text. No bibliography found in serious books on pottery making is complete without it, and every collection with any pretensions to balance should include it. A philosophic as well as technical presentation.

344. Long, Lois Culver. **Ceramic Decoration**. Indianapolis, American Art Clay Company, 1958. 59p. illus. index. (Book No. 1). $3.00pa.

Although primarily written as promotional materials for AMACO products, this booklet contains a great deal of information on decoration of ceramic pieces. There is information on the clay itself and methods of surface decoration, slips and engobes and methods of applying underglazes, glazes, and overglazes. A separate section suggests methods of making one's own mosaics and principles of composing a mosaic design. Additional chapters deal with glass colors and means of firing on glass, measurement of kiln temperature, and firing defects and remedies. A glossary of terms, a short bibliography, and a list of AMACO products are included. Excellent photographs throughout illustrate finished ware. A good instruction booklet for the beginner who is still at the stage of buying his materials ready-made.

345. Luisi, Billie. **Potworks: A First Book of Clay**. New York, Morrow, 1973. 154p. illus. $6.95; $2.45pa.

Good for today's amateur. All beginning aspects of potting are discussed (no throwing), as well as some of the practical problems of marketing and finding supplies. A glossary, a bibliography, and a list of suppliers are appended.

346. Nagumo, Ryu. **Japanese Pottery as a Hobby**. Tokyo, Japan, Toto Shuppan Company; distr. San Francisco, Japan Publications Trading Company.

The author of this book confines himself to describing hand modelling techniques. Emphasis is on those "hand methods long practiced in Japan which involve the use of the hands and only a few simple tools." In the first chapter the author introduces the reader to the history of the ceramic arts in Japan. Photographs, some in color, of beautiful simple pottery are distributed throughout this section. The second section is devoted to a description of the various types of pottery and the following section to a description of traditional Japanese clays and clay bodies. A step-by-step series of photos shows the construction of a simple kiln. The main body of the book, however, is devoted to the techniques used by the Japanese in hand modelling pottery. The techniques are not foreign to any American potter, but the sequential photos are very well done—a pinch pot, a pot using coiling techniques, and slab construction. The inventive technique of making a slab by using wire rather than rolling is very fast. There are sections on molding, relief design, and various texturing methods, as well as firing and glaze decorations. The techniques used here are all extremely easy and suitable for the beginner. However, the uniqueness of the Japanese touch conveyed in this text would be valuable to any American potter who is not already familiar with the Japanese manner. Highly recommended for all public libraries.

347. Nelson, Glenn C. **Ceramics: A Potter's Handbook**. 3rd ed. New York, Holt Rinehart and Winston, 1966. 331p. illus. index. $10.95. LC 66-18801.

This is a good handbook for the experienced potter and an excellent text for a course in pottery. The student who tries to use it as a self-teaching text, however, will feel the need of an instructor. There are good chapters on the history of ceramics and on contemporary ceramic arts in Japan and Europe, and the section on design is short but informative. Subsequent chapters provide information on clay and clay bodies, basic forming methods (throwing, coil, and slab construction), glazes, decoration, glaze calculation and formulas, kilns, mass production methods (slip casting, jiggering, press forming), and studio equipment.

The appendix provides tables of atomic weights of various elements, a list of common ceramic raw materials with their formulas, molecular and equivalent weights and the fired formula, an analysis of common clays and chemicals, feldspar, and a chart showing the water plasticity of various clays. Other charts provide data on pyrometric cones, glazes, body recipes, etc. There is a list of suppliers in the United States, Canada, and England, a short bibliography, and a glossary of ceramics terms. Recommended as a supplementary text in pottery courses and as a handbook for the already experienced potter.

An older work with more illustrations is Vincent A. Roy's *Ceramics: An Illustrated Guide to Creating and Enjoying Pottery* (McGraw-Hill, 1959. 278p. illus. $8.50. LC 58-14361) which, in addition to chapters on basic ceramic techniques, also includes a chapter on metal enamelling. A bibliography is appended.

348. Norton, Frederick H. **Ceramics for the Artist Potter**. Reading, Mass., Addison-Wesley, 1956. 320p. illus. $10.75. LC 55-7373.

Recommended by the publishers as a self-instruction text for hobbyists and as a text for ceramics courses. Mr. Norton's comprehensive work is designed for use as a teaching text and as a quick reference work on techniques. The first part, dealing with basic ceramic techniques, describes the complete range of operations from forming to firing. Hand forming, wheel forming, casting, and pressing are described and illustrated. Other sections deal with finishing, biscuit firing, glazing, underglaze decoration, ghost firing, and overglazing. The second part of the book is intended primarily to deepen the student's understanding of various aspects of the craft. There are sections on the history of pottery making, and on design principles and applications. Clays and non-plastic materials are discussed, as are ceramic bodies and their preparation. These and other sections that deal with the more technical aspects of pottery making are intended for instructional purposes (either self-instruction or classroom) and will be extremely valuable to both the student and the practicing potter. Technical data are presented in chart form, and there is also a directory of suppliers, a useful glossary of ceramics terms, and a bibliography. This is a basic text and handbook for the artist potter and the student. Contains over 450 illustrations integrated with the text.

349. Norton, Frederick H. **Elements of Ceramics**. Reading, Mass., Addison-Wesley, 1952. 247p. illus. $12.75. ISBN 0-201-05305-5.

In this text Mr. Norton deals with the more technical aspects of the ceramicist's craft. The book is designed to provide the serious potter with an understanding of the principles underlying "the various processes used in the ceramic field, with enough illustrations to make their application clear." In his treatment of all phases of ceramic processes, the author discusses various types of clay, their origins and properties, as well as non-clay materials. In addition, he discusses flow properties of ceramic pastes and slips, casting slips, forming methods, drying of ceramic wares, and ceramic bodies. Sections on firing include a discussion of thermochemical changes in clays and clay bodies, kilns and their setting, and glazes. One section deals with enamel on metal and others with coloring processes. There are 194 illustrations integrated with the text. An excellent work for the sophisticated practicing potter or amateur who is curious about the technical aspects of his avocation.

An even more advanced text for those who need to understand the "physical chemistry of ceramics, the characteristics of clays, and their qualities for making potteries" is Willis Grant Lawrence's *Ceramic Science for the Potter* (Philadelphia, Chilton, 1972. 239p. illus. index. $10.00. LC

72-4811). Dr. Lawrence is Dean of the College of Ceramics at Alfred University, New York.

350. Petterson, Henry. **Creating Form in Clay**. New York, Van Nostrand Reinhold, 1968. 112p. illus. $7.50. LC 68-22735.

This book, according to the author, has been structured and written specifically for the teacher, to assist "those who have the responsibility of solving the problems of group instruction in working with clay." His method is to stimulate both the teacher and the student by means of visual examples and thereby to stimulate fresh ideas. There is a short survey of processes used in the past, but the major portion of the book gives new examples of what can be done with clay. The author offers suggestions that should help the teacher urge his charges onward. Included among the chapters are sections on flat-slab-formed shapes, slab-coil-formed shapes, interior and exterior formed shapes, surface design, decorative firing, etc. The final chapter deals with classroom safety, and a useful glossary is appended. This could be a worthwhile text for the teacher or for anyone already familair with the fundamentals of clay work. The black and white illustrations are impressive. A good idea book for anyone involved in working with clay.

Another book of interest to teachers because of the step-by-step directions and the emphasis on useful and decorative objects (birds, animals, figures, teapots, etc.) is *Making Ceramics*, by Lis and Hans Lundkvist (Van Nostrand, 1967. 80p. illus. $4.95. LC 67-14158). Instructions are easy to follow, and photographs (some in color) and diagrams help the student in his progress.

351. Priolo, Joan B. **Ceramics and How to Decorate Them**. New York, Sterling, 1958. 144p. illus. $6.95. LC 58-12542. ISBN 0-8069-5026-9.

This is basically a book on decorating, though introductory chapters do treat briefly the fundamentals of clayworking—preparation of the clay, construction procedures by means of slab, coil, sculpturing and molding, and the process of firing. The major portion of the book deals specifically with glazing and decorating the already formed pottery object. There are chapters on planning the decorating, surface decoration, underglaze and glaze decoration, and the decoration of specific types of objects—figurines, animals, and birds. An additional chapter deals with forming and decorating ceramic jewelry, and there is a chapter on enamelling copper. A final chapter suggests means of producing pottery ware on a semi-production-line scale. An appendix provides designs for decorative motifs that may be traced or altered for individual treatment. This book might be useful to the beginning potter who is short on ideas and who needs non-technical instruction on the process of decorating. The artistic merits of the decorations are of dubious distinction, though an inventive student could use them as a point of departure.

352. Priolo, Joan, and Anthony Priolo. **Ceramics by Slab**. New York, Sterling, 1973. 48p. illus. index. (Little Craft Book Series). $2.95. LC 72-95195. ISBN 0-8069-5240-7.

A very basic introduction to potting. Using clay with grog (pre-fired particles of clay) to help prevent cracking when fired, and emphasizing the use of glazes that do not need to be fired, this beginner's book suggests more than a dozen simple projects, from a "house number plaque" to a round vase made with a glass jar as the guide. The glaze suggested is slate and concrete sealer, colored with oil paint. The attractive projects will appeal to children but also to beginning adults.

353. Rhodes, Daniel. **Clay and Glazes for the Potter**. Rev. ed. Philadelphia, Chilton, 1973. 219p. illus. (Creative Crafts Series). $12.50. ISBN 0-8019-5633-1.

This is a practical book for the potter, student, teacher, designer, collector, or industrial ceramicist who wishes to know more about the materials of the craft of pottery and the ways by which the varied colors and textures in ceramics are achieved. The origins of clay are discussed, and there are directions for blending various clays to get specific results in the finished piece. The characteristics and ceramic uses of the various kinds of clays are described. Numerous recipes for earthenware, stoneware, and porcelain bodies are included, together with methods for mixing, additives for different textures, and suggestions for firing. The author also tells how to test usable native clays.

The ingredients of glazes and methods of glaze calculation are fully described. In addition to information on methods of coloring, blending, testing, applying, and firing glazes, there is a good section on reduction firing and on reducing glazes and colors. The reader is told how to manage the kiln for reduction effect and how to achieve unusual glazes and colors—such as copper-red caladon, crystalline effects, and ash glazes.

The appendix offers over 30 glaze recipes designed for various temperatures and effects. The black and white photographs illustrate worthy examples of the potter's art from various periods of the past. The language of the text is simple and non-technical. The book is interesting reading as well as informative to those who are seriously involved with ceramics. Recommended for a basic ceramics collection.

354. Rhodes, Daniel. **Kilns: Design, Construction and Operation**. Philadelphia, Chilton, 1968. 240p. illus. index. $10.00. LC 68-57512. ISBN 0-8019-5358-8.

The definitive work on kilns. Mr. Rhodes brings together in this volume a great deal of material on ceramic kilns and firing, providing information about the history of the kiln from primitive times up to the present. Fuels, burners, refractories, masonry practice, construction details, temperature control, and measurement and safety precautions are thoroughly treated.

The various types of kilns are described and their advantages and disadvantages are discussed. The kiln designs include step-by-step information for their construction and their loading and firing. There are over 100 drawings by the author, plus numerous photographs showing design construction and firing of kilns from various countries of the world. This is an indispensable guide for the serious potter who wants useful information on how to construct his own kiln. It should also be of interest to anyone, collector or student, who seeks to deepen his knowledge of the potter's art.

355. Rhodes, Daniel. **Stoneware and Porcelain: The Art of High-Fired Pottery**. Philadelphia, Chilton, 1959. 217p. illus. index. $7.50. LC 59-15040.

This standard work gives a brief history of Oriental and European stoneware and porcelain from the potter's point of view and then proceeds to a lengthy and informative discussion of both stoneware and porcelain clay bodies. Decorative techniques are described at length, with practical suggestions on slip decoration, resist process, and various textural treatments. There is information on throwing and casting and other means of forming, as well as instruction for the design and construction of high-fire kilns and methods of firing. Additional information is given on materials and equipment, the shop, and methods of work. There are good black and white photographs of excellent examples of the potter's craft. Not for beginners in any sense of the word, but this book should be an essential part of any serious potter's library. Since it is not a highly technical work, the collector should also find this work of interest.

356. Riegger, Hal. **Primitive Pottery**. New York, Van Nostrand Reinhold, 1972. 128p. illus. $12.95. LC 75-184821.

Mr. Riegger is a professional potter who has taught pottery workshops. *Primitive Pottery* is directed to potters who wish to approach the origins—or at least the primitive mode—of their craft, thereby increasing their understanding and feeling for their pottery. This book, then, is a handbook for the primitive potter. Mr. Riegger discusses clays and earth minerals, providing information on firing ranges and plasticity. All of this is directed to the primitive potter using primitive equipment and tools. Forming methods are discussed, as well as simple glazes and firing with and without a kiln. Four pages of color photographs are included, plus numerous illustrations in black and white. Recommended for the practicing potter as well as the amateur with an experimental flair.

357. Riegger, Hal. **Raku: Art and Technique**. London, Studio Vista Publishers; distr. New York, Van Nostrand Reinhold, 1970. 136p. illus. index. $12.95. LC 77-102195. ISBN 0-442-36948-4.

Raku is one of the mysteries of the potter's art, since its inscrutably Oriental nature defies definition and can only be hinted at. Mr. Riegger attempts no real definition; if one does come away from this book with a knowledge of raku, it will be an intuitive grasp of the nature of the art, extrapolated from the text and the numerous photographs. The serious ceramicist will doubtless gain considerable depth of understanding here that will repay his curiosity—whether or not he understands raku. There are informative chapters on clay, drying, firing, kilns, and glazing, and a selected bibliography of standard works on the potter's art as well as on raku. Recommended whether or not you are a practitioner of Zen.

A new book on the subject is Finn Lynggaard's *Pottery: Raku Technique* (Van Nostrand Reinhold, 1973. 79p. $2.95pa. LC 72-12550).

358. Rothenberg, Polly. **The Complete Book of Ceramic Art**. New York, Crown, 1972. 276p. illus. (Arts and Craft Series). $8.95.

An excellent and comprehensive guide to the methods and styles of working in clay, illustrated with photographs. The availability and varied potential of today's commercial slips, glazes, etc., are investigated, as well as the influence of pottery from other cultures. In addition to the bibliography, there are also a glossary and a list of supply houses.

359. Röttger, Ernst. **Creative Clay Design**. New York, Van Nostrand Reinhold, 1963 (c.1962). 95p. illus. $5.95; $3.95pa. LC 63-8676.

A good elementary book on clay forming, this work offers only rudimentary notes at the end on ceramic processes. The author deals almost exclusively with handforming (slabs, coils, and sculpting), with many details on texturing. Text is minimal, the body of the book being devoted almost exclusively to excellent photographs of textures and forms that are accessible to even the beginning student. The objects shown have some artistic merit. This is recommended primarily as an idea book, though sufficient details are given to provide how-to information to the aspiring artist.

360. Sanders, Herbert H. **How to Make Pottery and Ceramic Sculpture**. Rev. ed. Menlo Park, Calif., Lane Books, 1964. 112p. illus. $1.95pa. LC 64-22657.

According to the author's foreword, this book is intended "as a manual of self-instruction for the beginner who will work at home, as supplementary material for both student and teacher in the classroom, and for use in the work of therapy and rehabilitation done in community centers and hospitals." It offers an introductory chapter on the pleasures of a ceramics hobby, a chapter on materials and tools of the craft, and additional chapters on techniques of working with clay (pinch, slab, coil, modelling, throwing, and casting) and on decorating, firing, and the construction of a potter's wheel. The instructions are clear and simple, with well-integrated photographs to help the student construct the simple projects that illustrate the techniques under discussion. Good illustrations of finished wares show what the diligent student may hope to achieve. Some recipes for mixing slips and glazes are included, and there are detailed instructions for firing. A good text for a novice who is not ready to invest a lot of money in a how-to book. Sufficient to get anyone started.

Another book by Mr. Sanders is *The World of Japanese Ceramics: Historical and Modern Techniques* (Kodansha, 1967. 264p. illus. $15.00). This is a collection of 213 black and white photos and 42 color plates of excellent examples of Japanese ceramics. In addition, there is a discussion of ancient and modern methods used by Japanese potters. Appendixes include glaze recipes and technical data. The author is a professor of ceramic art at California State University (at San Jose).

361. Seeley, Vernon D., and Robert L. Thompson. **Activities in Ceramics**. Bloomington, Ill., McKnight and McKnight, 1958. 82p. illus. index. $2.64pa.

Primarily directed toward self-instruction, but also intended for use in adult and high school craft courses. The authors provide a short introductory chapter with a glossary of common terms, a list of tools and equipment, and a description of the potter's techniques (including free form technique, press forming, build-up methods, slip casting, and wheel work). Each chapter includes projects that demonstrate the techniques discussed, with ample black and white photographs to guide the student. Subsections are devoted to glazing and various types of glazes. A short discussion of firing is included. A final chapter is devoted to the pottery industry with descriptions of several techniques used on an industrial level. A useful bibliography of books current at the time is appended, though many are now out of print. Although this is a useful introduction to ceramics, only beginning students will be able to profit from its brief treatment of techniques. Anyone seriously interested in ceramics will want to consult additional texts.

362. Seidelman, James, and Grace Mintonye. **Creating with Clay**. New York, Crowell-Collier Press, 1967. 56p. illus. $4.50.

A small book that covers, in step-by-step manner, all basic aspects of clay modelling, plus sections on firing, glazing, and painting. Methods are suggested for adapting the techniques to many different types of creative projects. Glossary.

363. Southwell, B. C. **Making and Decorating Pottery Tiles**. New York, Watson-Guptill, 1972. 126p. illus. $8.95. ISBN 0-8230-2988-3.

All aspects of the craft are investigated, from the making of cast and molded tiles to instructions for reglazing commercial tiles. There is a detailed discussion of using silk-screen printing to decorate tiles, plus a section on the uses of tiles. The list of suppliers is restricted to British firms, but the bibliography includes both British and American works.

364. Tart, Carlie. **The Beginner and the Wheel**. Indianapolis, American Art Clay Company, 1962. 33p. (Book No. 100). illus. $2.00pa.

This little booklet is a photographic essay on how to use the potter's wheel. All the operations associated with the wheel are treated in separate sections with photographs and accompanying step-by-step directions keyed to the photographs. The last ten pages give instructions for throwing different objects, bowls, plates, cylinders, etc. Some will say that one cannot learn to throw without a teacher, but this little book makes an excellent attempt.

365. Taylor, Doris W., and Ann Button Hart. **Creative Ceramics for the Beginner: Step by Step**. New York, Van Nostrand Reinhold, 1969. 120p. illus. index. $6.95. LC 68-9038.

This project book is intended basically for young beginners. Ignoring all but the most essential explanations of the craft, the authors plunge the beginner into a variety of projects that should appeal to young would-be craftsmen who want to see quick results. There are short introductory chapters on general procedure, supplies, and firing, but few technical details—just the bare essentials. The rest of the book is devoted to a wide range of projects that serve to introduce the various techniques of coil and slab work, forming, surface texturing, and glazing. Projects range from simplified finger formed bowls, to dollhouse foods, to bird houses and feeders, but most will appeal only to children—or perhaps to the less than artistic adult. Recommended for the teacher who needs simple ideas for young students.

366. Thorp, Harold E. **Basic Pottery for the Student**. Levittown, N.Y., Transatlantic Arts, 1970. 99p. illus. (Scopas Handbook). $6.75; $3.25pa. LC 73-88660.

This little handbook offers information, accompanied by photographs, on clays, pots, throwing, glazing, and kilns. The author, a teacher of ceramics, provides authoritative detailed instructions in all areas of the potter's craft. Included also is a brief historical introduction and numerous photographs of ceramic pieces dating from the prehistoric period to the present. Offered also in a paperbound edition, this handbook is recommended for classroom use and for public libraries.

367. Trevor, Henry. **Pottery Step-by-Step**. New York, Watson-Guptill, 1966. 127p. illus. index. $8.50; $3.95pa. (Ballantine, 1971). LC 66-13000. ISBN 0-345-02414-1pa.

Although many potters seem to think that books cannot teach one to throw clay on a wheel, authors continue to write books explaining the process. One section of this book is devoted to slab, coil, and mold casting of pottery, but the major portion is devoted to the wheel. There are, in addition, chapters on decorating, both by texturing and by glazing, and a section on setting up a studio. There is a listing of pottery collections (organized by state) for further ideas, a list of craft organizations devoted to ceramics, lists of pottery suppliers (organized by state), and a short bibliography that includes some journals. Photographs illustrate the techniques under consideration, and the text, which is minimal, is a running commentary keyed to the photographs. Photographs of excellent examples of the potter's art are distributed throughout. The treatment of throwing is quite good. This book is not recommended as a first book, but it would be a valuable supplementary text for a craft collection.

368. Villiard, Paul. **A First Book of Ceramics**. New York, Funk and Wagnalls, 1969. 175p. illus. $5.95. LC 68-56463.

Intended for the beginner, Mr. Villiard's book acquaints the student with a wide range of ceramic activities. As the author introduces the fundamental methods of the craftsman, he assumes little previous knowledge on the reader's part. Areas covered include hand modelled pottery, coil and slab work, the techniques of throwing, firing, and glazing. There is a good chapter on how to make molds and how to use them in slip casting, and a chapter on making an inexpensive and simple kiln will be useful to the impecunious craftsman. Though it is not as complete as John Kenny's book, *The Complete Book of Pottery Making*, Mr. Villiard's book is intended for the same audience; its illustrations are well integrated throughout, but they are not as copious as in Mr. Kenny's book. Certainly the beginner could benefit from reading both books. And if the price makes a difference, Mr. Villiard's book is slightly less expensive.

369. Wildenhain, Marguerite. **Pottery: Form and Expression**. New York, Van Nostrand Reinhold, 1962. 157p. illus. $9.95. LC 62-16374.

This is not a how-to book, though it will be technically instructive to both students and professional potters. The author's purpose is to deepen the potter's understanding of his craft, and this she does by discussing various aspects of the potter's craft in relation to the potter himself. Everything is directed to form, and the chapters discuss form in relation to the hand, the material, the function, technique, decoration, glaze, and expression in the pot itself. This book may well confirm the dedicated potter's commitment. Ms. Wildenhain, however, is not an encourager of mediocrity. Serious potters at all levels of ability will enjoy reading her collection of memoirs and philosophical essays, *The Invisible Core: A Potter's Life and Thoughts* (Pacific Books, 1973. 207p. $12.50). Black and white photographs of her work are included.

370. Willcox, Donald J. **New Design in Ceramics**. New York, Van Nostrand Reinhold, 1970. 119p. illus. $7.50. LC 77-126867.

There are over 200 black and white photographs, and eight pages of color photographs, in this book on Scandinavian ceramics. The compiler has attempted a visual gallery of contemporary work in Scandinavia. In each case he indicates the type of construction used for the piece photographed, the type of glaze, and the heat of firing. A short introduction describes the potter's place in Scandinavian society, the various schools in which the potter is educated, and the peculiar circumstances under which the Scandinavian potter works. The final page gives a short bibliography of literature on the subject, a listing of Scandinavian schools in which ceramics courses are taught, and a listing of Scandinavian design and handicraft societies and exhibitions. Good for indicating the range of expression in the medium of ceramics.

371. Winterburn, Mollie. **The Technique of Handbuilt Pottery**. New York, Watson-Guptill, 1969. 175p. illus. index. $10.00. LC 69-12494.

The author describes efficiently and with precision the various techniques used in handbuilt pottery. Beginning with preparation of the clay, she treats various techniques in separate chapters—pinch pot technique, coil, slabs for mosaics and three-dimensional work, mold making, and pulling. Additional chapters deal with decoration, glazing, and firing. A special section is devoted to projects, and the final chapter discusses potters and the teaching of pottery history. Photographs of completed works as well as sequential step-by-step series are distributed throughout the text. Excellent, simple descriptions make the text extremely useful to the beginner.

CERAMIC AND CHINA PAINTING

372. Sharp, Edith M. **China Painting: The Soft Look Technique**. Melbourne, Australia, Lansdowne Press, 1968. 96p. illus.

The author's aim is to teach the student to paint china, but she emphasizes the achievement of the "soft look." After an introduction advising the student about various aspects of the craft, the author provides a list of equipment and suggests methods of applying the design and of practicing the techniques described. The process used for painting five different firings are discussed in separate chapters, and there are also discussions of the kiln and firing. Two additional chapters treat the application of gold decoration and etched designs, and final chapters provide additional information on the choice of ware, care of brushes, markings, etc. A number of designs are illustrated, and there are color photos of finished pieces. Though Taylor and Hart's *China Painting* is a more thorough text on the general craft of china painting, those involved in the pastime may find Ms. Sharp's book of interest because of its special emphasis on the "soft look."

373. Taylor, Doris W., and Ann Button Hart. **Ceramic Painting: Step by Step**. New York, Van Nostrand Reinhold, 1966. 144p. illus. $8.95. LC 66-27525.

This well-illustrated book contains step-by-step directions for 10 projects in painting on greenware and bisque with translucent underglaze colors.

374. Taylor, Doris W., and Ann Button Hart. **China Painting**. New York, Van Nostrand Reinhold, 1962. 234p. illus. index. $9.95.

The first 40 pages of the text are devoted to basic principles of the craft. This includes a list of supplies, special notes on gold and metallic finishes, notes on background, and an excellent catalog of brush strokes that should be of enormous help to the beginner as well as to the advanced painter of china. An essential chapter on color completes the first section. The major part of the text is devoted to specific designs, each of which is illustrated in outline form with sections coded for reference to the numbered, step-by-step instructions. All the designs may be traced directly onto a plate or enlarged. Details are illustrated in separate plates that also provide information on brush strokes. The final part of the book provides instruction for firing, tips on designing, information on drydusting and enamels, a note on mending broken china, and a series of questions and answers on problems. A glossary of terms is appended. The authors have constructed an excellent step-by-step guide that is about as foolproof as a book of this sort can be. The designs are rather oldfashioned (Victorian flower and bird designs), but they will probably appeal to many china-painters. The principles outlined, of course, may be applied to china painting in general. Recommended for public libraries.

375. Wiggins, Hazel J. **How to Paint China**. Laguna Beach, Calif., Walter T. Foster, n.d. 40p.

In this large-format book the author describes how to mix and apply overglaze colors and discusses gold application, luster, and etching. Step-by-step photographs and drawings accompany the text.

SCULPTING IN CLAY

376. Dawson, Robert. **Practical Sculpture: Creating with Plastic Media**. New York, Viking, 1970. 111p. illus. index. $6.95. ISBN 0-670-57127-X.

Starting with a description of armatures, their purpose, and how to design and build them, this book then takes each "plastic" material in turn, describing its nature, showing how to prepare and manipulate it, and giving a wide-ranging description of applications. "Plastic media" for this author include all manipulatable materials, from clay to polyester resin reinforced with fiberglass. The most recent as well as the traditional methods are described. Materials discussed include clay, concrete, fiberglass-reinforced polyester resin, plaster, plasticine, and wax. Line drawings integrated with the text accompany the instructions. A separate section of black and white photographs is devoted to modern sculptures in the various materials. A good text that is especially appropriate for the beginner who wants instruction in basic materials. Recommended for a basic collection of how-to books on sculpture.

377. Di Valentin, Maria, and Louis Di Valentin. **Sculpture for Beginners**. Rev. ed. New York, Sterling, 1969. 192p. $4.95. ISBN 0-8069-5072-2.

This introductory text provides the essentials for modelling in clay. The beginning student is led step by step into the process, for this is basically a teaching text interspersed with how-to hints. First suggesting that the student become familiar with the clay by making a variety of small objects, the authors then point out what and how the student may learn from plaster casts of anatomical features. The student is then ready to make his own head, with the help of step-by-step instructions. There are several sections devoted to anatomy, after which the process of making a torso is described, with accompanying photos. Final chapters are devoted to casting, texturing, and caricatures. Although it is limited to the medium of clay and does not progress beyond the human form, this small text has a great deal to teach the beginning student.

378. Eliscu, Frank. **Sculpture: Techniques in Clay, Wax, Slate**. Philadelphia, Chilton, 1959. 192p. illus. index. $7.50. LC 59-7275.

Eliscu's book is a combination of written and photographic essays on the technique of modelling and sculpting. Beginning with clay, the author provides information on the medium as it concerns the sculptor. The step-by-step photos introduce a number of projects designed to familiarize the student with clay. Similar treatments are provided for wax and slate. A final chapter describes the process by which the author produced one of his own works—from inception to final installation of the bronze figure.

Clay, wax, and slate were chosen by the author because of their relative accessibility to the potential artist and because of the ease with which the basic techniques may be learned in these materials. The book is quite clearly organized; written comments on the photos are kept to a minimum, but they are sufficient. Examples of finished works (both ancient and modern) are illustrated throughout. An appendix illustrates a few sculptor's tools, though the text emphasizes using what is at hand. An excellent text for the beginning student or for anyone interested in sculpture.

379. Kenny, John B. **Ceramic Sculpture: Methods and Processes**. Philadelphia, Chilton, 1953. 304p. illus. index. $9.95. LC 53-5530.

This is a companion volume to the author's *The Complete Book of Pottery Making* (entry 340). It uses the same step-by-step technique as the former book, with copious illustrations well integrated with the text. Because the author assumes little on the part of his reader, this book is especially useful to the beginner. Advanced amateurs, however, will also find many suggestions here for saving time and money, since Mr. Kenny is a great believer in the do-it-yourself philosophy. Tools, equipment, and preparation of the clay are described, but the discussions have been adjusted and expanded here to apply to sculpting in clay, rather than to ceramics in general. After the initial chapters on fundamentals, the author turns to the principles of the human figure in clay, giving elementary physiological information to aid the craftsman. He then repeats the process with various animal figures. An additional chapter deals with portraiture and the modelling of the human head.

The second part of the book, largely technical in nature, concerns molds, materials, colors, kilns and their firing, and decoration. All of this information is applicable to all types of ceramic work. After the technical details the author again returns to the ceramic object, suggesting and giving instructions for making a variety of ceramic wares.

An easier text for beginners who must have more specific directions is the old but excellent little project book, *How to Make Pottery and Ceramic Sculpture: 20 Graded Projects*, by Julia Hamlin Duncan and Victor D'Amico (New York, Museum of Modern Art, 1947. 95p. illus. $1.95pa. LC 48-6372). Here the beginner will find directions for making 20 different ceramic objects, including bowls, boxes, toys, and animal figures.

380. Press, Fred. **Sculpture at Your Finger Tips**. New York, Van Nostrand Reinhold, 1962. 60p. illus. $4.95. LC 62-13690. ISBN 0-442-11066-9.

For the beginner, this offers the simplest imaginable list of tools and supplies: 10 pounds of plasticine, one smooth stick, and willing fingertips. The author then instructs the student in making a number of heads of his own design. Chapters proceed to human figures and from there to animal forms. Many of his figures are highly stylized and show a degree of sophistication that the less adroit student will perhaps not be able to imitate. Along with the numerous photographs are running comments and directions for constructing each type of figure shown. Though the beginner will not be able to aspire so high at first, it is at least refreshing to see examples of work that are appropriate to an adult reader. A helpful book for the beginner interested in modelling techniques.

TOYS

GENERAL

381. Alton, Walter George. **More Wooden Toys That You Can Make.** New York, Taplinger, 1972. 95p. illus. $6.50. ISBN 0-8008-5368-7.

Although this how-to book is British, the glossary that precedes the instructions helps bridge the language gap for American users. Projects, presented in graduated levels of difficulty, are clearly described, with diagrams and photographs to complement the text. The toys range from dominoes to busses, boats, and animals.

382. Caney, Steven. **Steven Caney's Toy Book.** New York, Workman Publishing Company, 1972. 176p. illus. $8.95; $3.95pa. ISBN 0-911104-15-1.

With over 100 photographs and line drawings, this book provides explicit and simple directions for making dozens of inexpensive toys. Projects are graded as to level of difficulty (some are for 11-year-olds and up, but others can be done by 6-year-olds alone, or even by 3-year-olds with help). Materials used include paper plates, string, clothes pins, etc. Some of the toys are for pretending, some for active outdoor, some for exploring nature. All are imaginative and appealing.

383. Joseph, Joan. **Folk Toys Around the World and How to Make Them.**
      New York, Parent's Magazine Press, 1972. 96p. illus. $4.50. ISBN
      0-8193-0598-7.

Published in cooperation with Unicef, this little volume presents
detailed instructions and diagrams for making 23 toys from all over the
world. Illustrations of the finished toys, many in color, are included. The toys
are interesting, unusual, and appealing, and information about the history of
the toy and the country of origin is provided. Construction ranges in
difficulty from simple to complex. Also included is an introduction
explaining the use of tools and materials, and a list of general sources where
various materials can be attained. Excellent for primary school children.

384. Lewis, Shari, and Lillian Oppenheimer. **Folding Paper Toys**. New York,
      Stein and Day, 1963. 93p. illus. $3.95.

Easy instructions show how to make action models that fly, sail, and
make noises as well as others that can be used in games and at parties. A
bibliography is included. Illustrated by drawings. Recommended for grades 1
to 6.

385. Pettit, Florence H. **How to Make Whirligigs and Whimmy Diddles and
      Other American Folkcraft Objects**. New York, T. Y. Crowell,
      1972. 349p. illus. index. $6.95. LC 78-175108. ISBN
      0-690-41389-0.

A project book providing authoritative detailed instructions for making
more than 20 authentic American folkcraft objects, including a carved
cherry-wood goose, a jumping jack, a colonial lanthorn (lantern), candles, a
pine cone cardinal (bird, not prelate), Christmas ornament, a quilt,
corn-shuck dolls, and others (including the ones indicated in the title). There
are also suggestions on how to select wood, sharpen a knife, and cut metal,
and how best to work with C-clamps, saws, paints, hand drills, braces and
bits. In her final chapter Ms. Pettit tells how to reduce, enlarge, and change
proportions of designs, and a glossary describes unfamiliar tools and
materials. Even the uninitiated, would-be craftsman should be able to follow
the detailed and simple instructions, which are supplemented by many
drawings and photographs. An excellent introduction to folkcraft projects, all
of which require few tools and little working space beyond what is found in
an average home. The projects themselves are charming.

386. Reeves, Robert. **Make-It-Yourself Games Book**. New York, Emerson,
      1964. illus. $4.95. ISBN 0-87523-152-7.

With more than 400 line drawings, this work provides directions for constructing 50 games and contests. There are projects designed for children as well as for young adults.

387.   Roth, Charlene Davis, with Jerome Roth. **Toys: A Step-by-Step Guide to Creative Toymaking**. New York, Lancer Books, 1972. 172p. illus. $1.95pa.

Numerous make-at-home projects, covering stuffed animals, puppets, mobiles, wooden toys, and papier mâché. Many of the items are simple enough for children to make, while others (especially among the wooden toys) will require parental help. Those who need a constantly revised supply of projects will find this a good book at the price. A more recent book on the general topic of toymaking is C. J. Maginley's *Toys You Can Build* (A. S. Barnes, 1973. $8.95).

388.   Schnacke, Dick. **American Folk Toys: 85 American Folk Toys and How to Make Them**. New York, Putnam, 1973. 219p. illus. $9.95.

Traditional folk toys made from wood and cloth are the focus of this how-to book. Besides the expected apple dolls and spool knitters, there are also lesser-known folk toys like the "flipperdinger." Directions for making 85 kinds of folk toys are included, with lists of the materials needed for each and step-by-step directions for making the toy. Mr. Schnacke owns a West Virginia shop that manufactures and sells folk toys.

389.   Slade, Richard. **Carton Craft**. New York, S. G. Phillips, 1973. 63p. $5.95. LC 73-1953. ISBN 0-87599-196-3.

Designed for youngsters, this crafts book suggests games and toys that can be made from cardboard cartons. Other household materials (such as plastic bottles) are used for some of the projects.

390.   Stevenson, Peter. **The Art of Making Wooden Toys**. Philadelphia, Chilton, 1971. 247p. illus. $9.95. LC 77-153136. ISBN 0-8019-5604-8.

A delightfully written instruction book, with details on making 23 projects—from four-inch trucks and cars to a child-sized pedal racer. In between are a bi-plane, a wheelbarrow (usable size), a grandfather clock, an elaborate dollhouse, racers and racing pits, a castle, and a "gypsy wagon." Each project is described in detail—cutting, assembling, and lumber list—with many photographs and line drawings. Patterns, full-size for the smaller projects, are included. In spite of the explicitness of the instructions, the author encourages individual initiative: "Try to look at the tape measure as little as possible when setting dimensions. If you're like us, when there's a tape too handy, you'll end up making something 5 inches long, when 5 17/32 inches would have looked better and would have been just as easy to cut if you hadn't known it was such an exotic measurement."

391. Waltner, Willard, and Elma Waltner. **Hobbycraft Toys and Games**. New York, Lantern Press, 1965. 142p. illus. $5.60. LC 65-12601.

Here the Waltners describe how to make a number of toys and games from easily available materials—bleach bottles, squeeze bottles, cardboard, scrap material, etc. Several can be made by small children, though many more will require the skill of parents or older siblings. The projects themselves should appeal to children from pre-school age up through the third grade. Projects include musical instruments, stuffed toys, dolls of spools and wire, a barn and farm animals, a wheelbarrow, and a rather nice little drawing board fitted with a roll of drawing paper. Clear instructions are given along with photographs of each toy. Recommended for general and elementary school libraries.

392. White, Alice. **Performing Toys**. New York, Taplinger, 1970. 131p. illus. $6.50. LC 72-126993. ISBN 0-8008-6280-5.

These toys, all of which can be made by children, are cleverly constructed so that, as the title indicates, they will "perform." Some are musical as well. Directions are extremely clear, materials are easily available, and the finished products are delightful.

DOLLS, DOLLHOUSES, AND STUFFED TOYS

393. Christopher, Catherine. **The Complete Book of Doll Making and Collecting**. 2nd rev. ed. New York, Dover, 1971. 290p. illus. index. $3.00pa. LC 76-102176. ISBN 0-486-22066-4.

A "revised republication" of the author's 1949 work, this paperback includes a new preface that updates the art of dollmaking and collecting over the past 20 years. Although the first three chapters tell how to make soft rag dolls, more advanced dolls, and costumes for dolls, respectively, the book is much more a guide for the collector than for the amateur dollmaker. The history of dolls and their costuming is covered from the point of view of the collector, but the information will also be useful to dollmakers whose interest is authenticity. The final chapters discuss "fitting backgrounds" for displaying dolls, making a dollhouse, and doll language and definitions. The patterns and unique dollmaking tips (e.g., how to model and cast doll heads) will be useful to those whose interests encompass both making and collecting dolls. A related book is Mary H. Morgan's *How to Dress an Old-Fashioned Doll* (Dover, 1973. $1.25pa.), originally published by Henry Altemus Company as *How to Dress a Doll* (1908).

394. De Sarigny, Rudy. **Good Design in Soft Toys**. New York, Taplinger, 1971. 239p. illus. $11.95. LC 71-164671.

As the title implies, this work emphasizes creative design in soft-toy-making. The first section of the book discusses proportion, design, and how to create soft toy patterns from pictures. The second section consists of patterns and directions for soft toys. The author assumes that the reader has a basic knowledge of sewing and embroidery.

395. Drew, Barbara. **Fashions for Dolls**. New York, Drake, 1973. 98p. illus. $5.95. ISBN 0-87749-237-9.

An irresistible book for anyone who loves dolls, this is simply a how-to book for a doll's wardrobe. The doll used as a model is 19-inch Kate (not a baby doll). Instructions are given for altering patterns to fit dolls with "slightly different" shape and measurements; presumably this means that Crissy, Sasha, Tressy, or any other 16- to 17-inch doll could be fitted—but that the standard "fashion doll" (Barbie) could not. The book consists of full-page pictures (one section of color plates) of Kate modelling her varied wardrobe, with lists of materials and directions for each outfit. There are directions for knitted items also (sweaters, long stockings, etc.).

396. Dyer, Anne. **Design Your Own Stuffed Toys**. Newton Centre, Mass., Branford, 1970. 117p. illus. $5.95. LC 75-105680.

Aimed at those who are no longer novices at making stuffed toys, this book provides the basic rules and instructions for design and pattern-making. Drawings accompany the text and help to illustrate principles. Another Branford book devoted to soft toys is Margaret Hutchings' *Modern Soft Toy Making* ($8.50. ISBN 0-8231-5007-0).

397. Gray, Ilse. **Designing and Making Dolls**. New York, Watson-Guptill, 1972. 96p. illus. $8.95.

Novices to dollmaking will find specific instructions for all types of fabric dolls, graded from the simplest sock dolls to double-headed dolls. Directions for miniature dolls and finger puppets are also included. Patterns are at the back of the book, and there is a selective bibliography.

398. Hollis, Nesta, with Valerie Janitch. **Top Outfits for Teenage Dolls: A Doll-Dressing Book Designed for the Popular "Teenage" Dolls.** New York, Taplinger, 1973. 110p. illus. $9.95. LC 72-7215. ISBN 0-8008-7768-3.

Those who have not grown disenchanted with Barbie and her friends will appreciate this book of patterns and instructions for 36 wardrobe items. Included, among other outfits, are a raincoat, bathing suit, pants suit, and the ubiquitous bridal gown. Outfits are illustrated with photographs (some in color).

399. Horne, Caroline. **Fashion Crochet for Your Doll.** New York, Drake, 1970. 112p. illus. $5.95. LC 77-175968. ISBN 0-07749-076-7.

Although basic crochet instructions are provided (including measuring and blocking), this book is best suited for an experienced crocheter who needs directions for making doll clothes. The wardrobe is designed for an 18-inch doll.

400. Ives, Suzy. **Making and Dressing a Rag Doll.** New York, Drake, 1972. 96p. illus. $5.95. ISBN 0-87749-248-4.

Includes patterns for a rag doll (female) and 11 outfits. Directions are step by step and illustrated, although the author assumes that the reader has a basic knowledge of sewing.

401. Johnson, Audrey. **Furnishing Dolls' Houses.** Newton Centre, Mass., Branford, 1972. 284p. illus. $16.50. LC 72-75079.

Ms. Johnson is the author of a number of related books, including *Dressing Dolls* (also published by Branford). This practical guide discusses materials and tools, then proceeds to its basic focus: late Victorian and early twentieth century English dollhouses. Exteriors are considered as well as interior furnishings and their period use. In addition to the 195 plates of drawings and patterns, there are 19 photographs.

402. Laury, Jean Ray. **Doll Making: A Creative Approach.** New York, Van Nostrand Reinhold, 1970. 135p. illus. $9.95. LC 79-126984.

A delightful treasury of dolls to make. Patterns are given for many, while photographs of the others will serve as inspiration. Many of the dolls pictured are not children's toys but are works of art definitely designed for adults. Techniques covered include single-shape dolls, jointed dolls, arch-shaped dolls, pillow dolls, faces and hair, stocking-face dolls (with unbelievably realistic results), and knitted and woven dolls. Essential for any crafts (or needlework) collection.

403. Lind, Vibeka, and Lis Albrectsen. **Dolls and Toy Animals**. New York,
     Van Nostrand Reinhold, 1973. 96p. illus. $5.50; $2.95pa. LC
     72-9377. ISBN 0-442-29968-0; 0-442-29969-9pa.

Inexperienced doll-stuffers will welcome the step-by-step instructions in this book. There are directions for drawing patterns, cutting, sewing, and stuffing. The toys are made not only from fabrics but from yarn and pipe cleaners. Among the project suggestions are Winnie the Pooh, Babar, a kangaroo, and a hobby horse. Designed for use by children as well as adults.

404. Moloney, Joan. **Dolls**. New York, Drake, 1973. 107p. illus. $4.95. LC
     73-1625577. ISBN 0-87749-078-3.

Includes detailed and illustrated instructions for making many kinds of dolls and their clothes.

405. Moloney, Joan. **Making Toys for Children**. New York, Drake, 1972.
     130p. illus. $6.95. LC 72-1259. ISBN 0-87749-255-7.

With patterns, good instructions, and diagrams, this book is an excellent guide to making a variety of toys, from soft toys for little children to toys made of wood, cardboard, and odds and ends.

406. Moore, Colleen. **Colleen Moore's Doll House**. Garden City, N.Y.,
     Doubleday, 1971. illus. $9.95. LC 79-125881.

A picture book, with text by Miss Moore. All dollhouse fans, silent movie fans, and collectors of miniature furniture will delight in the close-up photographs—most of them in color—of this elaborate dollhouse. Created with the help of all sorts of professionals (who were persuaded by Miss Moore to contribute their talents), this is the dollhouse supreme. A book to be pored over for hours.

407. Morton, Brenda. **Floppy Toys**. New York, Taplinger, 1971. 136p. illus.
     $5.95. LC 78-126981. ISBN 0-8008-2770-8.

An unusual approach to soft toys: the basic technique presented in the book consists of gathering up circles and threading them onto elastic. The British vocabulary is explained in a glossary. Will interest anyone who is tired of making the usual soft toys. Ms. Morton has also written *Mascot Toys* (Taplinger, 1969).

408. Morton, Brenda. **Soft Toys Made Easy**. New York, Taplinger, 1972.
     119p. illus $6.95. LC 79-184412.

A beginner will easily be able to make the charming toys in this book. In addition to detailed instructions for each item, there is also general information on fabric, stitches, patterns, and varieties of stuffing to use. The latest books by the prolific Ms. Morton are *Your Book of Knitted Toys* (Taplinger, 1973. $4.95) and *Do-It-Yourself Dinosaurs* (scheduled for November 1973, also with Taplinger. $6.95 tentative price).

409. Smith, Evelyn. **Nursery Rhyme Toys**. New York, Drake, 1972. 159p. illus. $7.95. LC 72-12042. ISBN 0-87749-328-6.

The stuffed toys in this book all represent, as the title suggests, nursery rhyme characters. Construction details provided are sufficient for those with previous sewing experience.

410. Tyler, Mabs. **The Big Book of Soft Toys**. New York, McGraw-Hill, 1973. 256p. illus. $8.95. LC 72-6420. ISBN 0-07-062952-8.

Soft-toy enthusiasts from kindergartners through adults will find appealing projects from among the 200 presented in this book. The how-to instructions are clear, and patterns and diagrams are included. Scraps of material, pipe cleaners, and sewing leftovers are used. There are 100 color photographs of finished projects.

411. von Boehn, Max. **Dolls**. Tr. by Josephine Nicoll. New York, Dover. 269p. illus. index. bibliog. $3.00pa.

This reprint, illustrated with over 250 photographs, is a history of all aspects of dolls and their uses (from little girls' toys to implements of black magic).

412. Worrell, Estelle Ansley. **The Dollhouse Book**. New York, Van Nostrand Reinhold, 1964. 126p. illus. index. $7.95.

Ms. Worrell's book, besides presenting photographs of some extraordinary antique dollhouses, provides detailed instructions for building and furnishing a variety of dollhouses of her own design with numbers of suggested variations. Plans of details (such as doorways, fireplaces, and decorative designs) are included, as well as instructions for making furniture of all types. Designs for appointments are divided into sections on seventeenth, eighteenth, and nineteenth century designs. There are innumerable suggestions for small furnishings, with line-drawing descriptions. Full details and instructions for making completed dollhouses are given.

413. Worrell, Estelle Ansley. **The Doll Book**. New York, Van Nostrand Reinhold, 1966. 135p. illus. index. $7.95. LC 66-27528.

In Ms. Worrell's first book, *The Dollhouse Book*, she described how to make and furnish dollhouses. In this 1966 work she tells how to make a whole family of dolls and how to dress them in period costumes of the seventeenth, eighteenth, and nineteenth centuries. There are patterns for the dolls and costumes, along with hints and suggestions. The costumes are marvelously detailed and the finished costumes shown in family group photographs are quite authentic. A directory of suppliers and equipment is included. In addition, Ms. Worrell provides us with an informative essay on period costuming.

414. Witzig, H., and G. E. Kuhn. **Making Dolls**. New York, Sterling, 1969. 96p. illus. index. $3.95.

The authors here show how to make a variety of dolls. The book begins with simple twig dolls, dowel dolls, and dolls made from gloves, handkerchiefs, and stockings; it progresses to fully jointed dolls with molded semi-hard and hard heads. There is information on body proportions, modelling materials, wire frame dolls, doll heads, and doll wigs. Some step-by-step series of drawings are included, and there are diagrams for making most of the dolls. This short book provides a good introduction. Most doll fanciers should be able to proceed alone after careful study of this book.

KITES AND PLANES

415. Barnaby, Ralph S. **How to Make and Fly Paper Airplanes**. New York, Scholastic Book Services, 1968. $3.50.

Captain Barnaby, who knew both Orville and Wilbur Wright personally, is an old-time paper pilot, and his thesis on the paper plane places him among his contemporaries, at least in comparison to Mr. Steidl (entry 422). But his horse-and-buggy paper planes are easily recognizable to even the most unsuccessful of us paper glider pilots, and he will tell us exactly what went wrong with all those millions of planes that didn't fly properly. Of course, we can defend Captain Barnaby because he did his work before the discovery of the all-important stick that is so prominent in Mr. Steidl's planes. And even with its discovery, it is heartwarming that Captain Barnaby had the integrity to ignore it.

416. Barwell, Eve, and Conrad Bailey. **How to Make and Fly Kites**. London, Studio Vista; New York, Van Nostrand Reinhold, 1972. 68p. illus. index. $3.95. LC 79-161974. ISBN 0-289-70228-3.

Although the book is designed for the beginner, with at least four very simple kites, some of the 18 projects are ambitious enough to interest the developing student of kiteflying. Kites range from simple two-stick to a Chinese dragon kite. The book opens with general directions for building kites (including notes on materials, techniques, etc.). Instructions for individual kites give specifics on tools and materials, line drawings to show proportions, methods, and steps, and photographs of the finished kite. Explicit directions and warnings about kiteflying conclude the book. Measurements are given in both centimeters and inches. Some of the warnings for kiteflying refer specifically to British law, but they are nonetheless useful as safety rules anyplace.

417. Brummitt, Wyatt. **Kites: A Golden Handbook Guide**. Racine, Wisc., Western Publishers, 1971. 120p. illus. index. $1.25. LC 70-134439.

This small handbook explains about kites, where they came from, how they fly, how they are built, and how to fly them. The author tells about wind, the flying line, launching and landing, and he describes the different kinds of kites as well as special types of kites and things that can be done with them in order to make them more fun. The appendix contains information on where to get kites and supplies. A short bibliography is also provided.

418. Hart, Clive. **Kites: An Historical Survey**. New York, Praeger, 1967. $12.50.

This is the classic work on the history of kites. Beautifully produced and comprehensive in scope, it should be in the library of anyone with a serious interest in kites.

419. Hunt, Leslie L. **Twenty-Five Kites That Fly**. New York, Bruce Publishing Company, 1929; repr. New York, Dover, 1971. 110p. illus. index. $1.25pa.

Three chapters of this reprint tell how to make plane surface kites, tailless kites, and compound kites. The final chapters describe techniques of flying and kite accessories, plus other useful information such as how to determine the altitude of the kite.

420. Jue, David F. **Chinese Kites: How to Make and Fly Them**. Rutland, Vt., Tuttle, 1967. 51p. illus. $3.25. LC 67-16412. ISBN 0-8048-0101-0.

Directions for making 10 beautiful kites (fish, butterfly, tree, house, the flying lampshade, etc.) conclude this little book. The introductory section provides notes on the history of kites, and on traditional Chinese kite-flying customs and legends. The suggestions for materials are extremely practical (the split bamboo called for comes from split bamboo window shades;

according to Mr. Jue, enough bamboo for 15 kites can be bought for under a dollar). An excellent introduction for young and old, with colorful and clear drawings.

421. Simon, Seymour. **The Paper Airplane Book**. New York, Viking, 1971. 48p. illus. $3.95.

Through diagrams and drawings the author instructs the young reader in how to make paper airplanes and how to alter the design for experimental manipulation of the aircraft. An excellent little book that illustrates scientific principles. Recommended for grades 4 and 5.

422. Steidl, Robert H. **Stick-Paper Airplanes**. New York, Abelard-Schuman, 1971. 255p. illus. $7.95; $4.95pa.

Although the publishers describe this book as treating the "art and craft" of making paper airplanes, it should more properly be described as detailing the engineering problems of the paper airplane. Mr. Steidl's approach is definitely a serious one, and the 50 designs he has come up with (requiring nothing more for construction than some balsa sticks, 70-pound paper, glue, and weights for balance) do actually fly. An excellent book for boys and their fathers; or for girls and their mothers, for that matter.

423. Wagenvoord, James. **Flying Kites**. New York, Macmillan, 1968. $6.95; $2.95pa.

Not only practical information is presented here, but thoughts on the aesthetics of kites.

424. Yolen, Will. **The Young Sportsman's Guide to Kite Flying**. New York, Nelson, 1963.

Will Yolen, master kiteflyer, prepared this book for the Nelson "Young Sportsman's Guides" series. His daughter, Jane Yolen Stemple, has written a kite book with an historical approach: *The World on a String: The Story of Kites* (World, 1969. $4.95). A new Yolen book, *Kites and Kite Flying* is scheduled for publication in 1974 by Simon and Schuster.

MASKS AND COSTUMES

425. Alkema, Chester Jay. **Masks**. New York, Sterling, 1971. 48p. illus. index. (Little Craft Book Series). $3.99. LC 75-151712.

Mr. Alkema's small book on masks is divided into three sections. The first gives instructions for making masks of paper, using paper bags, cylinders, cubes, and plates. Suggestions for painted and bas-relief details are included.

The second section details how to make papier mâché masks from a number of different molds—balloons, bowls, cardboard, etc. The final section deals with masks of cardboard with bas-relief details. Many different masks are illustrated, in both color and black and white. Many are highly imaginative and will provide inspiration for the young or adult mask-maker. Instructions for fashioning masks from the three materials are general but adequate for building masks like the ones illustrated.

426. Alkema, Chester Jay. **Monster Masks**. New York, Sterling, 1973. 48p. illus. index. (Little Craft Book Series). $2.95. LC 72-95208. ISBN 0-8069-5256-3.

The table of contents page also carries the words, "Breathes there a soul so dead / Who never to himself has said, / "I want to be a monster!" And monsters these are, indeed. Materials and techniques used range from drinking straws, yarn, and pipe cleaners to tinfoil bas-relief, tooled copper, clay, and even sandcasting. Some of the masks are for wearing, some only for decoration. Instructions are explicit as to technique, when necessary, but are quite general when discussing the design itself, to encourage the creator's ugly instincts. The numerous photos, both color and black and white, make the artist aware of the wide range of possibilities in making monster masks.

427. Cummings, Richard. **101 Masks: False Faces and Make-Up for All Ages, All Occasions**. New York, David McKay, 1968. 173p. illus. index. $4.50. LC 68-17510.

The author, a well-known West Coast puppeteer, has included in this volume instructions for making masks suitable for all ages and all artistic abilities. The volume is divided into six sections. The first is devoted to instant masks, which can easily be made by children from kindergarten to third grade. The "Rainy Day Masks" of the second section are somewhat more difficult but can still be made by children in the primary grades. The masks in these sections use readily available materials such as paper bags, stockings, paper feathers, etc. The largest section, "Professional Masks," deals with masks made of papier mâché that challenge the maker's ingenuity and talent. Two short plays requiring masks are included in this section (*The Elopement* is a *commedia dell'arte* production, and the second is "The Mad Tea Party" scene from *Alice in Wonderland*). Additional chapters are devoted to make-up faces (requiring paint, putty, crepe hair, and prostheses applied to the face), wall hanging masks of papier mâché, and novelty masks—a potpourri of suggestions. With the exception of this last section, sufficient instructions are given for each. All masks are illustrated in drawings and a few step-by-step series are included when necessary. This is one of the best books on masks with respect to both quantity and range. Recommended for public libraries, but especially for school libraries.

428. Grater, Michael. **Paper Faces**. New York, Taplinger, 1968. 134p. illus. $6.50. LC 68-14775.

With clear instructions and good illustrations, this book offers the reader an exceptional opportunity to make a variety of creative faces from paper. The faces range from simple to complex, but the basic technique is the same for all, requiring simple materials and tools. All are made by folding and cutting paper or light cardboard; details or special effects are added with paint, ink, or decoupage. The wide range of projects includes faces of people, animals, birds, clowns. An excellent book that should fascinate children and grown-ups alike. Applications of technique could be used in displays of all types. Highly recommended for school and public libraries.

429. Ives, Suzy. **Creating Children's Costumes from Paper and Card**. New York, Taplinger, 1973. 92p. illus. $6.50. LC 72-12431. ISBN 0-8008-1985-3.

Easy techniques of gluing, folding, cutting, and painting paper will result in masks and costumes to delight children. The introduction provides detailed and illustrated instructions for fundamental techniques of mask-making. The remaining sections cover more elaborate costuming—from a hippopotamus to a mouse.

430. Lewis, Shari, and Lillian Oppenheimer. **Folding Paper Masks**. New York, Dutton, 1965. 93p. illus. $4.45. ISBN 0-525-29999-8.

Provides instructions for making over 20 different masks including clown, owl, fox, and lion. Photos of decorated masks are included. Recommended for grades 1 through 8.

PUPPETS

431. Alkema, Chester Jay. **Puppet Making**. New York, Sterling, 1972. 48p. illus. index. (Little Craft Book Series). $2.95.

This publication provides practical information with detailed instructions on how to make puppets. The four sections are divided according to the material used. The first deals with paper puppets (from paper bags, folded paper, paper plates, cartons, etc.), the second with papier mâché (using various bases), the third with cloth puppets (including sock, mitten, and glove puppets as well as simple cloth monofold puppets), and the last with simple puppets made from whatever happens to be around the house (puppets made from food, from tongue depressors, puppets painted on one's hand, etc.). Directions are all adequate and the illustrations, some in color, will suggest more for the imaginative hobbyist.

A more specialized work scheduled for publication in Fall 1973 is Margaret Hutchings' *Making and Using Finger Puppets* (Taplinger. $8.50).

432. Baird, Bil. **The Art of the Puppet**. New York, Macmillan, 1965. 251p. illus. $19.95.

Presents a variety of information on puppetry as an art form and on the history of puppetry. The text is adequate, and the color illustrations are quite attractive. Children, teachers, and puppeteers will find this an informative book.

433. Böhmer, Gunter. **The Wonderful World of Puppets: Based on the Puppet Collection of the City of Munich**. Tr. by Gerald Morice. Boston, Plays, 1971. 156p. illus. index. $8.95. LC 76-107968.

This collection of photographs of puppets is a catalog of part of the collection of the Munich Puppet Museum, which owns one of the best collections of any museum of its kind. Divided into eight sections by types and geographical areas, the photographs are accompanied by short informative introductory notes. All photos are captioned. An excellent collection not only of academic interest but also of value in inspiring the puppeteer.

434. Crothers, J. Frances. **The Puppeteer's Library Guide: The Bibliographic Index to the Literature of the World Puppet Theatre. Vol. I: The Historical Background of Puppetry and Its Related Fields**. Metuchen, N.J., Scarecrow, 1971. 474p. $15.00. LC 71-149991.

The first of a projected six-volume index to the literature of puppetry, which will cover historical backgrounds, the puppet as an educator and entertainer, show production, puppeteers, and finally general material, sources, and indexes. Volume I is devoted to history, organizations, periodicals, festivals, and conventions.

435. Cummings, Richard. **101 Hand Puppets: A Guide for Puppeteers of All Ages**. New York, David McKay, 1962. 147p. illus. $3.95.

Like the author's *101 Masks*, this is an excellent book for hobbyists. The author tells how to make a variety of hand puppets ranging from the simplest sock puppet to complex puppets made from papier mâché and other materials. He describes in detail how to fashion all these puppets, using both text and his own illustrations. Few books on puppetry attempt the range presented in Mr. Cummings' text, yet all directions are simple enough for even the most inexperienced puppetmaker. Highly recommended.

436. Howard, Vernon. **Puppets and Pantomime Plays**. New York, Sterling, 1962. 108p. illus. index. $2.95.

This book is intended for the young puppeteer as a suggestion book on puppet plays. Instead of giving directions for making puppets, the author suggests briefly ways in which puppets can be made and then leaves it to the imagination of the child to continue from there. For the most part, the author discusses various ways of making puppets act and appeal to an audience. Suggestions for dialogue, action, and costumes are provided—suggestions which should inspire the puppeteer to use his own imagination. Recommended for elementary school and public libraries.

More detailed instruction on techniques of making puppets act is found in Larry Engler and Carol Fijan's *Making Puppets Come Alive: A Method of Learning and Teaching Hand Puppetry* (Taplinger, 1973. 192p. $9.95. LC 72-6623). Besides basic movements (with exercises suggested for perfecting these movements), this book discusses general theatrical techniques for puppetry: voice use, synchronization, dramatic conflict, improvisation, etc.

437. Kampmann, Lothar. **Creating with Puppets**. New York, Van Nostrand Reinhold, 1971. 76p. illus. index. $5.95. ISBN 0-442-24246-8.

Mr. Kampmann's book is in many ways an illustrated (mostly in color) guide to puppetry. Beginning with the simplest types of homemade puppet, the author illustrates and discusses the many varieties of puppets possible. Spoon puppets, puppets made from shoes, simple collage puppets, stick puppets, hand puppets, are all illustrated and discussed, as well as modelled heads from papier mâché and plastic modelling materials. Marionettes are covered, from the simplest to the most complex, and there is information on control devices. A section is devoted to the puppet stage in its most elemental form—a cardboard box. Following this is a short discussion of puppetry in the school, with observations on production. The photographs recommend this book most highly, suggesting as they do the enormous number of puppet types. A table indicating the grade level appropriateness of the puppets shown is provided at the end. May be of special interest to teachers of elementary grades.

438. Lewis, Shari, and Lillian Oppenheimer. **Folding Paper Puppets**. New York, Stein and Day, 1962. $3.95. ISBN 0-8128-1062-7.

The authors provide clear and simple directions for making 15 simple action models. All are excellent for teaching purposes. Some are original models. Recommended for grades 1 through 6.

439. Mulholland, John. **Practical Puppetry**. New York, Arco, 1961. 191p. illus. index. $4.95. LC 62-13448.

This is a "practical" handbook on all phases of puppetry. Although it was written for the amateur, it may also be informative for people who have considerable experience in this activity. In his first chapter the author discusses the history, the scope, and the many uses of puppets. Each additional chapter describes various aspects of the craft, beginning with simple puppets and progressing to glove and rod puppets, shadow puppets, and marionettes. Other chapters deal with technical aspects of production. There are discussions of visibility of the puppets on stage, construction of glove puppet stages and marionette theaters, lighting, special effects, plays and writing plays, etc. Instructions for making puppets are included in the chapters devoted to specific types of puppets, and suggestions and directions for operating puppets are given in detail. A well-balanced and mature treatment of all aspects of the puppeteer's art. Highly recommended.

440. Pels, Gertrude. **Easy Puppets: Making and Using Hand Puppets**. New York, T. Y. Crowell, 1951. 104p. illus. index. $3.95.

The author has taught puppetry in elementary school and has used puppetry in Girl Scout activities. Her book, primarily intended for children, uses diagrams and text to give directions for making a number of different hand puppets from inexpensive materials. Patterns are provided for making balloon, potato head, butterfly, and turtle puppets, along with many others, and trimmings required include feathers, buttons, bottle tops, and anything else available. Progressing to more ambitious projects, the young reader is eventually able to make papier mâché heads and to construct stages for puppet productions.

A new work devoted to small, easy-to-make puppets for very young children is Margaret Hutchings' *Making and Using Finger Puppets* (Taplinger, scheduled for September 1973. 96p. $8.50). There are suggestions for a puppet wedding and a Santa Claus, and plans for a Punch and Judy show.

441. Philpott, A. R. **Dictionary of Puppetry**. Boston, Plays, 1969. 286p. $8.95. ISBN 0-8238-0102-0.

This British dictionary defines terms, techniques, and types of puppets; it also includes the names of famous puppeteers and gives a history of puppetry. The author has written a number of other works on puppetry.

442. Rasmussen, Carrie, and Caroline Storck. **Fun-Time Puppets**. Chicago, Childrens Press, 1952. 41p. illus. $2.75.

This small book tells children how to make their own puppets. Directions are included for making puppets ranging from those of extreme simplicity (painted figures on a stick) to marionettes that will require adult supervision and aid. Directions for making a puppet theater are included, as well as suggestions for operating and acting. Even the most difficult puppets described are not terribly complex to make, but, because of its brevity, the book conveys little feeling of the artistry of puppets. Illustrated by drawings, both color and black and white.

443. Renfro, Nancy. **Puppets for Play Production**. New York, Funk and Wagnalls, 1969. 129p. illus. $6.95.

Two of the three sections of this book deal with puppetry as such—the first with construction of various types of puppets, the second with producing a puppet play. With numerous photographs of different kinds of puppets, the author provides instructions and suggestions for a wide variety of faces; all the puppets are basically simple and can be made by children in the primary grades. Materials are readily available in most homes. The second section deals with the production itself, making suggestions for stage and directing the reader in how to plan and perform a play. The third section is a discussion of the techniques of teaching puppetry to children. Materials and class plans are presented and there are suggestions for lessons in puppetmaking and acting. The author's enthusiasm for puppetry is evidenced everywhere in the book. Photos of finished puppets (most of them made by elementary school pupils) provide illustrations throughout. A short bibliography is appended, plus a list of puppetry organizations. Recommended for elementary school and public libraries.

444. Richter, Dorothy. **Fell's Guide to Hand Puppets: How to Make and Use Them**. New York, Frederick Fell, 1970. 202p. illus. index. $5.95.

After a brief history of puppetry, the author of this handbook gives instructions for making puppets. Chapters deal with human heads, animal heads, painting the head, and endowing it with hair. Costuming, the stage, and stage properties are discussed at some length. There are line drawings to depict the various topics under discussion and directions for making the various parts are specific. The discussion of puppetry in relation to the dramatic production deals with the voice; with lights, music, and special sound effects; with the actual production planning; and with the choice of a play. Chapters 13 through 17 provide five plays suitable for the puppet theater, with production notes for each one. The final chapter discusses comic routines for the puppets and gives a number of jokes of such vintage that even small children may blush. A bibliography is appended. Though not an inspired book, this is a practical one that teaches the basic elements of puppet making and theater production. As such, it is recommended for elementary school and public libraries.

445. Tichenor, Tom. **Tom Tichenor's Puppets**. Nashville, Abingdon Press, 1971. 224p. illus. index. $5.95. LC 76-147304.

Mr. Tichenor is a puppeteer of some distinction and wide experience, having been associated with local and national television for many years. In this book he manages to convey a sense of his own enthusiasm and love for the art of puppetry, while at the same time providing the beginner with practical information on how to get started and how to make puppets. The puppets here range from various types of hand puppets to marionettes. He tells how to make a puppet theater and includes seven plays for performance by both hand puppets and marionettes. Patterns for making puppets are included, along with many suggestions by Mr. Tichenor on puppets and puppet personalities. A charming section is the one devoted to biographical sketches of Mr. Tichenor's favorite puppets. An excellent book that will appeal to children and adults alike.

Dover has recently reprinted Helen Fling's four-volume *Marionette Hobby-Craft*. The title of the reprint is *Marionettes: How to Make and Work Them* (1v., $2.50pa.).

WOODWORKING AND CARVING

446. Adkins, Jan. **Toolchest: A Primer of Woodcraft**. New York, Walker, 1973. 48p. $4.50. LC 72-81374. ISBN 0-8027-6113-5.

Like Adkins' other books, this one is an enjoyable learning experience. It creates an interest in wood and tools, and it teaches basic facts about working with both. Inimitably written and illustrated by Mr. Adkins, it is highly recommended for anyone at all.

447. Bealer, Alex W. **Old Ways of Working Wood**. Barre, Mass., Barre, 1972. 231p. illus. $12.50.

Not specifically designed for woodcarvers, this guide will nevertheless have appeal for serious woodworkers. Techniques are described for felling trees, sawing, boring, chiselling, planing, and turning in ways that maintain old traditions. Traces the development of early woodworking and its tools, with line drawings to illustrate specific methods. Bibliography.

448. Borglund, Erland, and Jacob Flauensgaard. **Working in Plastic, Bone, Amber, and Horn**. New York, Van Nostrand Reinhold, 1968. 96p. illus. $4.50. LC 67-2491.

A sheet of plastic, a marrow bone, a cattle horn, and a chunk of amber are the raw materials of this book. Pictures and text in the book give clear instructions for the different techniques to be used with all these materials. In addition, a great many design suggestions are included for each material. The objects are, for the most part, easy to make, and some are quite handsome. A list of suppliers is appended. A good book for summer craft courses and for those interested in learning the fundamentals of working with these materials.

449. Burk, Bruce. **Game Bird Carving**. New York, Winchester Press, 1972. 242p. illus. index. $12.50. LC 72-79365. ISBN 0-87691-080-0.

This book launches the beginner on a simple carving project almost immediately. Detailed instructions and step-by-step photographs take him through his first attempt at shaping and painting, while projects of increasing complexity follow. The carver learns to plan and execute original carvings by understanding bird anatomy, by adapting his own drawings, and by careful planning. He is led on to advanced carving techniques—how to carve individual feathers, how to achieve the effects of iridescence. A special section is devoted to structural and dimensional characteristics of game birds, and the basic measurements and proportions for each species. Illustrated by more than 800 how-to photos and line drawings, with eight photos in color.

450. Campkin, Marie, ed. **Introducing Marquetry**. New York, Drake, 1971. 128p. illus. bibliog. index. $7.95.

The author describes the materials, tools, and techniques for making intricate marquetry pictures. There are descriptions of the most popular veneers used in this craft, plus notes, suggestions, and hints on design and adapting designs for interpretation in marquetry, hints on cutting and laying, glues and methods. Many photographs give step-by-step directions for performing preparations, while others show excellent examples of the craft; some of the photos are in color. This extremely good book, which covers many aspects of the craft, is highly recommended for the person who wishes to expand the possibilities of his work in wood. A short historical sketch of marquetry is included, along with a note on one of its outstanding modern practitioners. Appended are a short description of the Marquetry Society, suggestions for further reading, and a note on supplies.

451. Carstenson, Cecil C. **The Craft and Creation of Wood Sculpture**. New York, Scribner's, 1971. 170p. illus. index. $9.95. LC 72-162740.

The author begins with a description of tools and woods, then describes the carving of a simple mask. From this point he leads the craftsman to heads and figures and finally to large, involved sculptural works. An unusually practical work intended for beginners.

452. Cartmell, Ronald. **Wood Sculpture**. New York, Taplinger, 1970. 126p. illus. $6.50.

More than half of this text is devoted to photographs of wood sculpture; information provided for each includes attribution, size, and material, with some comments also on technique. The first portion of the book, however, provides some information on wood, tools, and techniques employed by the sculptor in wood. The sculpture of a bear is evaluated through diagrams and textual description. A one-page section provides notes on finishing, and precautionary notes are appended, as well as a short bibliography. For someone interested in obtaining information on the techniques and materials of wood sculpture, this would be a disappointing work. The text section, however, may be viewed as a technical introduction to the photograph section, in which case the book is more art than handbook. A newly announced title on the same subject is P. E. Norman's *Sculpture in Wood* (St. Martin's Press, November 1973. $5.95; $3.95pa.).

453. Endicott, Robert F. **Scrap Wood Fun for Kids**. New York, Association Press, 1961. 223p. illus. $4.95. LC 61-14181.

Written by a camp counselor, this book provides instructions and diagrams for making 100 simple projects from wood. It is intended for first instructions in woodcarving, whittling, and construction. Many of the projects are games or toys—ring toss game, kite string reel, racing car—but some are objects to be taken home to mother (recipe holder) or used by the child (pencil holder, jewelry box). The large format permits full-size diagrams for most of the projects. The introduction provides information that will be useful to the crafts director or teacher. Recommended for junior craft courses in camps, churches, and schools.

454. Flayderman, E. Norman. **Scrimshaw and Scrimshanders: Whales and Whalemen**. Ed. by R. L. Wilson. Published by the author; distr. Norwalk, Conn., Silvermine, 1972. 291p. illus. index. $19.95. LC 79-154305. ISBN 0-910598-09-6.

Expensive, but essential for those seriously interested in scrimshaw. A history of the art, a discussion of whalemen's lives, and an investigation of the techniques of scrimshaw are illustrated by some 450 examples of scrimshaw products.

455. Gottshall, Franklin H. **Woodcarving and Whittling Made Easy**. New York, Bruce, 1963. 128p. illus. $4.95. LC 63-10891.

In the first chapter of this book, the author provides information on tools, their care and maintenance. The second chapter describes the various techniques used in woodcarving, including line carving, low relief, carving in the round, and whittling. Chapter three describes briefly how to draw designs and patterns. The remainder of the book is devoted to 33 carving projects, all of which are illustrated by working diagrams and photos of the finished project. Commentary provides instructions for making each project and suggestions about woods. Projects range from relatively simple to complex;

beginners will be challenged from the start, and advanced carvers may pick up new ideas here.

456. Graveney, Charles. **How to Start Carving**. New York, Van Nostrand Reinhold, 1972. 68p. illus. index. $3.95. LC 71-161976. ISBN 0-289-70193-7.

Designed to encourage the development of manual skills in youngsters, this book provides information on wood and soap carving. The simple projects—which include folk toys as well as traditional carved objects—will acquaint the reader with some of the basic techniques used. Projects include a bird, paper knife, pastry roller, and jewelry, among others. Illustrations accompany the text, and a glossary of terms is appended.

457. Gross, Chaim. **The Technique of Wood Sculpture**. New York, Arco, 1966 (c.1957). 136p. illus. $4.95. LC 64-17382.

The author offers step-by-step advice for carving sculptural forms. Beginning with a short chapter on how he became a sculptor, he proceeds to a discussion of wood as a medium for sculpture, how and where to obtain wood, and how it is seasoned. Other chapters describe the workroom, the block, the idea of the sculptural piece, the initial steps in carving, abrading, and finally, sealing of the finished sculpture. Appendixes include information on tools, sharpeners, woods, the seasoning of wood, properties of specific sculptors' woods (arranged alphabetically), and a table of relative hardness and color of woods. Although the text will be of most value to the person already working in wood who desires more information on the subject, even the beginner will find valuable information that should help him to avoid costly mistakes. The author, a well-known wood sculptor, has taught courses in art schools. Black and white photos show techniques and various examples of wood sculpture by the author and others.

458. Hanauer, Elsie V. **Handbook of Woodcarving and Whittling**. New York, A. S. Barnes, 1967. 80p. illus. $4.95. LC 67-16959.

This book contains over 50 designs for carving, including birds, human figures, animals, guns, and plaques. Diagrams of all sides of the figures are provided along with dimensions and instructions for carving and finishing. The first section provides basic instructions in the art of carving and a description of tools. Detailed illustrations are in black and white. Recommended for libraries that have requests for how-to and project material. A more recent work by the same author and publisher is *The Art of Whittling and Woodcarving* (1970. $5.95).

459. Hennessey, James, and Victor Papanek. **Nomadic Furniture**. New York, Pantheon Books/Random House, 1973. 149p. illus. $8.95; $3.95pa. LC 72-3412. ISBN 0-394-47577-1; 0-394-70228-Xpa.

Not strictly speaking a crafts book, but a currently and deservedly popular do-it-yourself manual that is one answer to the problems inherent in the nomadic way of life. Hand printed, with detailed drawings (and a few photographs) of projects. After introductory chapters on nomads and human measurements, divisions include seating, eating and working, storage, sleeping, light, babies and children, and "etc." Extraordinarily useful suggestions for anyone short on space, anyone who moves often, anyone intrigued with modern design. Basic knowledge of building skills is necessary.

460. Hoppe, H. **Whittling and Wood Carving**. Tr. by Eric Greweldinger. New York, Sterling, 1972. 48p. illus. index. $2.95. LC 69-19488. ISBN 0-8069-5126-5.

Beginning with simple projects (the carving of a staff for decorative purposes), the author progresses to chip carving, veneer carving, ornamental carving, carving letter bowls and candlesticks, relief carving, sculpture (animal and human), puppet heads, and portraiture. There are special sections on tools and wood, and an interesting section on transferring measurements from clay to plaster to wood to stone. The illustrations offer instruction on techniques as well as numerous suggestions for designs. Treatment can hardly be comprehensive in 48 pages, but this small translation does offer the reader excellent beginning instructions.

461. Hunt, W. Ben. **Ben Hunt's Big Book of Whittling**. New York, Bruce, 1970. 182p. illus. $7.95. LC 78-140901.

This book has been compiled from two of Ben Hunt's earlier books—*Ben Hunt's Whittling Book* (1944) and *More Ben Hunt Whittlings*. All the whittling projects here are traditional favorites of hobby and craft enthusiasts, which means that they suffer somewhat from triteness. There are approximately 50 projects ranged within each subject heading, in order of difficulty. The subject headings include birds, Indian crafts, animals, faces, figures, and a section devoted to special projects. Detailed instructions, line drawings of each project, and photographs provide ample aid to the whittler. Despite the commonness of the various projects, they do have a certain naive appeal that may challenge the whittler's facility with the knife. Information is also provided on knives and sharpening. Especially recommended for boys' craft courses in camps and schools.

462. Johnstone, James B., and the Sunset Editorial Staff. **Woodcarving Techniques and Projects**. 2nd ed. Menlo Park, Calif., Lane Books, 1971. 80p. illus. glossary. $1.95pa. LC 72-157174. ISBN 0-376-04802-6.

Not a beginner's guide, but rather an introduction to the kinds of carving that can be undertaken by the neophyte. The first section covers choosing and seasoning wood, wood characteristics, etc., while the second is devoted to tools. Carved surface decoration, whittling, and carving in the round are the other major divisions of the book. The projects that serve as examples of these techniques include headboards, trays, doors, kitchen utensils, and a chess set, among many others. The last section is on techniques of finishing. Contains many useful hints, but a more detailed guide would better serve the rank beginner.

463. Kennedy, Monty. **Checkering and Carving of Gunstocks**. Rev. ed. Harrisburg, Pa., Stackpole, 1962. 336p. illus. $10.00.

With the help of more than 470 technical illustrations, some of the best craftsmen in the field discuss checkering and carving techniques and illustrate personal choices of patterns. Each pattern is full-size for easy transfer and use. Many checkering types—flat or English, French or skip style, sharp-pointed American, and combinations—are represented. For the carving buff, there are patterns for doing forearms, grip, and buttside, ideas for big game, game bird, animal, flower, and leaf and seed designs. Mr. Kennedy's long first chapter on checkering and carving describes the techniques and tools of the trade and is followed by observations on stock woods (by Tom Shalhamer) and numerous designs for various rifles described by the designer himself. Excellent for anyone interested in gun stock art, and very reasonably priced.

464. Matthews, John. **Creative Light Wood Carving**. New York, St. Martin's Press, 1971. 96p. illus. $3.95.

The author's approach to free-line shaping and carving of wood is intended to stimulate the pupil's interest immediately and to induce considerable enthusiasm and skill in creative work. It is suitable for secondary school pupils and should be of interest to anyone who wishes to begin to shape simple forms in wood. The author uses simple line drawings to illustrate the techniques of making handsome wall carvings, standing carvings, bowl carvings, and small wood sculptures. Patterns are given—some full size—and techniques for carving and finishing are fully shown. In addition, the pieces represented are extremely handsome and should make any pupil or adult proud of his effort. Recommended for crafts teachers especially.

465. Meyer, Carolyn. **Saw, Hammer, and Paint: Woodworking and Finishing for Beginners.** New York, Morrow, 1973. 128p. $4.95. LC 72-9927. ISBN 0-688-20069-9.

Girls and boys will learn basic techniques (measuring, cutting, and nailing) as they proceed from the first project to the progressively more difficult ones. Aspects of finishing are discussed in a separate section, and the project directions refer to this section when necessary. The simply presented text is augmented by drawings and diagrams. Projects range from a cheeseboard and a candlestick to a bookcase and a desk.

466. Rich, Jack C. **Sculpture in Wood.** New York, Oxford University Press, 1970. 155p. illus. index. $15.00.

Fully half of this essay is an alphabetically arranged description of the varieties of woods used in sculpture. In this chapter the author informs the student about where the wood is grown, its color and weight, its common names and characteristics. A second glossary classifies wood with respect to how easy it is to work with. Other chapters discuss toxicity of woods and seasoning. The first part of the book is a handbook on tools, carving techniques, care and sharpening of tools, joints, and glues. An excellent treatment for the amateur and professional sculptor who wants ready information on a variety of subjects relating to wood, including the tools and materials for working it.

467. Ritchie, Carson I. A. **Scrimshaw.** New York, Sterling, 1972. 48p. illus. (Little Craft Book Series). $2.95. LC 71-180454.

The author tells how to prepare and decorate whale teeth, elephant tusks, and any substitute for these. He tells how to incise a design on the tooth or tusk, and gives a short description of traditional designs. There is information on stippling and other techniques, and the last section describes Eskimo scrimshaw and primitive methods of working the material. Short but informative.

468. Sack, Walter. **Woodcarving.** New York, Van Nostrand Reinhold, 1973. illus. $5.50; $2.95pa. ISBN 0-442-299842; 0-442-29982-6pa.

Primarily for beginners, this book emphasizes the elementary aspects of woodcarving; use of simple tools, choosing and preparing wood, and basic carving techniques.

469. Tangerman, Elmer J. **Design and Figure Carving.** New York, McGraw-Hill, 1940; repr. New York, Dover, 1964. 289p. illus. index. $2.50. LC 64-18869. ISBN 0-486-21209-2.

This second volume by Mr. Tangerman is intended to "supplement and amplify" his earlier work, *Whittling and Woodcarving*—especially those chapters dealing with caricatures and in-the-round carving. It is graded in content, progressing from simple exercises to complex, and all designs in the first half are classified by tool "to assist in training, tool by tool." Thus, the first half, in addition to a chapter on present-day carving and design, has chapters dealing with the stamp, knife, gouge, saw, and all tools. The second half deals with specific carving problems, including inlay and marquetry, figures, heads and faces, the extremities, body in action, caricature, folk carving, and animals and birds. An appendix describes how to enlarge a design, and there is a bibliography. There are 1,298 photographs, drawings, plans, and layouts to aid the reader in his undertaking. Everything considered, this is a worthy complement to Mr. Tangerman's earlier work, and it well deserves the reputation it has maintained over the years.

470. Tangerman, Elmer J. **The Modern Book of Whittling and Woodcarving**. New York, McGraw-Hill, 1973. illus. $10.00; $7.95 spiral. LC 73-9994. ISBN 0-07-062670-7; 0-07-062676-9 spiral.

This latest book by Mr. Tangerman stresses modern designs. Among the 1,000 patterns presented in line drawings are those suited for beginners and for experienced carvers.

471. Tangerman, Elmer J. **Whittling and Woodcarving**. New York, McGraw-Hill, 1936; repr. New York, Dover, 1962. 293p. illus. index. $2.00pa. ISBN 0-486-20965-2.

In this book Mr. Tangerman attempts to establish a relationship between whittling and serious carving. Beginning with a history of whittling and woodcarving, the book progresses to basic information on woods and on knives (their selection and care, basic cuts and strokes). Succeeding chapters cover rustic work, windmills, puzzles, chairs, nested spheres, modelling ships in bottles, and caricatures. The second part of the book, which deals with carving proper, describes simple lines, woodcuts, low relief, pierced designs, sculpture in the round, inlay and marquetry, lettering, indoor and outdoor decoration, and style. The appendix adds information on finishing, repairs, and care of tools. Hundreds of illustrations complement the text; many of the illustrations show award-winning pieces. This excellent text is an invaluable aid to the carver, whether amateur or professional.

472. Waltner, Elma. **Carving Animal Caricatures**. Bloomington, Ill., McKnight and McKnight, 1951; repr. New York, Dover, 1972. 104p. illus. $2.50pa. LC 70-184691. ISBN 0-486-22813-4.

The author details the making of 24 different animal caricatures from wood. The first two have numbered steps accompanied by photos of the operation described, while the remaining projects illustrate only those operations that have not been described in detail previously. Illustrations include diagrams of each project and a photo of the finished animal. All the projects are appealing and should interest children, though the carving will require a mature hand.

473. Warring, Ron. **Balsa Wood Modelling**. New York, Sterling, 1973. 47p. illus. index. (Little Craft Book Series). $2.95. LC 72-95152. ISBN 0-8069-5252-0.

Like other books in the series, this one presents detailed instructions, with many patterns and line drawings, for specific projects. Boomerangs, boxes, a periscope, gliders, kites, ships, and yachts are among the projects. Full of general tips on modelling with balsa.

474. Wright, Lois A. **Weathered Wood Craft**. New York, Lothrop, Lee and Shepard, 1973. illus. $4.75. LC 73-5775. ISBN 0-688-41562-8.

Considering the current run on old barns, there is a large audience somewhere out there for things to make from weathered wood. Ms. Wright tells how to find the wood, clean it, and treat it, and she shows how to make many weathered wood items that are utilitarian and/or aesthetically appealing.

PERIODICALS

GENERAL CRAFTS

475. **All States Hobbyist**. 101 Chestnut Hill Lane East, Reistertown, Md. 21136. Bi-monthly. 1950. $2.00.

An idea-exchange publication sponsored by the All States Hobby Club. Covers a wide variety of hobbies.

476. **Craft Horizons**. 16 East 52nd Street, New York, N.Y. 10022. Bi-monthly. 1941. $2.00.

Covers most crafts fields (ceramics, metal, wood, jewelry, needlework, weaving, etc.). Published by the American Crafts Council, its audience includes all levels of craftsmen, as well as decorators, collectors, designers and architects, and teachers. Articles are not limited to the how-to approach; philosophy, materials, and techniques are also discussed. Highly recommended for libraries that serve craftsmen.

477. **Craftsman: L'Artisan**. 14–16 Elgin Street, Ottawa, Ontario, Canada. Semi-annual. 1968. $10.00.

Emphasis is on Canadian craftsmen and their work. Contains notices of exhibitions and activities. Many photographs.

478. **Creative Crafts**. Model Craftsman Publishing Corporation, 31 Arch Street, Ramsey, N.J. 07446. Bi-monthly. 1967. $3.00.

Any craft may be covered in the articles found here. Instructions are not step-by-step but they suffice. Regular features, in addition to the articles, include a question-and-answer column, a discussion of newly available crafts kits, etc. Illustrated with photographs of finished products as well as intermediate steps.

479. **Decorating and Craft Ideas Made Easy.** P.O. Box 9737, Fort Worth, Texas 76107. 10 issues per year. $4.00.

The thrust of this journal is the use of crafts for home decoration. Articles discuss specific projects that can be made from materials readily available in art and crafts stores.

480. **Design: The Magazine of Creative Art, for Teachers, Artists, and Craftsmen.** Reviews Publishing Company, Inc., 1100 Waterway Boulevard, Indianapolis, Ind. 46207. Bi-monthly. 1899. $4.50.

For teachers interested in the design possibilities of various media (ceramics, painting, glass, etc.). Discusses crafts techniques as well as theory.

481. **Good Housekeeping Needlecraft.** Hearst Corporation, 959 Eighth Avenue, New York, N.Y. 10019. Semi-annual. 1968. $3.00.

This periodical and *McCall's Needlework and Crafts* supplement and complement each other as "wishbooks" for homemakers interested in crafts. Both magazines emphasize needlework but also cover other crafts. Projects are usually either wearable, suitable for gifts and holidays, or designed to decorate the home.

482. **Handymanual.** 222 Park Avenue, South, New York, N.Y. 10003.

483. **Hobbies: The Magazine for Collectors.** 1006 South Michigan Avenue, Chicago, Ill. 60605. Monthly. 1931. $6.00.

Articles discuss antiques, collecting, historic items, etc. Copiously illustrated with photographs.

484. **Hobbies to Enjoy.** P.O. Box 2242, St. Louis, Missouri 63109. Semi-annual. 1945. $2.00.

This is the publication of the American All-Hobbies Association, a national group made up of many subsidiary, subject-oriented hobby clubs.

485. **Jaybee's Handicraft Magazine.** J. B. Printing, Box 39FT, Valley Park, Missouri 63011. Monthly. 1962. $4.00.

A folksy, how-to magazine filled with hints from fellow hobbyists and craftsmen. Patterns and instructions are included for some of the projects. A sample copy is available for $0.10.

486. **McCall's Needlework and Crafts**. McCall Pattern Company, 230 Park Avenue, New York, N.Y. 10017. Semi-annual. 1919. $1.25/copy; $6.00/two years.

Usually bought on the newsstand rather than by subscription, this is one of the most popular of the periodicals devoted to crafts for home execution. Needlework projects predominate, but stained glass, ceramics, paper crafts, etc., are also covered. A recent addition is a section devoted to "Nostalgia," which illustrates and provides instructions for crafts popular in the past (cross-stitched samplers, bead-work purses, etc.).

487. **Mobilia: For Furniture, Art Handicraft, Art and Architecture**. Mette Bratvold, 3070 Snekkersten, Denmark. Monthly. 1955. $25.00.

A beautifully illustrated periodical from Denmark that stresses design (furniture, crafts, architecture, etc.). Of greater use to the professional and the art teacher than to the amateur craftsman.

488. **Pack-O-Fun**. Clapper Publishing Company, 14 Main Street, Park Ridge, Ill. 66068. Monthly (September-June). 1951. $5.00.

Like the Pack-O-Fun books, this monthly is full of how-to instructions for projects made from leftovers. Particularly helpful for teachers and others who need a continual supply of new ideas for simple projects.

489. **Popular Science**. 355 Lexington Avenue, New York, N.Y. 10017. Monthly. 1872. $6.00.

Although the emphasis is on home workshop activities and on repairing and maintaining cars, hi-fi sets, etc., there are also articles on wood and metal projects and other crafts.

490. **Women's Circle**, P.O. Box 428, Seabrook, N.H. 03874. Monthly. 1958. $3.00.

For the housebound Hausfrau in need of new projects. Covers all sorts of crafts and needlework. Illustrated.

491. **The Workbasket and Home Arts Magazine**. Modern Handcraft, Inc., 4251 Pennsylvania Avenue, Kansas City, Missouri 64111. Monthly. 1935. $1.50.

How-to articles on crafts and hobbies, though needlework is stressed. Projects are similar to those in *Women's Circle*, *McCall's Needlework and Crafts*, and *Good Housekeeping Needlecraft*.

DOLLS AND PUPPETS

492. **Doll News**. 4035 East Kessler Boulevard, Indianapolis, Ind. 46220. Quarterly.

This is the publication of the United Federation of Doll Clubs, which is composed of 97 local and/or regional clubs of doll collectors.

493. **NIADA Newsletter**. National Institute of American Doll Artists, Ozone, Tennessee 37842. Three issues/year.

This is the newsletter for a professional organization of doll artists.

494. **Pelpup News**. Pelham Puppets, Marlborough, England.

Those interested in marionettes and puppetry can exchange ideas through this international club magazine.

495. **Puppetry Journal**. Box 1061, Ojai, Calif. 93023. Bi-monthly. 1949. $10.00; free to members.

Publication of the Puppeteers of America, which is an organization whose members include anyone interested in puppets, from children through the professional level. Publication includes book reviews and news of products and club members. Indexed annually.

GLASS

496. **The Glass Workshop**. 482 Tappan Road, Northvale, N.J. 07647. Bi-monthly. 1969. $4.00.

Published by the Stained Glass Club, which is a profit-making organization that sells supplies and custom-made stained glass lamps.

497. **Journal of Glass Studies**. The Corning Museum of Glass, Corning Glass Center, Corning, N.Y. 14830. Annual. 1959. $7.00.

For professionals working with glass. A scholarly approach to the art of glassworking from its earliest beginnings up to the present.

498. **Stained Glass Journal**. 3600 University Drive, Fairfax, Virginia 22030. Quarterly. 1905. $5.00.

This is a publication of the Stained Glass Association of America, whose membership is primarily professional craftsmen and manufacturers. Articles cover craftsmen, examples of recent and ancient work, and exhibits and competitions. Book reviews.

POTTERY AND CERAMICS

499. **Ceramic Arts and Crafts**. Scott Advertising and Publishing Co., 30595 West Eight-Mile Road, Livonia, Mich. 48152. Monthly. 1955. $6.00.

Designed primarily for those who buy greenware to paint, rather than for potters or others who create from clay. Within its limitations, it provides adequate instructions, lists of supplies, etc.

500. **Ceramics Monthly**. Professional Publications, Inc. 1609 Northwest Boulevard, Columbus, Ohio 43212. Monthly (September-June). 1953. $6.00.

Designed for potters at any level. Articles, which cover all aspects of the craft, are supplemented by photographs and drawings. Includes articles on glazes and on enamelling. Good popular magazine.

501. **Clay Chatter**. P.O. Box 39, Glen Burnie, Md. 21061.

Published by the National Ceramic Association, an organization founded in 1958 to promote and improve the craft.

502. **Hobby Teachers Manual**. P.O. Box 39, Glen Burnie, Md. 21061.

Another publication of the National Ceramic Association, this one is designed for those who teach ceramics.

503. **ICPTO News**. International China Painting Teachers Organization, 4125 N.W. 57th Street, Oklahoma City, Oklahoma 73112. Monthly.

Provides hints and suggestions for those interested in china painting.

504. **Popular Ceramics**. 6011 Santa Monica Boulevard, Los Angeles, Calif. 90038. Monthly. 1949. $7.50.

For teachers and potters. Includes how-to articles and technical articles on ceramics. Features include book reviews, a new products column, and news of shows and exhibits.

ROCKS AND GEMS

505. **Gems and Minerals**. P.O. Box 687, Mentone, Calif. 92359. Monthly. 1937. $4.50.

A how-to periodical that includes articles on field trips for gem collecting. For rock-hounds and amateur jewelry makers.

506. **Lapidary Journal**. Box 2369, San Diego, Calif. 92112. Monthly. 1947. $5.75.

Covers all aspects of gemcraft for the rock-hound: discussions of specific stones, projects, etc. Much advertising.

WOODWORKING AND CARVING

507. **Chip Chats**. 7424 Miami Avenue, Cincinnati, Ohio 45243. Bi-monthly. 1953. $3.00.

Published by the National Wood Carvers Association, this bi-monthly will be of interest to carvers and whittlers at all levels. Book reviews, articles on new products and technical advances, etc.

508. **The Family Handyman: The Do-It-Yourself Magazine**. Universal Publishing and Distributing Corporation, 235 East 45th Street, New York, N.Y. 10017. 9/year. 1950. $5.00.

Emphasizes do-it-yourself projects, including gardening and furniture-building; articles on decorating and woodworking would be of interest to craftsmen.

509. **Flying Chips**. Rockwell Manufacturing Company, 550 North Lexington Avenue, Pittsburgh, Pa. 15208. Bi-monthly. 1932. $1.75.

Primarily for those familiar with the use of power tools, this bi-monthly emphasizes furniture-making and similar heavy projects.

510. **Workbench**. Modern Handcrafts, Inc., 4251 Pennsylvania Avenue, Kansas City, Missouri 42111. Bi-monthly. 1957. $2.00.

For do-it-yourselfers. Emphasis is on home repair and maintenance, but some of the projects will appeal to amateur woodworkers as well.

OTHER PERIODICALS FOR SPECIFIC CRAFTS

511. **The Craftsman**. P.O. Box 1386, Fort Worth, Texas 76101. Bimonthly. $3.50.

Presents articles by leather craftsmen. Finished products illustrated by photographs, with line drawings where needed to supplement the instructions. Will be useful for teachers, professionals, and advanced craftsmen working in leather. Emphasis is on Western-style leatherworking.

512. **Kite Tales**. P.O. Box 1511, Silver City, New Mexico 88061. Quarterly. 1964. $3.00.

Published by the American Kitefliers Association for its members. Emphasizes kiteflying as an adult hobby; approach is generally scientific.

513. **Textile Crafts**. Box 3216, Los Angeles, Calif. 90028. Quarterly. 1969. $5.00.

Primarily, as the title indicates, for weavers and those interested in macrame, embroidery, and related textile crafts.

ORGANIZATIONS

All States Hobby Club, 101 Chestnut Lane, Reistertown, Maryland
21136.

This club is designed to provide a basis for the exchange of information among hobbyists. Over 200 different hobbies are represented in its membership. Publishes *All States Hobbyist*.

American All-Hobbies Association, P.O. Box 2242, St. Louis, Missouri
63109.

This national organization includes a number of auxiliary clubs devoted to specific hobbies (such as pets, stamps and coins, shells, travel, arts and crafts, and collecting). Semi-annual publication: *Hobbies to Enjoy*.

American Ceramic Society, 65 Ceramic Drive, Columbus, Ohio 43214.

American Crafts Council, 44 West 53rd Street, New York, N.Y. 10019.

The aim of this national organization is to promote an appreciation of the work produced by craftsmen in the United States. Founded in 1943.

American Kitefliers Association, P.O. Box 1511, Silver City, New
Mexico 88061.

The aim of this organization is to develop kiteflying in America as an adult sport. Its quarterly publication, *Kite Tales*, stresses the scientific aspects of kiteflying.

British Puppet and Model Theater Guild, 7 Lupus Street, London, S.W. 1, England.

Educational Puppetry Association (EPA), 23a Southhampton Place, London, W.C. 1, England.

International China Painting Teachers Organization, 4125 N.W. 57th Street, Oklahoma City, Oklahoma 73112.

An association whose aim is to promote excellence in china painting with lustres, gold, enamel, and other media.

International Kitefliers Association, 45 Tudor City Place, New York, N.Y. 10017.

This group was formerly the National Kite Association. One of its goals is the acceptance of kiteflying as an Olympic sport.

National Ceramic Association, P.O. Box 39, Glen Burnie, Maryland 21061.

The aim of this organization is to promote, standardize, and improve the activity. Members include manufacturers, dealers, teachers, and distributors. The organization sponsors seminars, meetings, and an annual convention; it publishes three periodicals: *Blue Book* (annual); *Clay Chatter* (bi-monthly); and *Hobby Teachers Manual*.

National Institute of American Doll Artists, Ozone, Tennessee 37842.

Professional club, with elected members from the ranks of patrons and professional doll artists. Promotes the recognition of original, American-created dolls.

National Wood Carvers Association, 7424 Miami Avenue, Cincinnati, Ohio 45243.

This organization provides whittlers and woodcarvers with a wealth of information: suggestions for projects, booklets on woodcarving, suppliers' names, etc.

Puppeteers of America, Box 1061, Ojai, Calif. 93023.

International organization for the exchange of ideas on the subject. Membership ranges from professional puppeteers through therapists and youth group leaders, on down to children interested in puppets. Publishes an annual directory and *Puppetry Journal* (bi-monthly).

The Society of Arts and Crafts, 69 Newbury Street, Boston, Mass. 02116.

This well-established organization is devoted to excellence in craftsmanship in the United States. Founded in 1897.

Stained Glass Association of America, 1125 Silmington Avenue, St. Louis, Missouri 63111.

Membership consists of professional craftsmen and manufacturers of stained and leaded glass windows, as well as windows made of hard metal and concrete. Organization sponsors competitions and provides a placement service for members.

Stained Glass Club, 482 Tappan Road, Northvale, N.J. 07647.

This organization makes and sells stained glass lamps to order. It also sells tools and supplies for stained glass craftsmen at all levels of experience. Publishes *The Glass Workshop*.

United Federation of Doll Clubs, 4035 East Kessler Boulevard, Indianapolis, Ind. 46220.

This is a national group made up of 97 independent doll collectors' clubs.

LIST OF PUBLISHERS

Abelard-Schuman, Ltd.
257 Park Avenue
New York, N.Y. 10010

Abingdon Press
201 Eighth Avenue South
Nashville, Tennessee 37203

Addison-Wesley Publishing Co.
Reading, Massachusetts 01867

American Art Clay Company
4717 West 16th Street
Indianapolis, Indiana 46222

Arco Publishing Company
219 Park Avenue South
New York, N.Y. 10003

Association Press
291 Broadway
New York, N.Y. 10007

Atheneum Publishers
122 East 42nd Street
New York, N.Y. 10017

A. S. Barnes and Company, Inc.
Cranbury, N.J. 08512

Barre Publishers
South Street
Barre, Massachusetts 01005

John G. Barrow
4509 Crestway Drive
Austin, Texas 78731

Charles A. Bennett Company
237 N.E. Monroe Street
Peoria, Illinois 61602

Bobbs-Merrill Company
4300 West 62nd Street
Indianapolis, Indiana 46268

C. T. Branford Company
28 Union Street
Newton Centre, Mass. 02159

Bruce Books   (An Affiliate of Crowell
Collier Macmillan)
850 Third Avenue
New York, N.Y. 10022

Childrens Press
1224 West Van Buren Street
Chicago, Illinois 60607

Chilton Book Company
Chilton Way
Radnor, Pa. 19089

Cornell Maritime Press, Inc.
Cambridge, Maryland 21613

Coward-McCann, Inc.
200 Madison Avenue
New York, N.Y. 10016

Thomas Y. Crowell
201 Park Avenue South
New York, N.Y. 10003

Crown Publishers, Inc.
419 Park Avenue South
New York, N.Y. 10016

F. A. Davis Company
1915 Arch Street
Philadelphia, Pa. 19103

John Day Publications
257 Park Avenue South
New York, N.Y. 10010

Doubleday and Company, Inc.
501 Franklin Avenue
Garden City, N.Y. 11530

Dover Publications, Inc.
180 Varick Street
New York, N.Y. 10014

Drake Publishers, Inc.
381 Park Avenue South
New York, N.Y. 10016

E. P. Dutton and Company
201 Park Avenue South
New York, N.Y. 10003

Educator Books
10 North Main Street
Drawer 32
San Angelo, Texas 76901

Emerson Books
251 West 19th Street
New York, N.Y. 10011

Exposition Press, Inc.
50 Jericho Turnpike
Jericho, N.Y. 11753

Farrar, Straus and Giroux, Inc.
19 Union Square West
New York, N.Y. 10003

F. W. Faxon Company
15 Southwest Park
Westwood, Massachusetts 02090

Frederick Fell, Inc.
386 Park Avenue South
New York, N.Y. 10016

Walter T. Foster
Laguna Beach, California

Funk & Wagnalls
Distr. by Thomas Y. Crowell

Golden Press
850 Third Avenue
New York, N.Y. 10022

Goodheart-Willcox Company
18250 Harwood Avenue
Homewood, Illinois 60430

Gousha/Times Mirror Co.
Box 6227
San Jose, California 95150

Government Printing Office
Washington, D.C. 20402

Great Outdoors Publishing Co.
4747 28th Street North
St. Petersburg, Florida 33714

Greenberg Publishers
Distr. by Chilton Book Company

Newton K. Gregg, Publisher
P.O. Box 452
Kentfield, Calif. 94904

Grosset and Dunlap, Inc.
51 Madison Avenue
New York, N.Y. 10010

Harcourt Brace Jovanovich
757 Third Avenue
New York, N.Y. 10017

Hawthorn Books, Inc.
70 Fifth Avenue
New York, N.Y. 10011

Hearthside Press, Inc.
445 Northern Boulevard
Great Neck, N.Y. 11021

Hill and Wang, Inc.
19 Union Square West
New York, N.Y. 10003

Holt, Rinehart & Winston, Inc.
383 Madison Avenue
New York, N.Y. 10017

Houghton Mifflin and Company
2 Park Street
Boston, Massachusetts 02107

House of Collectibles
220 Fifth Avenue
New York, N.Y. 10001

Indiana University Press
Tenth and Morton Streets
Bloomington, Indiana 47401

Ireland Magic Company
Magic, Inc.
5082 North Lincoln Avenue
Chicago, Illinois 60625

Japan Publications Trading Co.
1255 Howard Street
San Francisco, Calif. 94103

Alfred A. Knopf, Inc.
201 East 50th Street
New York, N.Y. 10022

Kodansha International/USA
599 College Avenue
Palo Alto, Calif. 94306

Lancer Books, Inc.
1560 Broadway
New York, N.Y. 10036

Lane Magazine & Book Company
Menlo Park, California 94025

Lansdowne Press
Little Bourke Street 37
Melbourne, Victoria, Australia

Lantern Press, Inc.
354 Hussey Road
Mt. Vernon, N.Y. 10552

J. B. Lippincott Company
East Washington Square
Philadelphia, Pa. 19105

Little, Brown, and Company
34 Beacon Street
Boston, Massachusetts 02106

Littlefield, Adams and Company
81 Adams Drive
Totowa, N.J.

Lothrop, Lee & Shepard Company
105 Madison Avenue
New York, N.Y. 10016

McGraw-Hill Book Company
1221 Avenue of the Americas
New York, N.Y. 10020

David McKay Company
750 Third Avenue
New York, N.Y. 10017

McKnight and McKnight
Box 845
Bloomington, Illinois 61701

Macmillan Company
866 Third Avenue
New York, N.Y. 10022

Julian Messner (A Division of
        Simon and Schuster, Inc.)
1 West 39th Street
New York, N.Y. 10018

William Morrow and Company
105 Madison Avenue
New York, N.Y. 10016

Nash Publishing Corporation
9255 Sunset Boulevard
Los Angeles, Calif. 90069

Thomas Nelson, Inc.
407 Seventh Avenue South
Nashville, Tennessee 37203

Oxford University Press
200 Madison Avenue
New York, N.Y. 10016

Parents' Magazine Press
52 Vanderbilt Avenue
New York, N.Y. 10017

Parker Publishing Company
West Nyack, N.Y. 10994

Penguin Books
72 Fifth Avenue
New York, N.Y. 10011

S. G. Phillips, Inc.
305 West 86th Street
New York, N.Y. 10024

Pine Cone Press
4847 Sedgwick Street, N.W.
Washington, D.C. 20016

Plays, Inc.
8 Arlington Street
Boston, Massachusetts 02116

Praeger Publishers, Inc.
111 Fourth Avenue
New York, N.Y. 10003

Prentice-Hall, Inc.
Englewood Cliffs, N.J. 07632

Professional Publications
P.O. Box 4548
Columbus, Ohio 43214

Putnam's Sons
200 Madison Avenue
New York, N.Y. 10016

Random House, Inc.
201 East 50th Street
New York, N.Y. 10022

Henry Regnery Company
114 West Illinois Street
Chicago, Ill. 60610

Resourceful Research
P.O. Box 642 FDR
New York, N.Y. 10022

St. Martin's Press
175 Fifth Avenue
New York, N.Y. 10010

Scarecrow Press
52 Liberty Street
Metuchen, N.J. 08840

Scholastic Book Services
50 West 44th Street
New York, N.Y. 10036

Charles Scribner's Sons
597 Fifth Avenue
New York, N.Y. 10017

Silvermine Publishers, Inc.
Comstock Hill
Norwalk, Connecticut

Simon & Schuster
1 West 39th Street
New York, N.Y. 10018

Stein & Day Publishers, Inc.
7 East 48th Street
New York, N.Y. 10017

Stackpole Company
Cameron & Keller Streets
Harrisburg, Pa. 17105

Sterling Publishing Company, Inc.
419 Park Avenue South
New York, N.Y. 10016

Taplinger Publishing Company
Room 1705
200 Park Avenue South
New York, N.Y. 10003

Transatlantic Arts, Inc.
Levittown, New York

Charles E. Tuttle Company
28 South Main Street
Rutland, Vermont 05701

Universe Books
381 Park Avenue South
New York, N.Y. 10016

University of Arizona Press
Box 3398
Tuscon, Arizona 85700

University of Washington Press
Seattle, Washington 98105

Van Nostrand Reinhold Company
450 West 33rd Street
New York, N.Y. 10001

Viking Press, Inc.
625 Madison Avenue
New York, N.Y. 10022

Wadsworth Publishing Company
  Belmont, California 94002

Walker and Company
  720 Fifth Avenue
  New York, N.Y. 10019

Watson-Guptill Publications, Inc.
  2160 Patterson Street
  Cincinnati, Ohio 45214

Franklin Watts, Inc.
  730 Fifth Avenue
  New York, N.Y. 10019

Western Publishing Company
  850 Third Avenue
  New York, N.Y. 10022

Albert Whitman and Company
  560 West Lake Street
  Chicago, Illinois 60606

Whitman Publishing Company
  Racine, Wisconsin

Winchester Press
  460 Park Avenue
  New York, N.Y. 10022

Workman Publishing Company
  231 East 51st Street
  New York, N.Y. 10022

INDEX

Index entries (for authors, titles, and broad subjects) refer to entry numbers and not to page numbers. Works that are mentioned in the annotations for other entries have the letter "n" following the entry number (e.g., "Art of Whittling and Woodcarving, 458n"). Subject entries are in boldface type.